THE ARCHAEOLOGY OF THE COLONIZED

This book focuses on the experience of the colonized in their landscape setting, looking at case studies from areas of the world not often considered in the postcolonial debate. It offers original, exciting approaches to the growing area of research in archaeology and colonialism.

The case studies used range from the pyramids of Old Kingdom Egypt to illicit whisky distilling in nineteenth-century Scotland, and from the Roman roads of Turkey to the threshing floors of Cyprus under British colonial rule. Dr Given uses the archaeological evidence to create a vivid picture of how the lives and identities of farmers, artisans and labourers were affected by colonial systems of oppressive taxation, bureaucracy, forced labour and ideological control.

This is the first book to integrate fully the archaeological study of the landscape with the concerns of colonial and postcolonial history, theory and scholarship. It will be valuable to anyone investigating the relationship between local community and central control in a wide range of historical and archaeological contexts.

Michael Given is a Research Fellow in the Department of Archaeology, University of Glasgow, and co-director of the Troodos Archaeological and Environmental Survey Project in Cyprus. His research interests include archaeological survey, landscape archaeology, imperialism and historical archaeology. He is co-author with A. Bernard Knapp of *The Sydney Cyprus Survey Project: social approaches to regional archaeological survey* (2003).

D0061114

First published 2004
by Routledge
2 Park Square, Milton Park, Abingdon, Oxon OX14 4RN

Simultaneously published in the USA and Canada
by Routledge
711 Third Avenue, New York, NY 10017

Routledge is an imprint of the Taylor & Francis Group

© 2004 Michael Given

Typeset in Garamond by The Running Head Limited, Cambridge

British Library Cataloguing in Publication Data
A catalogue record for this book is available from the British Library

Library of Congress Cataloging in Publication Data
Given, Michael, 1965–
The archaeology of the colonized / Michael Given.
p. cm.
Includes bibliographical references (p.) and index.
1. Archaeology and history. 2. Social archaeology.
3. Colonies–History. 4. Colonization–Social aspects–History.
5. Landscape archaeology. 6. Taxation–Social aspects–History.
7. Economic anthropology. 8. Peasantry–History. 9. Working
class–History. 10. Social control–History. I. Title.
CC77.H5G57 2004
336.2'009171'9–dc22
2003026273

ISBN 0–415–36991–6 (hbk)
ISBN 0–415–36992–4 (pbk)

CONTENTS

ILLUSTRATIONS

Figures

Table

ACKNOWLEDGEMENTS

The research for this book was carried out while I was an Arts and Humanities Research Board Institutional Research Fellow at the Department of Archaeology, University of Glasgow. I am very grateful to all the institutions, projects and individuals who have supported this work in so many different ways: the staff of the State Archives, Nicosia, and the State Archivist Effy Parparinou; the staff and residents of the Cyprus American Archaeological Research Institute; the directors, specialists and fieldwalkers of the Sydney Cyprus Survey Project and the Troodos Archaeological and Environmental Survey Project; the members of the Amheida Project, Egypt; the members of the Early Agricultural Remnants and Technical Heritage programme; and my colleagues and postgraduate students at the Department of Archaeology, University of Glasgow.

I am enormously grateful to the following for advice, ideas, information, references and help of many different kinds: Patricia C. Anderson, Fiona Baker, Alekos Christodoulou, J.J. Coulton, Füsun Ertuğ, Marios Hadjianastasis, Kristina Winther Jacobsen, Dorothy I. Kidd, A. Bernard Knapp, Valter Lang, Grith Lerche, Andriani Kosta Loïzou, Panayiotis Alexandrou Loppas, Iain MacGregor, Sturt Manning, Anna Marangou, Muriel McDonald, Robin Meador-Woodruff, Dimosthenis Milidhoni, Helen Murchison, Nikos Pampoulos, Luke Sollars, Sophocles Sophocleous, Catherine Steel, Marc Waelkens and Loïzos Xynaris. I would particularly like to thank those who read drafts of various chapters and commented on them so helpfully: Chris Dalglish, Julia Ellis Burnet, Angus Graham, Danielle Parks, Alison South and Peter van Dommelen. Special thanks go to Erin Gibson for the roads and paths.

Many different individuals and institutions have kindly given me permission to use material for illustrations. They are acknowledged in the captions to the relevant figure. All maps are my own except where otherwise indicated. I am grateful to Editions Gallimard for permission to quote in translation from *Triangle Bleu* in chapter 6; these quotations are copyright © Editions Gallimard, Paris, 1969. I would also like to thank Lt-Cdr Dairmid Gunn of the Neil Gunn Literary Estate for permission to quote from Neil M. Gunn's *The Serpent*.

High heaven save us from the symbolists, from the abstracters! Give us back the earth and the flesh and the lovely currents that flow in and between them!

(Neil M. Gunn, *The Serpent*, 1943, p. 67)

1

INTRODUCTION

Harvest time. Out in the wheat fields beyond the village the women and men wield their iron sickles, grasping a handful of stalks with their left hand, pulling the curving blade sharply across them with their right. Behind them more women and the older children gather up the swathes and tie them rapidly with a few twisted lengths of straw, and the sheaves are bundled and strapped onto both sides of a donkey. Almost hidden underneath the family's livelihood, the little line of donkeys is led down the path towards the village.

Each threshing floor is heaped up with the family's income for the year. This is not stalks and ears, or an abstract number of kilos or litres. This is bread, porridge, gruel, lumps of cracked wheat and yoghurt dried and stored for making soup in winter. They spread out their harvest across the threshing floor with pitchforks, and bring on the threshing sledge. Two oxen, or a horse and a donkey, or a mule and an ox are hitched to it, and an old man or a couple of children are placed on top of it, sitting on an old wooden chair. There is a constant swish and hiss, like the waves on a shingle beach, as the sledge passes over the harvest and its myriad stone blades cut the grain and straw rolling underneath it.

With a prayer to the appropriate deity or saint – in Cyprus it was the Prophet Elijah – a winnowing wind springs up. With a regular rhythm they shovel the threshed harvest into the air, and let the straw, chaff and grain fall into different fractions across the threshing floor. You hear the crunch of the wooden shovel going into the pile, then a patter and whisper as the grain and straw fall to the ground. Everywhere is the wonderfully rich smell of fresh grain and straw. The grain must now be sieved to clean it further, but the chaff is kept for the chickens and the chopped straw for the family ox. They can now be taken into the family's courtyard for storage.

That leaves the pile of grain sitting on the threshing floor (Figure 1.1). This is the very substance of nourishment, prosperity, and the family's livelihood throughout the year. Pick up a handful, and let the pale kernels dribble through your hand. This is not a symbol of life, or a substitute for money, or a representation of family wealth, pride and prestige. It *is* that life and wealth, in its ultimate tangible, edible form.

1

Figure 1.1 Threshing floors heaped with grain outside Nazareth, Palestine, in the early twentieth century. Source: Dalman 1933: plate 12.

And then two strangers come into the village. They come straight to the cluster of threshing floors on the village edge, and begin their work. They are officials; that is immediately clear from the way they dress, and the way they look at the villagers. They might have a uniform or fez or just a badge, as well as smarter clothes and an air of smug self-importance. They go to the first threshing floor, and begin measuring the grain in an old, worn measuring bin. The family and some friends and neighbours stand in a nervous semi-circle, watching every movement as the bin is filled and emptied, filled and emptied. Are they under-filling the bin, these two men, to pretend that there are more measures of grain than there really are? Are they counting the number of bins properly? Will they really take away a third of the harvest as they say, or could the family lose as much as half of its year's sustenance? What are they like, this year's tithe collectors? Will they listen to stories of starving children, or perhaps take a bribe in return for a lower count?

The officials finish measuring, and this is the time for negotiation, protest, argument, pleading. But a third or more of the family's crop is loaded onto government donkeys and taken away to some distant tithe store, never to be seen again. In return, the family receives a piece of paper. The tax men tell them that this paper speaks, and that they must not lose it as it says they have paid their tithes. They look at it uncertainly, and watch the government donkeys carrying away their food.

This is where the experience of being colonized really comes home. It is not so much the pageant of imperialism that affects people's lives, or the restrictions on speech and political action, or the arrogance of foreign elites. The most direct involvement of ordinary people with imperial rule is when their hard-won food is removed from in front of them and taken right out of their family, their community, and often their country. As well as the loss of livelihood, there is the personal humiliation, the knowledge that they are being cheated, if not by the tithe collector then certainly by the regime.

It makes no difference if the colonizer is a distant imperial power, a foreign landlord who has been given ownership of their village, or a central government supporting its bureaucrats and yes-men by sucking the peasants dry. They are all alien, external, and they all survive by extracting food and labour from their subjects. This is colonialism, as experienced by the great majority of people who lived under it. Tribute begins at the threshing floor.

The archaeology of the colonized

The subject of this book is the experience of colonized peoples, as far as we can reconstruct it from archaeological and other sources. It is not concerned with the rulers or elites who gained by exploiting them. The problem is, of course, that the colonized tend to be 'invisible' and 'voiceless', only becoming part of history when their rulers decide to write about them. Official statistics and government reports reduce them to numbers in boxes or dots on the map, while foreign travellers filter them through a wide array of assumptions and agendas. Only in a very few cases can their actual voices be heard, transcribed, for example, by courtroom clerks recording their accusations or defences.

What happens if we want to go beyond these elite sources and occasional courtroom records? What if we are dealing with a society where there are no such records? This is where archaeology comes in. People experienced colonial rule in specific situations and actual places, such as the threshing floors of my opening narrative. In many cases these can be visited, described and mapped. Encounters with imperial officials centred round structures and artefacts such as state granaries and measuring bins, which once again can be found and analysed. Even forced labour can leave unintended monuments to the attitudes and experiences of the labourers in the form of the actual structures and public works that they built.

When archaeological material such as this is carefully analysed in a framework based on the theories of postcolonialism and agency, then it does indeed become possible to reconstruct the experience of colonized people, even without historical records. For many periods, of course, the archaeological sources can be combined with historical sources such as taxation records, official documents, historical photographs, ethnography and oral history. When this is possible, it gives a broad array of evidence, with the archaeology compensating for the elite bias of the historical sources.

Colonialism is now a popular subject in archaeology, and has a century-long heritage in studies of ancient Greek colonies and the Roman Empire. This long heritage is in fact one of the problems, as the long-standing focus on elite monuments and art work makes a body of published literature which is very biased towards the rulers rather than the ruled. Farmsteads, illicit whisky stills and labour camps are far more interesting and instructive than palaces, villas and temples, but they are grossly under-represented in the archaeological literature. The increasing popularity of intensive survey and landscape archaeology in the last 20 years has begun to redress the balance, and to focus interest on rural structures and societies. Even so, this study of the archaeology of the colonized must remain to some extent preliminary.

I take a broad view of the term 'colonized'. In its most restricted sense it refers to people who are controlled and exploited by a group who come from another 'country', a term redolent of late eighteenth- and nineteenth-century nationalism. For the colonized themselves, what matters is that they are being ruled by a group they see as being alien: coming from outside, speaking a different language, or belonging to a radically different culture. There is little alienation in giving food as a contribution to your chief's feasting, or in paying taxes to support the local services which you clearly need. It is very different when you are forced to give food, money or your own labour to build a fortress which prevents you from rebelling, or to glorify an imperial metropolis to which you will never go. Clearly there are many different stages and combinations in the long spectrum from identification with your rulers to alienation from them. For the purposes of this book, it has proved more helpful to include a wide range of situations than to exclude those which fall on the wrong side of an arbitrary division.

Words and chapters

The power relations between colonizer and colonized, in all their different degrees and manifestations, are played out in specific situations, whether on the threshing floor, in the government office, or in the labour camp. It is in their actual practice that people dominate, resist, negotiate, compromise. The same applies to archaeologists and academics. We are part of a long tradition of legitimizing colonial rule through providing imperial precedents or stereotyping native character. It is through our own practices that we can reinforce or challenge that heritage. Academic neo-colonialism is not an abstract ideology, but a series of actions and statements that are played out in specific and very real contexts: taking part in a big project abroad; talking to the mixed participants of a conference session; shaping the class dynamics between lecturer and student; reading or writing a book.

In all of this, the words are crucial. Are they alienating and jargon-ridden, intended to display the power and knowledge of the author rather than to achieve any sort of communication? Do they claim to be totally objective and omniscient, and so end up dismissing any alternative voices? Or are they condescending, pointing out the reader's inferior knowledge and skill? In a book or article, these power relations are played out in the details of the word-smithing.

One small way of trying to create communication and understanding is by narrative. It provides the beginnings of a relationship between a reader and a book, through identification and sympathy, feeling an atmosphere rather than trying to penetrate a logical maze. When the little girl goes exploring in the state granary at Karanis (chapter 6), what she finds is in fact the stuff of site reports and transverse sections. Evoking it through her experience, though, allows readers to lift their eyes from the page and go exploring independently of the author.

Wandering narratives without any structure or theoretical underpinning, of course, are recipes for a confused and frustrated reader, and just produce a different sort of alienation. My theoretical framework is built round four headings: 'resistance – agency – landscape – narrative' (chapter 2). Focusing on resistance and agency highlights the active and dynamic role of colonized people in making their own decisions and forming their own communal and social structures, even when that has to be done in the face of colonial oppression. The landscape context is essential for understanding the experience of any group of people, particularly given the importance of dispersed rural activities in resisting colonial rule. Because of narrative's useful role in the communication of context and experience, its background and function need to be fully explained.

The struggle between the colonized and their rulers over agricultural surplus lies at the heart of the colonial experience. 'The archaeology of taxation' (chapter 3) is a new area of archaeological research which investigates this. Archaeological evidence for taxation can be seen in the areas such as threshing floors where crops were processed, in the standard measures that were used, in storage facilities, and in the various seals, stamps and receipts used in the administration of taxation. To demonstrate that this approach can be used even in a prehistoric period, a case study examines the management of the olive oil crop in the valleys of southern Cyprus in the Late Bronze Age.

Colonial rule affects people's lives in many more ways than just by removing their surplus food. The first thing they had to endure when their area was taken over by a new external regime was 'the settlement of empire' (chapter 4). A complex machinery of roads, communications, military forces and administration had to be set up, including of course the facilities for the assessment, collection and processing of taxes. An excellent example of this is the settlement of the Roman provinces of Asia Minor, ancient Anatolia. For people travelling or living 'on the road', there were constant duties of forced labour and forced hospitality, as well as regular military posts along the roads themselves. Many people chose to exploit these new situations, and a large and prosperous pro-Roman elite grew up in the cities. Many others chose to stay 'off the road', and either lived as bandits or groups in semi-permanent rebellion, or else continued with their rural lives with only a minimum of intrusion from the Roman administrators and officials.

The common colonial obsession with census, survey and mapping meant that for many the experience of being colonized was one of 'living between lines' (chapter 5). This was particularly the case for Cypriot forest villagers and goatherds under British colonial rule in the late nineteenth and early twentieth centuries. To protect the forests, the British forestry department mapped out the boundaries of state forests and marked them with white-washed masonry cairns. They directed a battery of regulations and exclusions against the Cypriots, who responded with an equally wide range of activities. These ranged from maintaining their detailed knowledge and understanding of the forest landscape to downright disobedience and arson attacks.

For many, the experience of colonial rule was a very physical one, and every blow was felt in 'the dominated body' (chapter 6). This was the case even with something as apparently mundane as the processing of the grain tax in Roman Egypt. Farmers and their families had to deliver the grain to the state granary themselves, as well as undergoing a wide range of other unpaid and highly laborious duties. In all the towns, along the roads and along the rivers were a series of gates and barriers which controlled their physical passage from one place to another. For all the impressiveness of monumental architecture, it can also be an unintended monument to the labour of thousands of people, often forced labourers. This can be seen in the contrasting cases of the pyramids of Old Kingdom Egypt and the Nazi building plans for Nuremberg and Berlin. Is participation in such massive projects intended to incorporate people into a new state, or alienate them through punishment?

Resistance to colonial rule is often played out in people's conversations and stories, and can centre on figures such as the Cypriot Saint Mamas, 'the patron saint of tax evaders' (chapter 7). In the Medieval and Ottoman periods his story and the many landmarks associated with him encouraged people in their attempts to grow food for themselves and their families without the knowledge of their rulers. The evidence for this can be seen archaeologically in remote production areas such as threshing floors and pitch kilns, which were clearly operated away from the knowledge of the colonial regime. Sometimes archaeological survey can find whole settlements which seem to have escaped the colonial surveyors and tax assessors.

Social changes in the highlands of Scotland in the eighteenth and nineteenth centuries stimulated some very striking examples of 'landscapes of resistance' (chapter 8). Before the highland clearances and agricultural improvements, people in the farming townships had an intimate knowledge of their local landscape and the rhythms of rural life which bound together themselves, their settlements, and their environment. Those rhythms were broken when they were expelled to unproductive coastal sites and forced to become labourers, fishermen, or to emigrate outright. In contrast to the picture of depressed and passive acquiescence given by many eyewitness accounts and modern historians, an archaeological study of the landscape shows that there was a wide range of activities that allowed people to maintain their pride and identity and their knowledge of an integrated landscape. One of these was the production of illicit whisky, which became an enormous industry in the late eighteenth and early nineteenth centuries.

This book includes a wide range of case studies, from Old Kingdom Egypt to post-Medieval Scotland, and from Roman Anatolia to Nazi Germany. They are intended to illustrate an approach which can be applied to many different societies, and to suggest ways of understanding social relationships and experiences at a local level where historical sources are few or unhelpful. The voice of the colonized may be drowned out by elite sources or ignored by generations of archaeologists, but it is always there.

2

RESISTANCE – AGENCY – LANDSCAPE – NARRATIVE

It is a little before midnight in the summer of 1885. An August moon shines across the threshing floors which run down a spur below the village of Mitsero in central Cyprus. On one of the floors stand two women, talking and laughing quietly as they sieve the winnowed grain. All around them lie the other threshing floors, with heaps of unthreshed sheaves, long piles of grain and the assortment of shovels, pitchforks and sledges which are needed for processing the harvest. As they shake and tip the heavy sieves the women glance down occasionally at a spare sieve lying beside them, stilling their conversation for a moment. A winnowing breeze from the north brings a first hint of coolness, and begins to dry the sweat on their chaff-encrusted arms. From a threshing floor down below them come the loud snores of a man, a foreigner from outside the village, sleeping amidst the sheaves with a half-empty goatskin of wine beside his limp right hand. The women pause and listen, smile at each other as they hear the snores, and continue their work.

What is going on? Why are these two women sieving at night all on their own? Who is the sleeping man, and why are they careful not to waken him? Is there someone missing who ought to be using the spare sieve? More to the point, what is a clearly fictional piece of narrative description doing in a supposedly scholarly book, particularly at the beginning of a theory chapter?

This chapter is intended to be a guide to interpreting the actions, experience and material culture of the colonized. It is theoretical, in the sense that it is generalized and derives from a wide body of abstract writing in archaeology and the social sciences. My purpose, though, is a very practical one. The theory which I explain in this chapter will be applied to concrete material and situations: state granaries, military roads, forest boundaries, illicit whisky stills. Like the moonlight on the threshing floors, theory can reveal patterns we would otherwise not notice. But those patterns are composed of human actions and material culture; they are the phenomenological realities which are the goal of my investigation (cf. Gosden 1994: 108).

Examining resistance is one of the keys to understanding the experience of colonized people, as some 40 years of postcolonial theorizing have demonstrated. This is a welcome alternative to the usual one-sided emphasis on elites

Figure 2.1 Sieving the threshed grain in Cyprus. Source: Tarsouli 1963: plate 54.4 (reproduced with permission of the Holy Archbishopric of Cyprus).

and modes of domination that still characterizes much archaeological writing. As we are focusing on the actions and decisions of individuals and particular social groups, it is clearly important to make use of agency theory. How can we use material culture such as tools, structures and waste materials to investigate how the colonized chose to resist, subvert, or accommodate colonial rule? Examining its context is crucial: it is not enough to pick out a few items or sites which seem to suit a particular argument. People's actions need to be understood across the whole landscape, to include their farming, hiding and travelling just as much as their living in the 'sites' to which archaeology often limits itself.

There is one more major component of my theoretical discussion. The judicious use of narrative can highlight the importance of human experience and decision-making, and greatly facilitate the communication which is so essential to any analytical exercise. The story of the two women on the threshing floor, for example, suggests that they have decided to process their crop in secret. As I will explain later in the chapter, examining this sort of activity is central to understanding the experience of the colonized. First, however, we need to scrutinize the concept of resistance, and develop a method of applying it to archaeological material.

Resistance

No longer can we lump together the colonized and stereotype them as passive, unthinking machines whose actions are determined by their masters. A range of ethnographic and historical studies and an ever-increasing body of post-colonial theory have demonstrated their rich, active and varied lives, in constant negotiation with the structures and officials of the colonial regime (e.g. Gosden and Knowles 2001; Scott 1990; Singer 1994). This is not to deny the staggering impact of extortionate taxation, official brutality, forced labour, and the regular and public humiliation of everyday colonized life. In many situations, the power and invasiveness of colonial regimes and regulations can severely limit people's freedom to act (Scham 2001: 199). However savage the oppression, nevertheless, there are always stories and parodies, little acts of resistance, the creation of alternative meanings and symbols, and the ability to find space for new social powers.

Understanding power is one of the problems. In our effort to interpret the world around us, it is all too easy to reduce the complexities of lived experience into binary pairs: power and incapacity; domination and resistance; colonizer and colonized. On one side is total, monolithic power, which manufactures dominant ideologies to convince the masses of its legitimacy. On the other is a mass of undifferentiated ciphers who have been oppressed out of any individuality or agency, whose only resistance, if it exists, is a passive reaction to the initiatives and ideologies of the powerful.

This binary world view is a denial of the complexity and richness of human dynamics, and a clear falsification of every colonial situation (Meskell 1998b; van Dommelen 1998: 24; 2002: 122–6). Worse than that, it is a continuation of colonial attempts to define the powerful self against the native other. European colonial societies of the nineteenth and twentieth centuries were fractured at every point, as can be seen not just in current postcolonial theory but in the newspapers of the period. Officials competed with private businessmen and among themselves, women and men had differing interpretations of the society round them, and 'poor whites' were considered almost as bad as natives (Given 2001; Paynter and McGuire 1991; Stoler 1989).

The same applies to the colonized. To see them as heroic defenders of their freedom and authentic culture is romantic and wildly unrealistic, little better than the noble savagism of an earlier generation of western writers (Ortner 1995: 176–80). Different social and ethnic groups competed and often fought among themselves, and individuals could choose whether they wanted to resist, ignore, accommodate or exploit colonial rule (Scham 2001: 191–2). The Senussi in North Africa, for example, quite happily taxed and oppressed their Bedouin subjects at the same time as leading them against the Italians who dominated them both (D. Atkinson 2000). Whether or not people chose to resist depended on a wide range of factors, including personal inclination, the ability of the colonized society to work together, and the availability of resources (Morrison 2001). 'Resistance' is multifaceted and complex, more a range of decisions and negotiations than a single activity.

One version of this stereotyping is the idea that resistance consists of clinging tenaciously to your traditional culture in the face of attempted assimilation by the colonizers. This is a tempting option for archaeologists, as they can detect continuity of material culture, social hierarchy or settlement patterns, existing alongside imperial styles and artefacts. Plantation slaves in South Carolina, for example, clung to their original African food-ways and pottery styles (Ferguson L. 1991). Greek elites maintained their local loyalties and residence patterns in spite of the ideological power of their Roman masters (Alcock 1997). In both these cases, of course, people are still making active decisions and self-definitions. Yet 'continuity', 'tradition' and 'survival' are dangerous terms, used extensively in the archaeological and anthropological literature of the nineteenth and early twentieth centuries to characterize colonized societies and so justify the rule of 'dynamic' and 'progressive' Europeans (Adas 1995; Paynter and McGuire 1991: 1–3).

Part of the problem is that postcolonial theory and political correctness have combined to make 'resistance' an enormously trendy and popular term in anthropology and, increasingly, archaeology (M.F. Brown 1996). This book is a characteristic example. Resistance is everywhere, in what we eat, how we talk, when we arrive for work. The frenzied search for resistance in every aspect of daily life can lead to the neglect of other important explanations, such as survival strategies, collaboration, or ritual or social activities which might be largely unrelated to the experience of colonial rule. This is ultimately producing ethnographic 'thinness', a lack of context in our understanding of particular societies (Ortner 1995).

Another result of this proliferation of studies is that the term 'resistance' now embraces an enormously wide range of activities. At one end of the scale is outright and overt armed rebellion, often well-documented in the historical texts. At the other lie unconscious patterns of everyday behaviour which do not quite add up to what the rulers expect of their subjects (L. Ferguson 1991: 28). Somewhere in the middle of the scale lie deliberate but discrete acts of defiance such as tax evasion and pilfering, as well as boasting about them in safe locations. This broad spectrum of meanings seems to be making the term 'resistance' increasingly meaningless. Applying this spectrum, however, can actually provide a more contextual and nuanced understanding of the experiences of colonized people.

Many actions from the middle of that scale may not be very bold or ambitious, but they still constitute active decision-making on the part of the colonized. They are actions targeted directly at the colonizers, and so are acts of deliberate disobedience or avoidance. At this level, resistance is indeed made consciously and deliberately (cf. van Dommelen 1998: 27–8). Winnowing and sieving your grain at night to avoid it being measured by the tax collector is one example; hiding the bones of meat pilfered from your masters in the root cellar of your house is another (chapter 7).

James C. Scott's 'hidden transcripts' are not just the wistful stories told in the privacy of the home or alehouse about answering back the bailiff or punching the landlord in the face. They are also practices such as secret meetings, parodies, petty crime and tax evasion, which take place in arenas away from the elite's surveillance (Scott 1990: 120–4, 187–92). Many of these practices are based on material culture, involving such things as hiding-places, tobacco pipes, alcohol bottles, and secret crop-processing facilities (Casella 2001; Hall 1992: 384–6). At this level, resistance is expressed in a range of activities which do have their correlates in the archaeological record.

Yet the precise motivation for such activities can be hard to identify. When we find evidence for the production of moonshine whisky, for example, that is clearly an example of deliberate defiance and resistance. But is it motivated by political dissent, a thirst for profit, or merely a vague desire to continue what your parents did before you? And who are you resisting? The local exciseman in person, the imperial government and all it stands for, or some vaguely conceived 'them' who get the blame for everything? Even though secret cultivation or hiding grain from the tax collector has to be a deliberate act of resistance at some level, it might be a straightforward survival strategy rather than a political protest against an exploitative regime (Adas 1986: 69; Fegan 1986: 104).

So how do we go about investigating such activities in the archaeological record? Before we even start, of course, we need a clear theoretical framework, with an ongoing deconstruction of our own assumptions, particularly when so many of them in the analytical literature derive from the western colonial experience. A fully contextual 'thick description' of the society under study will help to avoid giving to some explanations ('resistance', 'hegemony') more weight than they actually deserve, and also help us to interpret the meanings and motivations behind particular patterns of activity (Ortner 1995: 174, 190; van Dommelen 2002: 126–7).

When it comes to the actual material, the problem is of course that archaeology has traditionally focused on elite structures, monuments and public activity, at the expense of the non-elite and private. To look for acts of resistance, we need access to the secret arenas and hidden transcripts (Paynter and McGuire 1991: 13). The recent impressive growth in landscape archaeology provides evidence for a much wider range of activities, in much better context than that provided by the excavation of isolated sites. The other related approach is to look for the evidence of daily practice: the activity areas, refuse and artefacts from which we can interpret labour patterns and experience (Silliman 2001b: 384). These are the arenas where resistance took place, and where the colonized led their active and individual lives.

Agency

One of the main aims of postcolonial theory is to re-empower the colonized, at least in the analytical literature. Above all, we need to allow them individuality, choice and an active role in society. This is the task of agency theory. As with resistance, my use of agency theory is eclectic and firmly practical: it is intended for the very specific project of investigating the active role of the colonized. I am interested primarily in the ways in which groups and individuals choose to act in particular circumstances, and in doing so create their own identities and give meanings to the social and physical world round them (Dobres 2000: 141–3).

One thing I am not doing is hunting for named or known individuals, as identified from the material remains of themselves or their activities (Johnson 1989: 190). It is all too easy for this kind of study to slip into a study of the 'big men' who changed history, or else of a 'typical' person who is somehow a microcosm of society (Meskell 1998b: 157–8). The first is a retreat into elitism, and the second denies the subject any agency. Information from burials can sometimes demonstrate the varied experiences of life and death which create individual world views and identities within the same society (e.g. Hodder 2000; Tarlow 1999). For my purposes, it is more profitable to use contextual information to reconstruct the mechanisms by which the living created their own roles in society.

Whether or not it is possible to give names to specific people, we are dealing with real experiences of embodied people, rather than the dehumanized objects that critics have variously termed 'faceless blobs' (Tringham 1991: 94), 'cultural dopes' (Giddens 1979: 52) and 'uninhabited bodies' (Meskell 1998b: 140). There were certainly major constraints on how people acted, some of them imposed by colonial powers, for example, and the results of people's actions may not always have been as they intended. But they were still deeply involved in creating their own interpretations and identities. We may not know the names and faces of the Cypriot women sieving grain at night, or the Egyptian family bringing its wheat to the state granary, but we can still reconstruct their real, bodily experiences in the localities that they have made meaningful.

Agency theory, like all such trends, is very much a product of current concerns and conditions, and it is important not to impose anachronistic experiences on the people of other cultures. A particular danger of agency theory is projecting modern, western ideas of the free-thinking individual onto the past (Dobres and Robb 2000: 13). Some agents would explain past realities and their own decisions as determined by fate, or God (D. Carr 2001: 162–3). For some societies, groups such as the family or community are seen as the primary unit which takes decisions and establishes identities; in nineteenth- and twentieth-century rural Greece, for example, it was the peasant household (Forbes 1989: 88, 96). As with resistance, it is critically important to examine the entire social context.

13

Examining people's practices is an appropriate way of investigating agency and deliberate acts of resistance. The routine practices of everyday life are an expression of how people organize their society and personal relations. These bodily actions are often picked up unconsciously during childhood, and in normal circumstances seem to be relatively consistent and homogeneous (Bourdieu 1977; Dobres 2000: 136–8). Even so, it is through such bodily engagements with the world that people create meanings and identities for themselves: a skilled carpenter; a sharp trader; a cheerful worker. In particular, it is through working in a team and cooperating in a series of physical movements and personal relations that people create their place in the social network.

This is the concept of the *chaîne opératoire*, which has been much written about in the context of technological processes, particularly the manufacture of artefacts (e.g. Dobres 2000: 153–5; Gosden and Knowles 2001: 18–19). It applies equally well on a building site. By participating in a state building programme on the scale of the Giza pyramids or Hitler's planned reconstruction of Berlin, workers were playing a role in the social and political fabric of that state (chapter 6). On a smaller scale, a project such as a grain harvest incorporates all workers into an elaborate mesh of interactions, exchanges and initiatives that constitutes the community at the most intensive stage of its annual cycle. Abujaber's description of the harvest in early twentieth-century Jordan illustrates the sheer complexity of such a project (1989: 54–60). Archive footage and photographs of traditional agricultural tasks such as winnowing, flailing or scything vividly portray the skill, teamwork and pride of these groups of virtuoso labourers (Figure 2.2; Lajoux 1966). The pattering rhythm of flails striking the ground or scythes swishing in unison through the stalks of wheat can become an aural expression of agency, teamwork and community.

Normally the social and political relations that such practices create are not explicitly recognized or discussed. So when they include heavy labour for a landlord with no direct return, that unequal relationship becomes implicit within people's understanding of the world (Silliman 2001b: 383). This is not to say it is always accepted or seen as 'natural', just that it is part of people's everyday experience of the world. When a routine practice is suddenly challenged or disallowed, then unthinking routine becomes conscious thought, and the agent will suddenly face the decision of whether to submit, protest or resist (Gosden 1994: 125–6). An incompetent reaper might be mocked by a colleague, a building labourer whipped by an overseer, a villager pauper's right to glean suddenly taken away by a stingy landlord. All of these break the routine, and provide arenas and opportunities for active and deliberate change to the social order.

With this understanding of agency, it is clear that the colonized can play a major, active role in constituting their world and even the structure of the colonial society. They are constantly seizing, maintaining and enlarging the

Figure 2.2 Winnowing at Karavas, Cyprus, in the first half of the twentieth century. Photograph: Ververis (copyright, 'TO MATI' Collection, the Leventis Municipal Museum of Nicosia).

space in which they have power, and negotiating their position with the different representatives of colonial authority (Scott 1990: 132). One of the most common arenas for this negotiation of power is against that most ubiquitous and invasive of colonial operations, tax collection (chapter 3). Even without resorting to bribery or evasion, there is always considerable space for argument, negotiation and even exemption (e.g. Brand 1969: 44–5; Singer 1994). Attitudes to authority, of course, are as wide-ranging as a classroom full of schoolchildren. But there is always active negotiation, appropriation, transformation and resistance, and these take place in particular arenas which can be investigated archaeologically as well as historically.

The farmer confronts the tax collector; the agent confronts the colonial structure. All of these negotiations happen in very concrete arenas of activity: it is through material culture and at meaningful localities in the landscape that such negotiations take place (Johnson 1989: 199–200). Precisely because they are meaningful, these arenas in turn influence the relationship between agent and system. Places carry memories, precedents and counter-examples, and the availability of tools and raw materials limits people's choices and actions. This is why archaeology is so much more than a substitute for history or ethnography when other sources are not available. By focusing on patterns of artefact use and the attribution of meaning to structures and landscapes, archaeology is central to understanding the active role of the colonized in constituting their own society.

The reconstruction of routine practices and labour patterns through the patterns and distribution of tools, processing areas and waste is a standard archaeological technique (e.g. Lightfoot *et al.* 1998; Silliman 2001b). Agricultural tools, for example, can be the central focus of the elite's attempts to control production and subordinates' strategies for transforming this attempted control to their own advantage. Paola Tabet argues that in many societies men systematically create a technological gap between themselves and women. Women are under-equipped; their labour is restricted to what they can do with their own bodies. Men, by contrast, have access to machinery which allows them to transcend their own physical limitations, and they are the ones who control the manufacture and use of weapons (Tabet 1979). Similar strategies can be used by colonizers, by restricting access to labour-saving machinery and using forced labour to create an image of the perfect, controlled ant-like society (chapter 6).

Yet this rather structuralist schema does not allow for the complexities of the colonial situation, or for the active role of the colonized in creating and maintaining the structure of their society. It may be that the authorities actually restrict the use of manual tools: it is easier to control and tax a harvest if it is being processed in central facilities owned and policed by the landlord. Conversely, the colonized often deliberately choose to use manual tools or apparently outmoded technology. Scottish landlords of the eighteenth century tried to ban the use of hand grinding mills, as tenants were refusing to have their grain ground at the landlords' mills where they had to pay dues (chapter 8; Dodgshon 1998: 116). Filipino tenants in the twentieth century continued to use outmoded foot-powered means of threshing, because it was quieter and they could thresh secretly without the overseers hearing them (Fegan 1986: 98). These are not merely matters of practicality for exploited tenants struggling to keep enough food for their families to survive. The deliberate use of old materials and technologies can be an active move on the part of the colonized to create their own cultural space and identity in the face of new, imposed artefacts and techniques which they associate with the colonizing power (Silliman 2001a: 201–4).

Contextual study is clearly vital here. A single hand mill is not evidence for secret grinding or the construction of an anti-colonial identity. We have to understand the whole system of agricultural practice and social control, and work out the range of choices and dilemmas faced by the people who lived in that society. Only then can we detect the exceptions, tensions and anomalies in the pattern (Dobres 2000: 135). This applies at a range of different scales, all of which are relevant when using daily practices to investigate the ongoing creation and maintenance of society (Lightfoot *et al.* 1998: 202–3). As well as materials and technologies, this approach works well for domestic architecture, particularly when there are a few clearly idiosyncratic structures

(E.R. Carr 2000), or when a period of social and stylistic transition creates a broad range of opportunities for individual choices and solutions (Johnson 1989: 196–206). At the broadest scale, we will only understand social patterns and exceptions to them by investigating practices and human agency across the entire landscape.

Landscape

Landscape studies are currently hugely popular within archaeology. There is widespread agreement that this is an appropriate scale at which to investigate a broad range of archaeological issues such as social organization, rural economy and sacred space (Anschuetz *et al.* 2001; Knapp and Ashmore 1999). As far as the archaeology of the colonized is concerned, it seems obvious to investigate labour, agency and resistance across the landscape, particularly because of the rural and non-elite nature of much of this activity (Paynter and McGuire 1991: 7). In spite of the vast literature, however, there is little agreement on what 'landscape' means in an archaeological context, and almost nothing on how we can use data such as site descriptions and pottery density charts to answer these perhaps ambitious questions.

A common-sense approach to landscape is to divide it up into analytical categories which can be identified from the material remains: economic (farms, mines); social (settlements); political (forts, palaces); and cultural (sanctuaries, memorials). Although rarely expressed as baldly as it is here, this is the commonest principle underlying archaeological discussions of landscape. However convenient and intuitive, this scheme is clearly an imposition of the modern western habit of pigeon-holing, and is totally inadequate for dealing with apparent contradictions such as sacred cities or bureaucratic palaces, let alone the sophisticated and often holistic conceptions that many past societies had of their worlds.

Another modern dichotomy is that between the physical and cultural landscape. Mountains, ore bodies and fertile soils are taken for granted as always in existence, and they are exploited or built upon to create a cultural landscape of fields, roads and buildings. At its most extreme this is environmental determinism, in its new guise of Geographic Information Systems analysis showing the relationship between site locations and natural resources (Blanton 2001: 629; Gaffney and van Leusen 1995). A more sophisticated version couples the constraints of the physical landscape on human society with the impact that people have on that landscape. People are attracted to well-watered hillslope soils, for example, but fail to protect them against erosion. This leads to a new physical landscape of denuded slopes and heavily sedimented plains, which provides its inhabitants with a new set of constraints (van Andel *et al.* 1986). This approach sets up a useful dynamic between people and their environment, but it still separates the two, and makes no allowance for perception or the individual creation of meaning.

An approach which is much more sensitive to the different cultures we study is the investigation of 'ideational' or 'associative' landscapes where people associate features in the natural and built landscape with their own memories, meanings or emotions (Alcock 2001: 326–7; Knapp and Ashmore 1999: 12–13). This is particularly appropriate for sacred landscapes where hilltop monuments, holy trees or whole vistas carry very specific associations for the people who live and move among them. Ethnographic information can provide a wealth of meanings for such elements of the landscapes. The elders of the Western Apache, for example, associated a series of didactic narratives with the rocks, trees and streams of their landscape, and used them for the instruction of their children: 'wisdom sits in places' (Basso 1996). Detecting such associations from purely archaeological data is much more of a challenge, requiring clear patterns of structures, dedicatory offerings or art work in a range of equivalent locations (Bradley 2000).

Our experience of the landscape is much more intense even than this. Climbing a mountain, feeling the weather, labouring together in the fields – all are physical and biological experiences by embodied individuals in real and meaningful places (Tilley 1994: 26). Our choices and previous experiences affect which of those places become or remain meaningful. As we continue to move, work and live we interact with our landscape, and its meanings constantly change and develop (Basso 1996: 83; Tilley 1994: 23). These changes are brought on by different people acting in different contexts, and even by ephemeral features such as haystacks, the colour of the crops and weather patterns (Brassley 1999). The experiences of hearing, smelling and touching can be as significant as seeing, and are often possible to reconstruct from the archaeological record. These are the sorts of meanings that we are looking for in the archaeological record: the arrays of related activity which Ingold refers to as 'taskscapes', and the linear experiences which are created by following paths and tracks (Ingold 1993: 158, 167; Tilley 1994: 27–31).

Tilley's phenomenological approach to prehistoric monuments (1994), while hugely stimulating, has been criticized for its poverty of contextual information, and its assumptions that prehistoric and modern viewers of monuments share the same cultural attitudes and perceptions (Brück 1998; Fleming 1999b). Ingold (1993) proposes more of a 'thick description' of a landscape of labour, though his example is a painting rather than real archaeological landscape data. Agricultural work and the many activities associated with it are clearly central experiences in the landscape. Through such experiences people build up a network of personal identities, stories and associations with the landscape. This is the field where my father broke the village scything record; this is the road where the bandits robbed the government tithe wagon; this is the cave where we distil our secret whisky.

The landscape, then, is an arena for social agency. 'Arena' is a better metaphor than 'stage'. There are still performers and spectators, but for the participants, the gladiatorial combats and wild animal hunts enacted there are very real dramas indeed. Activities such as harvesting and tool-making unfold in meaningful locations with constant interaction between people and material culture, in the context of family, community and society (Anschuetz *et al.* 2001: 161; Dobres 2000: 127–8). This is how people create their identities as skilled workers or clever tax avoiders, and how experiences of oppression, hard labour and successful resistance become embedded in a local culture.

The landscape is an arena for resistance. As with any other activity, resistance consists of a series of actions, stories and associations by which particular places are given meaning. Historical resistance movements tend to be associated with specific regions, often remote areas away from the centre of power where an alternative set of meanings can be built (Paynter and McGuire 1991: 15). Mountain areas and broken-up terrain can provide ample opportunities for autonomy and distinct local identities (chapter 4), though it is all too easy to slip into a simple deterministic framework of law-abiding farmers in the plains and bandits in the mountains (e.g. Shaw 1990). Landscapes of resistance are created by the actions and decisions of specific people and groups.

The 'public transcripts' and 'hidden transcripts' by which people choose their occasions for submitting to authority or protesting against it have clear spatial correlates; they are materialized in the landscape (Scott 1990: 120–4). The village square and infields, and the threshing floors during tithe division, can be associated with obedience and submission. Remote fields and working-class cafés – and the threshing floors at night – become associated with resistance and a different, more powerful and proactive identity. Because of its privacy, the home or courtyard can also provide an arena for the hidden transcript (Silliman 2001b: 385).

As the case of the threshing floor shows, the same location can have different meanings at different times and for different people. Features in the landscape may carry narratives of resistance to colonial rule, such as the stories of Saint Mamas in Cyprus which I will tell in chapter 7. But they are not universally legible; they are told to some but not to others. This particularly applies to natural features such as rocks. Just outside the village of Spilia in the Troodos Mountains of Cyprus is a large perched boulder, with a strikingly flat surface where it sits on the bedrock beneath it. To a visiting colonial official or other outsider, this is merely a curious rock. To a member of the community, and those they wish to share the story with, it is the millstone on which the Virgin Mary ground to death a plague which had attacked the village. Different social groups, particularly colonized and colonizers, experience alternative landscapes; they participate in 'rival geographies' (Sparke 1998: 305).

There remains the challenge of interpreting these experienced landscapes using archaeological data. The key here is 'activity'. Different activities leave different traces, in terms of artefacts, waste products, structures and alterations of the terrain. These all need to be mapped systematically and carefully.

In the context of an intensive Mediterranean survey project, this might involve the locating and analysis of hundreds of structures, thousands of lithic artefacts, and tens of thousands of sherds. Above all, such work must cover the entire landscape, and include the low-density scatters and minor features which are still being dismissed at the expense of major, elite sites (Alcock *et al.* 1994; Given and Knapp 2003). This includes working in upland zones where terrain and ground visibility are challenging, and features often hard to detect (Cherry 1994: 99). Even so, paths, threshing floors and cultivated terraces tell us more about the experience of the landscape than any amount of elite urban architecture.

However detailed and systematic, archaeological survey on its own does not constitute landscape archaeology (Finlayson and Dennis 2002: 225–6). To reconstruct people's experience in the landscape requires a major interpretative operation. The first stage is to put the artefacts and structures in their full context (Gaffney and van Leusen 1995: 375, 378). This involves the integration of as much information as an interdisciplinary team can extract from the landscape, covering areas such as geomorphology, botany, historical documentation, ethnography, and remote sensing. Broader study of the periods and issues in question provides cultural context for the tentative interpretations of the survey material.

When that has been done, we start seeing patterns of activity in the landscape which seem culturally meaningful. Threshing is done beside the villages, not in the fields; whisky distilling is carried out half an hour's walk from the nearest settlement; military roads follow routes which are highly visible. We also see the exceptions and anomalies which can be the result of specific decisions and choices. Occasionally threshing is, surprisingly, done in the fields; some whisky stills are grouped together in prominent positions; one particular track creeps along the bottom of a side valley. Keeping carefully within the cultural context, we can reconstruct the experiences that accompanied these varied activities, by following paths, examining views, establishing patterns of sound and smell, and estimating participation. Only when we have done all this do we begin to hear the stories of the colonized.

Narrative

In a sense, all archaeological writing is narrative. It has a strong chronological emphasis, often with an explicit sequence of events or styles. These are presented as related to each other, whether causally or by sharing the same context, and each archaeological text has some sort of internal coherence and leads naturally to a conclusion. By describing the geographical and cultural context, archaeological writers provide a background against which the processes they are studying are set. According to this very broad definition, there is no need for narrator or audience. A 'narrative' is a textual structure, not a human experience. A table of factors or a list of bullet-pointed conclusions can be a narrative.

When focusing on human agency and experience, it is helpful to define narrative more closely as a story (Pluciennik 1999: 654). A story has a story-teller and an audience. The audience can respond to the characters in a number of ways – by identifying with them, reacting against them, or taking up any other emotional stance. The series of events or revelations draw the audience in; they create narrative drive. Such stories can be the subjects of archaeological analysis, when we try to understand people's choices and actions. They can also be an analytical technique in themselves. In this section I aim to show that incorporating narratives into archaeological writing is not an 'indulgence' on the part of a conceited author, or 'light relief' to spice up an otherwise tedious text. Narrative is an integral and necessary part of the analysis of human experience and its communication to others.

Most human experiences are explicitly sequential (Dobres 2000: 156–7). The stages in making a tool or processing the grain, the progression from childhood to puberty to adulthood, the changing outlook when walking along a track; in each case the protagonist undergoes a chain of related experiences. The archaeologist's aim is to reconstruct that narrative, and so to focus on real experiences rather than depersonalized generalizations and 'macro-processes' (Hodder 2000: 30–1; Meskell 1998b: 156; 2000: 424). We are not dealing with numbers in a matrix. People, groups and communities have their own trajectories through landscape and society.

The natural progression of knapping a scraper or sieving the wheat is often interrupted: by a piece of poor quality chert, by the tax collector, by a storm, or by any other of the accidents and contingencies of everyday life. These contingencies play a major role in human decision-making and experience, and are part of the ongoing creation, maintenance and transformation of society and community. The meanings which are given to artefacts or places or experiences can change, depending on who is experiencing them, what the context is, and what else has happened previously. Understanding people's lives and experiences as fluid narratives, rather than as rigid analytical structures, gives us a much more sophisticated and nuanced understanding (Hall 1992: 377).

If we want to understand people's lives as narratives and communicate that understanding to others, it is clearly appropriate to use narrative ourselves. This allows us to focus on people and human actions, the indeterminacies that affect them, and the whole 'drama of deliberation and choice' (D. Carr 2001: 163). Narrative is particularly useful as it examines events and societies from the point of view of the agents, rather than with the hindsight of the historian (164–5). The decision about whether to fight a battle or dodge a tax collector is a real dilemma for the agent, but not for the historian who knows the outcome.

One important function of narrative is to link together a series of disparate elements so that they are coherent and intelligible, and allow the narrator to suggest an interpretation or explanation (Pluciennik 1999: 658–9). For the two women winnowing their wheat at night, we have their actions, and the location of those actions on the threshing floors and adjacent to the village. The tools used by them and others are all relevant, as are the wind, the light and the temperature. The reader really needs to know more about the social structure of the community. Why is it the women who are doing the threshing? Where are the men? Why is the sleeping man a 'foreigner'? What do the village authorities think about this?

All of these different elements need to be incorporated into a fully contextualized 'thick description' of the situation, and therefore of the society in action. It is exactly this that narrative allows. When this is done, the narrator can suggest to the audience that there is a point to the story. This is what it feels like to resist imperialism, for example; these are the fault lines within a colonized society. One particularly successful example is Clifford Geertz's famous narrative of the police raid on a Balinese cock fight and its ramifications for his relations with the villagers (Geertz 1972: 412–17).

So there is a general equivalence between narrative in the present and human experience in the past which makes it an appropriate analytical tool. There is a further equivalence between the telling of a story and the experience of hearing that story which makes narrative a particularly effective means of communication. And what use is research without communication?

Academic archaeological writing has been characterized as 'dry, uninspired, uninspiring, uncreative, unimaginative, cold, inhuman, perverse' (Boivin 1997: 106). Jargon and convoluted sentence structure set up barriers rather than try to cross them. Such writing is intended to advertise and defend the academic territory of the writer, rather than contribute to shared knowledge and understanding. Quite apart from the criminal waste of deadening what should be an exciting and challenging engagement with past lives, this is a poor return on the money invested by public and private institutions, and on all those archaeological sites destroyed by excavation.

Against this, more and more academic articles, and a few actual narratives, are emphasizing the importance of the immediate and vivid communication of the results of our research to students (Conkey 2002) and to the general public (Gibb 2000, and commentators). The advantage of narrative, in the sense of using a measure of explicit storytelling in academic archaeological prose, is that one of its primary goals is to promote communication with the audience or readership. Readers are drawn into the situation, can identify with the protagonists or oppose them, and respond in accordance with their own personal context and feelings. They become agents, not blobs. They are engaging in a dialogue with the narrator, rather than enduring a monologue in silence (Joyce 2002: 9). Jargon-ridden academic prose is a 'readable' text, which imposes a single meaning on readers and leaves no room for their own interpretations. Narrative is a 'writable' text, in that it allows readers to create their own meanings and follow their own paths (Eagleton 1983: 137–8).

These issues of communication are very relevant to foreign archaeologists working in postcolonial countries. A particularly unpleasant stereotype declares that western archaeologists are theory-based, in contrast to their empiricist local colleagues. This is exacerbated unnecessarily by the deliberate obscurity of much theoretical writing, and the lack of its clear application to empirical data. Even those who use postcolonial theory can fail to examine the context of their own writing and the relationships it sets up between themselves and their readers. The postcolonial theorist Homi Bhabha argues that political theory should not be seen as an elite western preserve, divorced from the 'real' political activism of the third world; both are hybrid forms of political engagement which enable and support each other (Bhabha 1994: 19–22). This is undeniable; the same applies in the archaeological field. What he seems blind to is that his argument is expressed in desperately difficult and alienating language, which can only deepen the divide he is trying to bridge.

Narrative is no panacea for epistemological and political difficulties, and undoubtedly has its own problems. With the postcolonial focus on 'people without a voice', it is all too easy to claim that by creating characters and stories we are giving a voice to the voiceless (Joyce 2002: 17; Sparke 1998: 308–10). This would be tantamount to colonial representation, the attitude that colonizers know more about the colonized, including their histories and identities, than they do themselves (Given 1997; Said 1978: 31–41). But we can use narratives to imagine a lost perspective, form new questions and stimulate new thought.

Narratives tend to provide meaning and closure, and in their effort to interpret the world can end up delivering a reality that is excessively neat and apparently complete. Human experience and social dynamics rarely have such neatness, of course, so it is important to use narrative techniques such as irony and paradox to subvert such constructed realities. Narrators can always turn the focus of the story to themselves, and this reflexive quality is particularly effective at showing how ideologies and meanings are rhetorical creations in particular situations for particular purposes (Callinicos 1995: 49–52). By juxtaposing a story about archaeological field survey with the academic results of that survey, for example, it is possible to demonstrate how the archaeological data were generated and then transformed into a set of confident and coherent conclusions (e.g. Given and Seretis 2003).

This is precisely the opposite of setting up the 'archaeologist-as-hero' myth, which legitimizes all the ethnocentric and imperialist activities of archaeologists in the past two centuries (Silberman 1995: 251–2). It is particularly important to undermine the 'metanarratives' or 'grand narratives' by which events lead inexorably to an ideologically inspired conclusion, such as progress, world rule or the classless society (Pluciennik 1999: 655–6). Once again, the ironic and reflexive capabilities of narrative are ideally suited to this.

This book is not dedicated to large-scale storytelling with the creation of major fictional truths, however worthy a goal that might be. My use of narrative will be judicious, with brief paragraphs at salient places, as well as the occasional sentence or fictional example ('this is where we distil our whisky'). Such narratives can still adhere to scholarly standards of evidence and argument. In chapter 7, for example, I will discuss and give references for the evidence that lies behind the story of the sieving women with which I began this chapter. By using these techniques I aim to embody the dilemmas and decisions of social agents in my text, and to engage you, the reader, in specific social contexts and landscapes.

*　　*　　*

The same moon that highlighted the women on the threshing floor was throwing sharp shadows on the mud-plastered wall of a courtyard within the village. Among the winnowing shovels and the sacks which would be used for bringing in the grain, a third woman turned and looked up unhappily at the wall where she usually hung her sieve. On each side of her courtyard was a jumble of houses and walls and other courtyards, with intrusions and angles where one had been built into another or a door blocked up or a wall torn down. She could see her cousins and aunts and friends in every roof and doorway or tumbled-down wall, where a wedding or a death or a new son had altered the fabric of her village.

She turned back and hesitated before the doorway which led out into the alleyway. Her two friends would be down at the floors by now; she could tell that from the angle of the moon. Her sieve was already down there, left during the afternoon in readiness. But she had married outside the village, and that tithe collector down there was the cousin of her husband. And she was always conscious of the village headman, her sister's father-in-law, who complained loudly that anyone taking wheat before it had been measured would be bringing punishment onto the whole village, and especially onto his, the headman's, own head. Her husband snored inside the house; he certainly didn't approve.

She turned again and looked at the clay-lined pits where they would store the family's grain for the coming year. Another dry winter like the last, and her children would starve. And here she was, giving away a good third to that pompous tithe collector who loved to bang down his measuring bins in the middle of each threshing floor and flick the pages of his receipt book as he looked contemptuously round at the anxious family. And most of it would go to those dogs who used it to grow fat in their palaces in Nicosia . . .

It never finishes, she thought, as she sighed and looked round her courtyard and home. Perhaps she would go and sieve a sack or two. But then it would be the same problem next year; a different harvest, probably a different tithe collector, but the same insecurities and problems. Perhaps she would be so angry by then that she would go and do it just to spite them. But then there would be another year, and new people. The story never ends, she thought, and looked up at the moon to see if there was still time to go out to the floors.

3

THE ARCHAEOLOGY OF TAXATION

A measuring jar is of little use when it is so worn that its original rim has entirely disappeared. That was the problem in 1697, when an 80-year-old wooden measuring jar was at the centre of a confrontation on the remote and windswept island of St Kilda, some 55 km west of the Outer Hebrides in the Western Isles of Scotland. It was the annual visit of the steward, the sub-chief of Clan MacLeod who visited the island each year with a retinue of up to 60 followers to collect the rent. He claimed that the original size of the jar could be estimated by putting your hand against its side, and heaping the barley up to that level. This clearly gave him more barley to take back to his chief's headquarters at Dunvegan on the Isle of Skye. The islanders, naturally, disagreed, and ended up voting to send their representative to Skye to put their case to the chief himself (Fleming 1999a: 189–90; Martin 1698: 267–8).

Taxation lies at the heart of the experience of being ruled. In anything other than an entirely egalitarian society, people are forced to give part of their income to the empire, the state or the chief. The rulers can try to justify it, with promises of protection or public works, and make the payment of taxes or rent seem as inevitable and natural a part of the annual cycle as the harvest or a religious festival. For those who were taxed, though, this was the most personal and direct contact with the state, in the person of the steward, tithe collector or revenue official. This particularly applies to tax in kind. The fruits of your year's work, which will support you and your family through the coming year, lie there in the barn or on the threshing floor. As you watch, helpless to do anything other than protest at any apparent unfairness, your crop is measured, divided, and a significant proportion removed.

The extraction of surplus, of course, takes many different forms, from rent in kind to income tax on a payslip. In an imperial province conquered in war, tribute is drawn from the province to the metropolis, and by definition is intended to benefit the rulers at the expense of the ruled. Even when the colonizing society claims to spend some of the tax on paved roads or schools, there is still a sense of alienation. People might not see any use in the roads, or be suspicious about letting their children learn what the rulers want to teach them. In a chiefdom society such as western Scotland in the sixteenth and seventeenth centuries, people still had to give food to their chiefs. But there was less alienation. They were giving hospitality to their respected kinsman, and in return they received not just help in time of crisis but a sense of kinship and identity, even their name, and a place in the social landscape (Dodgshon 1998: 31–50).

In this chapter I propose an archaeology of taxation. This will involve examining the role of food surplus in complex societies, and in particular the control of that surplus. To demonstrate that taxation is visible in the archaeological record, I will review some examples of its material culture: food processing areas, measures, storage, administration and infrastructure. A case study from Late Bronze Age Cyprus will put these ideas into practice, investigating the management of olive oil in the valleys of the south coast.

Surplus and society

Complex society needs surplus food. It feeds the craft specialists who can devote their time to tool production or the creation of prestige goods, rather than being bound to subsistence agriculture. It gives those who control it wealth and power, and so supports the divisions and hierarchies of a ranked society. It provides a commodity which can be easily measured and exchanged in the form of cash, prestige goods or staples, and so allows trade and the integration of distant communities.

Surplus refers to what is left over after sustainable agricultural production. The basic needs are a minimum supply of food for the cultivators, seed for next year, feed for any animals, enough to pay for any equipment or materials that need to be repaired or replaced, and enough to fulfil any social needs such as weddings or hospitality. In a simple, egalitarian society production can stop there; there is no need to continue working when the basic needs of life are met. In any form of complex society, the producers must give up a proportion of their income, and so are forced to intensify their methods, work longer hours, and produce a surplus (Wolf 1966: 2–6).

To explore the relationship between surplus and complex society, I will follow a logical progression from the beginnings of inequality and control over surplus to the sophisticated multi-ethnic empires of the historical period. This is often a chronological progression, of course, but not always. There is nothing inevitable about the increase in social complexity, and its forms vary hugely. I will take most of my examples from Greece, not because it can stand for the rest of the world, but because its highly variable and often challenging environment provides a microcosm which highlights the development of social complexity and the control over surplus.

The struggle for control over surplus begins with the need for risk-buffering. Most regional climates have an element of unpredictability. Some, particularly in the Mediterranean, are notoriously variable. On Crete, for example, the rainfall in any one place can vary from well under half the annual average to almost twice that average (Rackham and Moody 1996: 35–6). This variability has a huge effect on crop yields. Even if a farmer's land produces enough for basic needs in a normal year, it just takes an unusually low rainfall, a torrential downpour at the wrong time, or a sudden attack of locusts to threaten entire families and communities with starvation.

The solution to this climatic variability is risk-buffering, the putting aside of some extra food in case of a bad year. Most simply, this can be done by producing more than is necessary, processing it so that it will keep, and storing it. If stored in anaerobic conditions, wheat and barley can keep for a couple of years. Similarly, fruit can be dried, olives can be made into oil, and a wide range of spices and preservatives will prolong the life of meat. An unusual example of this form of direct storage lasting into the twentieth century comes from Methana in southern Greece, where what was effectively an untaxed subsistence society relied on the long-term storage of grain and oil and a range of emergency measures (Forbes 1989). Storage can also be indirect: by feeding agricultural surplus to livestock, it can be stored on the hoof, and eaten as meat whenever required.

Storage is only one way of risk-buffering. Others are particularly suited to Greece, where steep mountains, narrow valleys and a multitude of tiny islands make a patchwork of topographical zones and microclimates. A farmer can grow different crops in different areas. If one type of crop fails or one field is hit by a very localized hailstorm, the other crops or other areas are more likely to survive. This diversification is one explanation for the fragmented land holdings of many pre-modern Mediterranean farmers, often criticized as being inefficient or wasteful of time (Christodoulou 1959: 83–7). More drastically, people can move from a drought-stricken area to another area which happens to have received better rainfall, again exploiting the local variation of climate.

Another way of evening out local shortfalls and abundances is by means of exchange. In the simplest cases, a surplus of wheat in one area can be exchanged for a surplus of olive oil in another. Where there is very great regional variation, such as in much of central and southern Greece, these exchanges can happen over relatively short distances (Halstead and O'Shea 1982: 96). In contrast to overproduction and storage, which tend to create isolated and self-sufficient farming units, exchange as a method of risk-buffering tends to integrate separate communities into networks of agreements, procedures and negotiations (O'Shea 1981: 168–9). Exchange can be carried out in prestige goods and labour as well as staple goods. Instead of the direct storage of grain or olive oil or the indirect storage of livestock, people become involved in the 'social storage' of surplus. They can exchange surplus for prestige goods, for example, and sell them back again for food when necessary (Halstead and O'Shea 1982).

This is where control over the surplus becomes crucial, and brings about social inequalities and hierarchies (Halstead 1994). Some farmers might have more skills or experience than others, or have particularly well-watered land which survives dry years better than neighbouring areas. In a normal year, everyone produces enough to live on. In a bad year, the farmers with the better land and skills are the only ones to have a surplus, which they can then give to their less fortunate colleagues in exchange for labour, materials, prestige goods, or any other agreed social or economic obligations. After a string of bad years, such farmers have become an elite, controlling surplus and labour and displaying their superiority in monumental architecture or prestige goods such as jewellery and table ware.

In this control of agricultural surplus lie the seeds of taxation. The elite give up farming themselves, and support their increasingly ostentatious lifestyle by extracting more surplus in good years and more labour and other obligations in bad years. By investing time and skill in the manufacture of tools and the development of skills and techniques, they embed this relationship in the society and economy, until a regular payment of agricultural surplus to the local or regional elite becomes an integral part of every farmer's life. Apart from periodic bad years of low returns, the 'normal surplus' produced by a relatively intensive agricultural system in reasonable conditions provided plenty of substance for the elite to convert into status and authority (Halstead and Jones 1989: 54).

This development is what took place in broad terms between the Late Neolithic and Early Bronze Age in mainland Greece, as analysed by Paul Halstead (1992; 1994; 1999). People colonized more and more marginal land, they specialized in particular aspects of agriculture and support services such as tool manufacture, and they intensified agricultural production, above all through the introduction of draught animals and the plough. By the Middle and Late Bronze Age in southern Greece the end result was a series of large-scale political and economic entities based on hierarchical rule and the sophisticated administration, storage and redistribution of surplus; in other words, states.

The logic of this argument is not intended to represent a deterministic progression leading inevitably from small surpluses to the superstate. The collection, storage and redistribution of surplus can be just as central to a chiefdom as to a state (Strasser 1997: 92–3), and the increasing complexity of social organization can give rise to a series of competing or co-existing heterarchies, rather than a single central hierarchy (Keswani 1996). My point is simply that the control of agricultural surplus is central to the operation of a complex society. It is true that taxation often supports a dominating elite, but the central storage and redistribution of surplus can also integrate a wide territory with varying topography, resources and communities (Morrison 2001: 267). It can even form the focus of a struggle against central authority. Local leaders in nineteenth-century Jordan used their control over surplus to maintain their own power at the expense of the Ottoman governor (Rogan 1999: 40–1).

Taxation is the appropriation of more than surplus. When an administrative elite extracts a proportion of people's grain or dairy produce, it is also removing their self-subsistence and autonomy. No longer do they control their own risk-buffering or indirect storage. In time of drought or emergency they must turn to state, landlord or patron, and show every gratitude when they are given back a fraction of what they originally cultivated. This is supported and legitimized by a battery of paternalist ideologies. The Ottoman sultan was the 'father of the peasants', and was presented as taking a direct personal interest in their well-being (Singer 1994: 123). The Russian 'tsar-deliverer' was a similar figure, encouraging oppressed peasants to blame not the tsar or the system but the 'disloyalty' of local officials (Scott 1990: 96–8).

In other situations the ideology was less benign. The extraction of surplus could also be a punishment for societies that had been conquered in war, as well as a prize for the victors. One of an empire's first tasks in the 'settlement' of a newly conquered province was to put in place a system for the collection of tribute (chapter 4). It was clearly efficient to use as much of the existing system and officials as could safely be done. For the British or the Ottomans, this meant sending in survey teams to carry out a census, document the existing tax system, and adapt it to their own imperial structure. The Aztecs, by contrast, separated the subject state from the tribute provinces, often to the extent that they had different boundaries. This allowed them to deal with subject rulers as if they were colleagues and allies, and so maintain their political loyalty, while extracting a heavy tribute from the common people as a completely separate process (F. Hicks 1992).

There was a range of ideologies justifying such payments of tributes. The tribute demands of both the Aztec and the early Islamic empire were considerably lower for provinces which had surrendered. Such ideologies, however, could also be manipulated by the subject states. In the first century BC, for example, the inhabitants of Segesta in Sicily claimed that they were descended from the Trojans and so related to the Romans. That argument from history won them freedom from tribute (Lintott 1993: 71). During the first three centuries AD, municipal magistrates throughout the Roman Empire devoted considerable time and thought to constructing elaborate arguments for their right to freedom from imperial taxes, and so control of their own surplus.

The material culture of taxation

The imperial ideologies I have just been discussing seem very remote from the lives of specific farmers. They did indeed participate in such ideologies, whether by petitioning the sultan, seeing their surplus disappear to some foreign imperial capital, or benefiting from their city's winning tax free status from Rome. But to investigate the ways in which people experienced and often resisted this loss of surplus, we need to focus on the material culture and the real lives that can be inferred from it.

This approach is suggested by the agency theory that I discussed in chapter 2, but it is also supported by historical studies of taxation at a grass-roots level. Taxation may have seemed like a highly organized system with a sustaining ideology, and that is certainly how it appears in the contemporary documents justifying it. On the threshing floor, however, where tax collector and peasant family stand opposed on either side of the grain heap, taxation is a morass of disagreements, partial payments, negotiations, claims and counter claims (Singer 1994: 87–8; Wolf 1966: 49). The focus of their interaction is above all the food that has been produced, but also the material culture that is part of the taxation process. For the St Kildans standing before the MacLeod steward, the whole struggle for control over their surplus is embodied in that worn wooden measuring jar.

In this section I will give some examples of the main aspects of material culture which play a role in taxation: the locations where the crops are processed; the measuring containers used to assess the crop and the state's or landlord's share; and the facilities used for storing taxed or untaxed produce. Taxes in kind are particularly amenable to archaeological analysis, as the handling of large quantities of produce requires large-scale and specialized equipment. My examples will mainly concern cereal production in the eastern Mediterranean where the data are relatively abundant, though it is an approach which is widely applicable. Historical sources are also useful in demonstrating the role of material culture in its social context.

Processing areas

In the long and complex process of harvesting the crop and transforming it so that it can be eaten or stored, there is an ideal stage for the authorities to measure it and extract their share. This must be late enough so that impurities have been removed and the crop is at its lowest bulk and highest value, but not so late that it has already disappeared into people's private homes or stores. Olive oil is most easily taxed after the crushed olive pulp is pressed, and dairy produce after it is turned into the durable form of cheese or butter. For cereals, this comes after threshing, winnowing and sieving. The clean grain is easily measured and transported, and the tithe collectors do not have to deal with the bulky straw and chaff.

This stage of the crop processing happens in very specific places and uses specific tools. Olive presses, butter churns and threshing floors are easily identifiable in the archaeological record, and are far more central to their society than the usual studies of agricultural techniques imply. For peasant cultivators, this is where the family can see in material form the success of the harvest, their health and prosperity for the year and, for many, the results of their prayers. But it is also where the state or landowner exercises the greatest control and supervision, and where the conflict and negotiation between the two groups is the most intense.

The threshing floor is a particularly good example of an arena where the dramas of food-processing and tax collection take place, and I will return to them in many parts of this book (Figure 3.1). In the hot, dry summers of the Mediterranean the grain can be processed in the open air, and the threshing floor provides a clean, level surface for threshing, winnowing and sieving. Threshing floors from the fourth millennium BC have been excavated in the Negev desert in Israel (Avner 1998). The Minoan 'Assembly on the Hill' fresco from the West House in Thera shows what is most likely a circular threshing floor (rather than an animal fold), with a low stone wall round it to catch the chaff during winnowing and shaded by two trees (Sarpaki 2000: 665). The documents from Roman Egypt are full of references to threshing floors (chapter 6), and abandoned twentieth-century threshing floors are a familiar site in Cyprus and elsewhere in the Mediterranean (chapter 7).

Historical records and ethnography show that threshing floors meant far more to their users than just being the location of food processing. After the harvest they held the grain heap, which embodied the family's entire livelihood for the year. In southern Indian villages in the mid-twentieth century the threshed grain was heaped up in the middle of the threshing floor, decorated with flowers and formally worshipped. Offerings were made to it, and then were distributed to the crowd. Only after that had been done did all the many claimants from the community come up to receive their share, from the blacksmith and the barber to the moneylender and the headman who took the family's tax payment. What was left could then go into storage (Beals 1974: 71).

For any creditor, landlord or tax collector, the greatest need was for surveillance and control. In sixteenth-century Palestine, the villagers had to announce to the district judge that the crop was ready to harvest. It was then sampled and measured, so that the authorities could estimate the size of the harvest and so of the tithes, and then the whole process from reaping to threshing and sieving was supervised and watched closely by an official. The climax came with the measurement and division of the threshed grain on the threshing floor, with a whole range of arguments, negotiations and protests (Singer 1994: 92–7). It is hardly surprising that the threshing floor also becomes the arena for violent resistance. On the threshing floor of Jaba', for example, between Jerusalem and Ramallah, an Ottoman tax collector was knifed while loading the tax grain (Singer 1994: 105).

Even when locations such as threshing floors no longer survive, the site of the food processing can be detected in the landscape by mapping the tools or waste products. The usual threshing implement in the Mediterranean and Middle East from the Early Bronze Age to the 1950s and beyond has been the tribulum or threshing sledge. This consists of a wooden board whose underside is set with rows of chipped stone blades (Anderson and Chabot 2000; P.C. Anderson 2003). It is pulled round the threshing floor by draught animals, usually with someone standing or sitting on it to weigh it down. By

Figure 3.1 Abandoned twentieth-century threshing floor at Mitsero, Cyprus, after cleaning. Photograph: Michael Given.

cutting and crushing the crop it separates the grain from the straw and chaff and simultaneously cuts the straw into appropriate lengths for animal fodder.

Clearly, not many threshing sledges are found in situ, even from very recent periods. The chipped stone blades, however, are very distinctive, and intensive survey can investigate the spatial distribution of threshing by mapping the blades (Given and Knapp 2003: 309). Does all the threshing take place in easily controlled areas round the settlements, for example, or is there food processing taking place in secret beyond the control of the tax collector (chapter 7)? In many complex societies there is a clear tension between centralization and control on one side, and dispersal and resistance on the other.

Measures

With farmer and tax collector both concerned with their share of the produce, it is clear that the equipment used to measure the harvest will be a central focus. The example from St Kilda at the beginning of this chapter is a prime instance. Both sides watch the measuring process like hawks, to see if they are being cheated in any way. The size of the measuring jar, the particular unit of measurement being used, the degree to which the grain is packed down or heaped up, how worn the measuring jar is — all of these become objects of intense scrutiny and negotiation.

Once again an ethnographic example gives the material culture some social context, and demonstrates the enormous cultural and social impact of the taxation process. Gustav Dalman's observations of agricultural processes in Palestine in the early twentieth century give a wealth of detail and thick description (Figure 3.2; Dalman 1933). The whole measuring process is watched by the farmer and the representative of the tithe collector; if there is any disagreement, the measuring must be done again. The best times are midday or sunset. The man doing the measuring must be ritually clean, and kneel facing Mecca, beginning the process with the invocation, 'In the name of God, the compassionate, the merciful'.

The measure itself is made of wood with iron bands, and holds one *sa'* of grain which, depending on the local version being used, is equivalent to between 12.5 and 15.0 litres. After being admonished, 'measure according to God's law!', he fills the measuring jar with both hands, and shakes it sideways to settle it. When it is full the grain is pressed and the jar shaken again to settle the grain, then it is heaped up, usually scraped across the top, and poured into the waiting sack. As in Medieval England, cutting the grain across the top of the measure was generally felt to be more accurate (Brady 1996: 68). The man doing the measuring counts each measure out loud, so it is honoured by God, and everyone else listens in silence (Dalman 1933: 149–51).

In this description the concern with accuracy, fairness and consistency is palpable. The whole operation is conducted in the same way as formal worship and is overseen by God himself, who is witness to any attempts at defrauding the farmer or, presumably, the tithe collector. Dalman's account is somewhat idealized, as if he has asked his informants the proper way of doing the measurement, rather than observing a series of actual measuring operations. Singer's analysis of sixteenth-century court records for the same area shows that the reality could often be much more contentious (1994).

Measuring jars have the enormous archaeological advantage of having consistent sizes. Where there were already standard-sized containers for a particular commodity, these could be reused as measures, such as the 18-litre olive tin used for measuring the grain on the Greek island of Amorgos, observed in 1980 (Halstead and Jones 1989: 46). Others were made specially for the particular measure being used, such as the *sa'* in Ottoman Palestine.

Even without the actual measuring jars, standardized storage or transport containers show that there was careful control over the amounts of produce. During the Late Roman and Byzantine periods transport amphorae were made with increasingly precise and consistent capacities, with separate metric systems for red wine, white wine and oil. Much of this was due to increasingly centralized control over surplus for supplying military bases, though it would certainly have also helped the management of the state *annona*, the collection of taxes in kind (van Alfen 1996).

A similar standardization can be seen in the storerooms of the first-century AD fortress of Masada, on its 360-m high plateau above the Dead Sea (Yadin

Figure 3.2 Measuring wheat on the threshing floor with a wooden *sa'* measure, in the village of el-Bīre, Palestine. Source: Dalman 1933: plate 34.

1966: 96–7). Different storerooms held specific types of storage vessels, depending on their contents, particularly wine, oil and flour. Many of them had Jewish names inscribed on them in ink or charcoal, belonging presumably to the Zionists in their final defence against the Romans in the early 70s AD. As well as the names, several had the Hebrew letter 't', which seems to stand for *truma* or 'priestly due'. Along with another inscription referring specifically to a 'priestly tithe', these suggest that the defenders of the fortress were still paying tithes to their priests, each jar labelled with the tithe-giver's name.

Storage

One of the most striking features about the Masada storerooms was how closely controlled they were, with only a single point of access. In the fortress's previous phase, when it was rebuilt by Herod, a gateway at this point gave access to the storerooms, a large administrative building with its own storage rooms, and to a bath house and Herod's northern palace-villa (Yadin 1966: 103). This demonstrates another vital aspect of the material culture of taxation. Once the produce has been measured and divided, the tithe that is then taken must be stored somewhere both central and secure. As with the location of the crop-processing area, there is a tension between the central control of storage and dispersed resistance and autonomy.

The storage of surplus food clearly plays a central role in complex society. At the most basic level it allows survival through the non-productive seasons of the year, as well as extra risk-buffering. When the surplus is appropriated by an elite they can either hold it for redistribution when needed, use it to pay or feed their support staff, or exchange it for prestige goods. This means that the actual foodstuffs and the mechanisms of their movement and storage are crucial to the relationship between different social groups. When taxes in kind are extracted they must be stored centrally in a state granary or tithe barn, before being redistributed, sold or used for paying members of the state bureaucracy.

Storage has the enormous advantage of being archaeologically visible. Containers, pits and specially designed structures can usually be readily identified, though there are times when the term 'storage' as an explanation for a mysterious pit comes to be almost as used indiscriminately as the proverbial 'ritual' (Strasser 1997: 93). Assuming proper identification, changes in social and economic relations can be charted by means of changing storage patterns. A good example is the gradual integration of semi-nomadic societies on the Kerak plateau in western Jordan into a broader regional economy in the mid-twentieth century (Kana'an and McQuitty 1994). In the late nineteenth and early twentieth centuries, the principal function of settlements such as Al-Qasr was for storage of grain and lentils, while the population took their flocks to warmer areas in winter or to wherever there was good grazing. The buildings of this period are dominated by large-scale storage facilities, many of them built into the structure and filled by pouring grain in from the roof. By the 1940s markets for grain across Transjordan and Palestine were increasing and communications improving. As the societies of the Kerak Plateau were integrated into this economic system, there was a very visible decrease in the capacity of their storage facilities.

Just as important as the functional and economic aspects of storage is its social and moral effect (Hendon 2000). Stored food is a concrete expression of people's role in society. It can embody a head of household's prudence and care, or the power of an elite over its subjects, or the proud memory of a family's hard work during the harvest. We need to see storage not as a narrowly defined economic function of providing risk-buffering, but as a series of practices by which people create their identities within society.

A common social function of storage is that of display. The massive architecture and central location of estate barns in Medieval England demonstrated the authority and wealth of their landlords. Some were up to two and half times the size of what was actually needed: they were commonly the largest and most extravagant building on the estate (Brady 1996: 143–59). This is no static monumentality. The power and wealth of the owner was acted out at each harvest as he or his bailiffs stood at the massive barn entrance, scrutinizing the lines of heavily laden peasants and checking that the barn was properly filled and the correct amount of tithe put aside. Conversely, peasant unrest often focused on this embodiment of oppression and exploitation (Brady 1996: 163–6).

Such domineering architecture is easy to find in the archaeological record, and in chapter 6 I will examine the impact of the massive state granaries of Roman Egypt on the farmers who had to bring their tithes there. So important is the control over storage, however, that it could also be considered to be secret knowledge, and so carefully kept hidden. Maya society shows an interesting tension between these two ethics of storage (Hendon 2000: 45). The lower and middle strands of society displayed most of their stored food in separate, highly visible buildings outside their homes, while the elite keep theirs inside and out of sight. The control of storage has been transformed into a control of knowledge, and only the elite know the resources of both groups.

The converse of this is that people can resist elite control over surplus by hiding some or all of their food stores (chapter 7). African-American slaves used 'root cellars' in their quarters to hide a range of stolen or forbidden foods from the plantation owners and overseers (Kelso 1986), and there are various stories of secret grain pits in early twentieth-century Palestine, Syria and Cyprus, to hide grain from the tithe collectors. This is a natural extension of secret food processing, and is one more aspect of people creating their own social and economic system in the face of imperial or state exploitation.

Administration

Even in pre-modern societies, taxation was often a large-scale and complex operation. Its bureaucratic procedures required a battery of specialized equipment: tax registers, receipts, measuring jars, stamps and seals, offices and warehouses. On top of that was the infrastructure of roads, bridges, harbours and police stations needed to manage the collection and movement of large quantities of tax in kind. All of this material culture became part of people's everyday experience, and was drawn into the oppression, negotiation and resistance that made up taxed society. The emotional impact of an oversized measuring jar or a receipt you could not read was immense, and a contextual study of this material culture is essential to understanding the experience of taxation.

For the state, taxation was an exercise in knowledge. By counting and classifying its subjects it could establish how much surplus it could extract from them, and simultaneously demonstrate its total knowledge and therefore its control. This is the function of an imperial census: ostensibly to assess each community or individual's tax assessment, but actually to impose a grid of unambiguous, restrictive identities (Anderson 1991: 164–70; Given 2002: 3–5).

The material correlate of this control is the tax register. In the famously bureaucratic Byzantine Empire the register for a particular community consisted of a series of 'line-entries', which recorded the person's name, land-holdings, the amount of tax and any exemptions (Brand 1969: 47). Where they survive, such as the *defters* of the Ottoman Empire, such documents are invaluable sources of information about specific communities, the rural economy, and a host of other historical and archaeological issues. But they are also material culture in their own right. The late tenth-century Marcian taxation treatise shows that when a taxpaying individual or institution such as a monastery or old people's home managed to achieve a tax exemption, their line-entry was 'entirely cut out by the roots and cast out of the register of parcels' (quoted in Brand 1969: 51). The material embodiment of its taxable status, in other words, was physically removed.

Writing is clearly central here. Greek mountain villages which managed to avoid being registered by Ottoman census takers were called *agrapha*, 'unwrit-ten' (chapter 7; Clogg 1986: 21). At a much earlier period, the Late Bronze Age palaces of southern Greece equally relied on written records, with the contributions of various subject groups and individuals being recorded on clay tablets (Chadwick 1976: 15–33). Produce paid to the palace became embroiled in the complex machinery of writing-based bureaucracy, which at Pylos in the last year of the palace's life was run by something like 40 literate officials, judging by the numbers of handwriting styles. Tablets counting the same category of products were kept in the correct order in baskets, with the most recent tablet in the series on top of the pile, recording the total of all the others.

Any member of a large state has experienced the alienation caused by bureaucracy and apparently pointless procedures and regulations. This was even greater when only the official elite were literate. It is unclear how directly farmers or shepherds of Late Bronze Age Greece experienced the power of the incomprehensible, all-important tablets. The archives room at Pylos is immediately beside the main entrance and so accessible to those who were not allowed to enter the palace itself, which suggests that the scribes and officials did deal with visitors and those bringing tax payments.

The alienation is much clearer in that other tool of the bureaucratic machine, the receipt. A peasant family has to give up perhaps a third of the crop it has laboured over for a year, and all it gets in return is a piece of paper or, in Roman Egypt, a broken piece of pot, with a series of unintel-ligible signs on it. Perhaps the family is being cheated by the tithe collector. Perhaps a local judge will declare their receipt invalid, and demand they pay their taxes again. They hold the artefact in their hand but are still at the

Figure 3.3 Grain stamp from Kızılkaya, Turkey. 15 cm square. Photograph: Füsun Ertuğ.

mercy of the officials and tax collectors. That receipt is the materialization of the power of the state to rob them of their livelihood.

The enormously rich field of Ottoman archaeology has produced another artefact used in the administration of taxation, which was a tool for the outward display of control and appropriation. This little-known implement is a wooden stamp variously called *çeç mühürü* (grain stamp) in Turkish, *khitm* (stamp or seal) in Arabic, and *sfrayi* (seal) in Greek (Figure 3.3). Such stamps were used by Ottoman tax collectors and harvest supervisors in Anatolia (Ertuğ-Yaraş 1997: 262, 275; Koşay 1951: 13; Yakar 2000: 172), Palestine and Jordan (Abujaber 1989: 63; Dalman 1933: 166–7), and Cyprus (Loïzos Xynaris, Mitsero, interviewed by the author 8 July 1999).

The stamp, typically about 15 cm square, had either an abstract pattern on its underside or, as recorded in Jordan, Koranic phrases such as 'There is no God but God'. This was used to 'seal' the heap, stamping the pattern all over, or else in a strip all round the pile a few centimetres from the bottom. It was immediately obvious if anyone had broken the seal to remove some of the grain before it had been measured and assessed. For those who had produced the grain, it was an outward demonstration that their produce was already in the control of the state.

Variants on these stamps included making patterns by hand, or using the side of a wooden shovel to make a spiral. After the abolition of tithes, such stamps remained in use as protection against thieves, though they may also have had associations with fertility. Similar objects have been found in Early Bronze Age contexts in eastern Anatolia, and these may have had the same functions of controlling the crop, or else producing fertility (Koşay 1976: 190).

For the state to deal with large quantities of tax in kind required not just the administration and control of the crop but its physical movement. It was always a major issue whether the tithe was transported by the taxpayer, by state officials, or by state-paid entrepreneurs. For a farmer of Roman Egypt, a large part of the experience of taxation involved the laborious transport of the tithe to the state granary in the town, or to the harbour on the Nile (chapter 6). Even when the state exchanged the tithe for cash, there had to be facilities for collection, storage and redistribution. A society taxed on a large scale, then, is characterized by a major infrastructure of roads, bridges, harbours, police stations and control posts. For the great imperial organizers such as the Romans and the British, setting up the infrastructure for extracting the tax was the most important part of the 'settlement' of a new province (chapter 4).

The prehistory of taxation: Late Bronze Age Cyprus

With all these processing areas, measuring tools, and the large-scale storage and transport of tithes, the mechanics of taxation should be clearly visible in the archaeological record. To test this, I will examine a prehistoric example from Late Bronze Age Cyprus (c. 1550 to c. 1050 BC). Much of the literature on the organization of society during this period focuses on the role of copper production and the foreign contacts that the copper trade encouraged (Keswani 1996: 219–20; Keswani and Knapp 2003; Knapp *et al.* 1994: 419–29). The recent excavation of central facilities for crop processing, storing and administration, however, suggests that control of agricultural surplus may also have played a major role in social organization.

One commodity which had an economic and social importance as great as that of copper was olive oil (Hadjisavvas 1992). The significance of Cypriot olive oil in the eastern Mediterranean is clearly demonstrated by the number of references to it in Linear B tablets and Akkadian and Ugaritic documents (Knapp 1997: 66–7). Olives require very different work patterns from cereals, and so, like pastoralism, they make an excellent supplementary crop for providing surplus for exchange or taxation (Forbes 1993). They grow well on thin soils and hillslopes which are not as suitable for cereals, and are harvested during late summer, after the cereal harvest but before ploughing.

The peak of the Late Bronze Age in Cyprus, from which most of our data

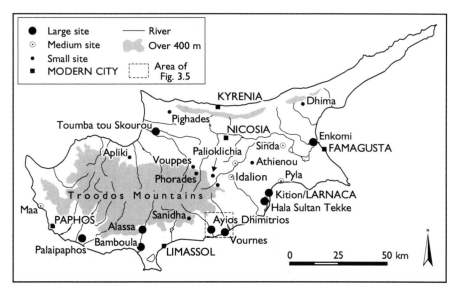

Figure 3.4 Map of Cyprus with Late Bronze Age sites. Source of archaeological data: Knapp 1997: 54.

come, is the Late Cypriot IIC period, running roughly from the late fourteenth to the late thirteenth century BC (Manning *et al.* 2001). The period is characterized by elaborate city plans, extensive trade contacts across the eastern Mediterranean, mass production of copper, and a complex settlement hierarchy. Yet rather than being one single large-scale state, the island was divided into a series of urban centres, each controlling the territory round it (Figure 3.4). Even within many of these polities, authority may have been based on a 'heterarchy' of different elite groups. At Enkomi, for example, the most fully excavated of these centres, there was a series of separate administrative, religious, and industrial compounds; they were not integrated into a single, coherent hierarchy (Keswani 1996: 221–6). A similar heterarchy has also been argued for Middle Minoan II Malia in Crete (Schoep 2002).

Along the south coast of the island the pattern may be rather different. At Kalavasos-Ayios Dhimitrios there is a single, massive administrative building or 'palace' – though only a small percentage of the urban site has been excavated. The same centralized hierarchy is suggested for Alassa and Maroni-Vournes/Tsaroukkas, though in both cases, neither of them by any means fully excavated, separate complexes of administrative buildings have been found a few hundred metres apart (Keswani 1996: 229–33). There are other ways of identifying hierarchy or heterarchy in the material record, and at these south-coast cities there seems to be a real break with the ostentatious and competitive burials of the preceding Late Cypriot IIB period. Many of those tombs were deliberately destroyed and major administrative buildings constructed over them. The memory of aristocratic rivalry is obliterated, and replaced by unified authority with total control over production (Manning 1998a).

Various writers have suggested that local economies in this period depended on staple finance, with agricultural surplus being paid in the form of tribute or tithes to regional centres. Longer-distance payments were probably wealth-finance, in the form of high-value goods (Cadogan 1989: 50; Keswani 1993: 79; Webb and Frankel 1994: 18–19). This is supported by the settlement pattern, with a site hierarchy consisting of urban centres, intermediary settlements for collection and redistribution, and local production sites (Keswani 1993; Knapp 1997: 48–50). Rural sanctuaries may have had a role in legitimizing and controlling this flow of surplus (Knapp 1996; 1997: 54), but it is hard to see any significant spatial patterns with only three examples from this period.

Can an archaeology of taxation help us to understand the mechanics of Late Bronze Age society? What was the experience of the agricultural workers who produced the olive oil and cereals that these hierarchies and heterarchies were based on? Did the elite administrative structures in the urban centres control all the agricultural surplus of their territories? To try to answer these questions I will look at the valleys of the Vasilikos and Maroni rivers on the south coast (Figure 3.5). Both have urban centres with major administrative facilities, and both have been investigated by archaeological survey projects, the Vasilikos Valley Project and the Maroni Valley Archaeological Survey Project respectively.

The area consists of a series of chalk and limestone plateaux which have been cut to form deep valleys and gorges. There is a clear scarp on their southern edge, and below it a broad and flat coastal plain. Within the Vasilikos Valley the river has formed a narrow plain just north of Kalavasos village, but then runs through a gorge which only widens out again just north of Ayios Dhimitrios (Todd *et al.* 1978: 163–4). The rivers run only from late October to early May, and the annual rainfall is typically 400 mm on the coast and 800 mm in the higher reaches – comparatively generous by the standards of the Mesaoria plain in the centre and east of the island (Todd *et al.* 1982: 71–2).

Figure 3.5 shows the settlement hierarchy of the Late Bronze Age, based on the preliminary results of the two survey projects. Almost all sites which have been dated precisely flourished in the Late Cypriot IIC period, and it is highly probable that most of the rest also include components from this period (Todd and South 1992: 203). The Vasilikos Valley Project surveyed its area by means of 19 east–west transects 500 m apart, with two to four people zigzagging across a 100-m wide strip. This was complemented by intuitive, extensive survey (Todd *et al.* 1982: 63–5). The more intensive Maroni Valley Archaeological Survey Project covered 50 × 50 m grid squares with four evenly spaced walkers, mainly east of the river between Tsaroukkas and Maroni, and just north of Psematismenos (Manning *et al.* 1994; 1997: 126–8).

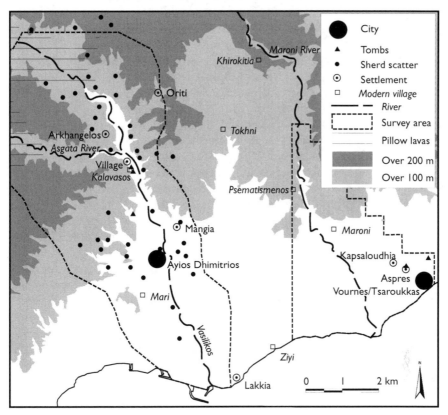

Figure 3.5 The Late Bronze Age in the Vasilikos and Maroni river valleys, south
coast of Cyprus. Sources: Manning 1998a; 1998b; Manning *et al.* 1994;
South 2003; Todd 1988; 1989; Todd and South 1992; Todd *et al.* 1982.

The highest level of the settlement hierarchy is abundantly clear. Kalavasos-
Ayios Dhimitrios was an urban centre up to 450 m across, with domestic
and monumental buildings following a highly organized town plan, including a straight street 3.8 m wide and at least 150 m long (South 1996; 1997).
The most impressive structure to have been excavated is Building X, a monumental building for administration and elite display with extensive olive oil
processing and storage facilities. The two excavation projects of Maroni-
Vournes and Maroni-Tsaroukkas may belong to one large urban centre at
least 500 m across. There are several distinct activity areas: extensive processing and storage facilities for olive oil, cereals and textiles; monumental ashlar
structures; an anchorage; a settlement area; and burials (Cadogan 1989; 1992;
Manning 1998b; Manning and Monks 1998).

The intermediate level, which I have labelled as 'settlement' on the map, is
characterized by substantial evidence for food processing and storage, and

by a settlement of sufficient size to represent a complex of habitations and agricultural installations. Trial excavations at Maroni-Aspres showed part of an olive press and large storage jars, while surface finds from nearby Kapsaloudhia included storage jars, stone tools for grinding or other types of processing, and architectural debris (Manning 1998b). In the Vasilikos Valley there are at least four such sites. That of Arkhangelos, which seems to be continuous between that locality and neighbouring Malouteri, includes a broad and dense scatter of storage jar sherds, of the same type as those found in Building X at Ayios Dhimitrios (Todd 1989: 43). The eight Late Cypriot II tombs at Mangia probably accompanied an agricultural and domestic settlement at Mangia V (Todd and South 1992: 197–8). Oriti is a substantial scatter of local and imported fine ware and pithos fragments of the same types as at Ayios Dhimitrios, well up into a tributary valley of the Vasilikos river (South 2003). Three Late Cypriot II tombs and some structures have been discovered in the modern village of Kalavasos (Todd 1988: 134).

The lowest level of the settlement hierarchy consists of a series of Late Bronze Age sherd scatters of widely varying sizes in the Vasilikos Valley. Some of these may represent farmsteads (South 2002: 62–3, 66; Todd 1988: 135). Others consist of a handful of Late Bronze Age sherds noted during the survey of substantial settlements from other periods. Experience elsewhere in the Mediterranean suggests that there may be similar very low densities of Late Bronze Age sherds in other parts of the survey area, which were not noted because they did not lie among significant sherd scatters from other periods (Bintliff *et al.* 1999). The sherd scatters marked in the Vasilikos Valley may not represent a map of farmsteads, but they do indicate a minimum distribution of rural activity such as cultivation, movement and small-scale or intermittent settlement.

The key to interpreting this distribution is the control of resources. Some activity is clearly associated with the copper ores in the pillow lavas to the north-west, though part of this area was inaccessible to the surveyors. There is a coppersmith's workshop in Building IX at Ayios Dhimitrios and a certain amount of slag throughout the settlement, though nothing on a large scale has been discovered (South 1989: 320). Much more obvious is the focus on agricultural resources, both on the coastal plain and in the upper, broader part of the Vasilikos Valley north of Kalavasos. These are areas of alluvial soils, reasonable water flow, and easy access, much of it suitable for cereals and all of it highly suitable for olives (Christodoulou 1959: 172). Given the survey's east–west transects, the pattern of sherd scatters keeping to the lower slopes of the valley is likely to be a real one; it is particularly pronounced in the central part of the Vasilikos Valley.

The south coast of Cyprus is often suggested as an example of urban centres controlling resources directly, rather than via distant intermediaries (Cadogan 1989: 49; Keswani 1996; Muhly 1989). This clearly applies to copper mining, as the ore sources in the pillow lavas are in most cases much

Figure 3.6 Kalavasos-Ayios Dhimitrios: north-east area (LCIIC). Circles are pithoi
and pithos bases; grey walls are robbed out; hatched walls pre-date
LCIIC. Source: Alison South.

closer to coastal cities than they are in the north or east. For agriculture,
the key question is where the processing and storage was taking place. In
eighteenth-century Scotland, there was a clear hierarchy of grain mills, with
large mills equipped with vertical wheels serving wide areas, smaller horiz-
ontal mills based in townships, and individual households using rotary
querns. Which of these you used depended on how closely the estate controlled and taxed the processing of the grain (Dodgshon 1998: 217).

In the Vasilikos and Maroni Valleys, the usual assumption is that the
processing of olive oil was controlled by the urban centres. Buildings X and
XI in Ayios Dhimitrios certainly have facilities on a large scale (Figure 3.6;
South 1992; 1997). Building X is a monumental, well-built structure for

45

administration, storage and elite residence. The most striking elements are the two large halls in the south-west and north-west containing over 65 giant storage jars, each with a capacity ranging from 580 to 1,200 litres. Gas chromatography of 19 samples shows that some or all of these jars contained olive oil, with a total capacity for the building of something like 50,000 litres (Keswani 1992). The two olive presses were in a room between the two halls and in Building XI immediately across the street to the west. The remains consist of a press weight, fragments of grinding and crushing equipment, numerous carbonized olive pits, and pebble floors with rough channels leading into a collection tank. The tank from Building X has been robbed out, but that in Building XI is cut from a single piece of sandstone weighing about 3.5 tons and holding 2,065 litres.

The precision of these capacity measurements allows some calculations about production and consumption rates. The excavator suggests that both installations working intensively during the harvest season could have produced far more than the 50,000 litres the building could store (South 1996: 43). If so, it would be tempting to see the building as providing pressing facilities for the whole Vasilikos Valley and taking a proportion of the oil as payment, as was done by the church-owned olive presses of the Ottoman period. This does not seem to be substantiated by the figures. David Mattingly has reviewed ethnographic sources, Roman writers and the remains of Roman period olive presses in North Africa, and it is clear that a large lever press worked intensively could produce no more than about 10,000 litres of oil a year (Mattingly 1988a). Assuming the Late Bronze Age presses at Ayios Dhimitrios were smaller, less efficient, and were worked less intensively, even the two presses working together would fill only a quarter of the building's storage jars.

How many olive trees could these presses support? Again, Mattingly's figures allow some very rough calculations (1988b: 37). In a good year the two presses could perhaps produce as much as 15,000 litres. Historical and ethnographic yield measurements vary from 3.4 to 28 litres of oil per tree, which would mean between 535 and 3,750 trees. With unintensive production and the possible use of some wild olive trees in the Late Bronze Age, the number is likely to be at the lower end of the scale; say 1,000 trees. Taking a very low density figure of 20 trees per hectare, this is only 50 hectares, or a circle with a radius of 400 m.

Clearly, the area serviced by the two olive presses could have been much larger or smaller than 50 hectares, depending on the precise circumstances of Late Bronze Age olive cultivation. Equally clearly, there is no way in which the presses of Buildings X and XI could have serviced the entire Vasilikos Valley. This suggestion that production units were relatively small is supported by the archaeological evidence. There are small presses in two other buildings at Ayios Dhimitrios, probably for olives, and substantial concentrations of pithos sherds in other parts of the site. Buildings X and XI were not the only centres within the town which were processing olives from the valley.

Olive presses have also been found at Vournes, Tsaroukkas and the smaller settlement of Aspres (Hadjisavvas 1992: 21; Manning 1998b: 45–6, 50–3). None of the other settlements have been excavated, but all those marked on Figure 3.5, other than the structures and tombs found in Kalavasos village, have extensive scatters of large storage jars. As the map shows, they are typically 1 or 2 km from each other, which implies an agricultural catchment of about the scale I am suggesting. The urban centres did not have a monopoly on the processing of olive oil or other agricultural commodities.

There is also the question of scale. Were Building X at Ayios Dhimitrios and the similar Ashlar Building at Vournes really 'palaces' with 'kings', which controlled the production of mini-kingdoms, just like Middle Bronze Age Knossos and Late Bronze Age Mycenae in Greece (Karageorghis 1998: 48)? Or were they just two out of many small-scale individual estates? Or perhaps they were something in between, small-scale polities with substantial towns and a relatively complex social organization (South 2002: 67–8).

Some figures from the Medieval period provide some interesting comparisons with Building X's 50,000 litres of storage. When Guy d'Ibelin, the bishop of Limassol, died in 1367, a complete inventory was made of his property. Liquids were stored in giant storage jars, not unlike those of the Late Bronze Age, and his main residence in Nicosia and his three small rural estates had a total storage capacity of 65,671 litres, of which 44,969 were specifically for wine (Richard 1950). Similarly, the substantial rural estate of Psimolophou stored 53,436 litres of wine in 1318 to distribute to its staff (Richard 1947: 129, 144). Ayios Dhimitrios Building X seems to be about the size of an average Medieval estate.

The 'heterarchy' suggested by Keswani for other parts of Late Bronze Age Cyprus may also be applicable to the Vasilikos and Maroni Valleys. Vournes and Tsaroukkas show several processing and administrative structures separated by 500 m, which is not dissimilar to Enkomi, with its imposing self-contained ashlar mansions dispersed across the city (Keswani 1996: 224–7). Based on the excavator's estimate of the total city area, only between 7 and 10 per cent of Ayios Dhimitrios has been excavated (Todd *et al.* 1989: Figure 2). Even from this small percentage, there are traces of at least four other ashlar structures across the site, though the best examples seem to be in the north-eastern area, including Building X (South 2003). The same pattern of individual estates spreads across the landscape, with intermediate level sites such as Arkhangelos and Kapsaloudhia controlling local agricultural production.

Once again, Medieval Cyprus provides a useful parallel. The main cities, Nicosia and Famagusta, each had many imposing complexes where a host of different noblemen and prelates controlled the produce of their estates and led ostentatious lifestyles: the king, the church, the Templars, the Hospitallers, particular monasteries, private individuals. This was mirrored by another series of estates in the countryside, similarly controlled by the state, the church, the religious orders, or private landowners. The royal palace was only one 'palace' out of many.

So there is no evidence from the Vasilikos and Maroni Valleys in the Late Cypriot IIC period for centralized state-controlled taxation. This is a major contrast to the palaces of Mycenaean Greece, and explains why no archive rooms full of tablets recording taxation income have been found in Cyprus. This does not mean, however, that there was no taxation, or that there was no struggle for the control of surplus.

The 50,000 litres of storage in Building X represent a substantial surplus, assuming in normal years that the producers were allowed to keep enough of their produce for their own subsistence. A few inscribed stone lids for storage jars suggest that the bureaucrats were labelling and keeping track of the contents (South 1989: 322). A set of bronze and stone weights discovered in Building III shows that the inhabitants of Ayios Dhimitrios may have participated in one or more Near Eastern metrological systems (Courtois 1983: 128). Elsewhere on the island, there are intriguing stamped impressions on storage jars from sites associated with the control of agricultural produce, such as the rural estate of Analiondas-Palioklichia or the olive oil processing plant at Maa. These seem to be associated with controlling a proportion of the surplus reserved for particular individuals or institutions (Webb and Frankel 1994: 18–19).

The farmers and fieldworkers of the Vasilikos and Maroni Valleys clearly had to surrender much of their surplus to the elites who controlled the monumental administrative buildings. They did not have to transport the heavy produce any further than 500 or 1,000 m, assuming that was the purpose of the processing and storage facilities at intermediate settlements such as Malouteri and Kapsaloudhia. Even so, for those whose produce was controlled by the elites of Ayios Dhimitrios, Vournes and Tsaroukkas, it meant a trip with animal-loads of olives or grain into the imposing, straight streets of the town and up to the monumental walls of the ashlar building that controlled their subsistence and well-being. As with the grain farmers of Ottoman Palestine or the islanders of eighteenth-century St Kilda, the results of their labour were taken, measured and processed, and then poured into the vast storage jars in the ashlar halls.

4

THE SETTLEMENT OF EMPIRE

In the mountains of southern Phrygia, just beyond the headwaters of the Maeander river, a man and a boy were leading a string of laden mules along the edge of a stone-paved road. Some fifteen kilometres behind them was the city of Apollonia, location of a regional customs office. Another fifteen kilometres in front of them was the city of Apamea, a major market town, assize centre and communications hub. The mules' hoofs beat dully on the dusty track that ran along beside the broad margin stones of the imperial paved road.

The boy looked up from the track to the ridge line in front of them, and saw a deep notch where the engineered road cut through the crest, and up above it on its left, a tall pillar or cairn. As they came slowly closer, he could see that the cutting was only just wide enough for the paved road, sending their track curling up to the left. They followed it up and stood by the stone pillar, looking westwards at the wide vista which was suddenly revealed to them. Just beyond the further ridge was Apamea, their destination, but in front of it there were marshes filling the entire basin. The road skirted around the edge of it to the right. A garrison at the narrowest point was full of Roman soldiers, who were all too happy to plunder anyone passing along the road.

The boy turned and looked up at the massive pillar towering above them. It stood on a three-stepped base 2 metres across and 1 metre high, with the pillar itself another 2 metres above that. In its central section was a flat panel into which had been carved 17 lines of Greek letters, each of them 4 cm high.

'What does it say?', asked the boy, his eyes wide with awe and curiosity. The man glared suspiciously up at the lines of marching letters. 'It says,' he growled, 'may the gods protect us on our way, and bring punishment to all bandits, soldiers, and toll collectors.'

An imperial power which has just acquired a new province faces the huge task of organizing the territory and implementing its power. In the British Empire, particularly as it incorporated the princely states of India into the Raj, this was known as 'settlement' (Cohn 1996: 3–8). Once the new imperial power has quelled any substantial military resistance, it needs to carry out some sort of census or survey to evaluate what it has acquired, make sure that necessary communications systems are in place, and above all set up a system for the extraction of surplus by means of taxation. This 'settlement' is the material face of the colonial project as a whole: the creation of order, government and infrastructure, often with the ideological trappings of paternalism and altruism.

In this chapter I will examine the impact of imperial control on the landscape, as expressed in communications, settlement patterns and land use. Most of it will be taken up with the roads, settlements and rural spaces of south-western Anatolia under the early Roman Empire, during the first two centuries AD. In particular, I wish to show how imperial domination was experienced by the people who actually lived and worked in the landscape. What did it mean to travel on (or beside) a new Roman road, or see a temple dedicated to the Roman emperor dominating the skyline of your city? What were the opportunities, challenges and constraints of becoming a provincial in someone else's empire, rather than being at the centre of your own world?

Becoming provincial

One constant reminder of an external power was the road that led there and brought its representatives into your world. At the most practical level, road networks allow imperial troops and administrators access and penetration into their new territory. After the Jacobite uprising of 1715, for example, the English general George Wade constructed a network of military roads and barracks across the Scottish Highlands. Thanks to the efficient communications and troop movements that they allowed, he was able to implement the English government's disarmament orders and carry out what his original instructions referred to as 'the good settlement of that part of the Kingdom' (Taylor 1976: 17–23).

There is much more to an imperial road than the troop movements that take place on it. Its military construction and use can make it a symbol of occupation and oppression. Many highlanders refused to use Wade's roads: they walked through the heather beside them, and waded across the river beside the bridges (Taylor 1976: 125). My discussion of the theories of agency and practice in chapter 2 is relevant here. Individual agents can choose to travel on a road, or beside it, or along a different route entirely. Are people habitually commuting to their fields along paths and tracks radiating out from their nucleated village, as in Medieval Europe or the tells of Bronze Age Mesopotamia? Have they appropriated the military roads of their occupiers for their own purposes of travelling and trade? Do they deliberately avoid them, or ambush those who travel on them? These are the sorts of experiences that we need to reconstruct from the archaeological and historical record.

The experience of travelling through an imperial landscape is punctuated by points of control: garrisons, forts, checkpoints, customs posts. Many are intended as powerful reminders of raw military power. The fortified garrisons that Wade built across the Highlands in the 1720s were standardized in plan and immediately recognizable. The impact these made is very clear in the case of Ruthven Barracks near Kingussie, sited prominently on a spur above the road. Smaller facilities such as checkpoints or border posts can also interrupt the experience of travel and subject the traveller to the machinery of imperial control: from the checking of papers and identity cards, to the extraction of numerous tolls and customs dues, to the technically illegal but still common extortion of bribes. As with the imperial roads, people can decide to attack them, exploit them for their own purposes, or just avoid them entirely.

After establishing military control, the biggest single imperial effort was the construction of the machinery for extracting surplus wealth. This was totally dependent on the communications system. Officials and inspectors needed access to the main nodes of tax collection, while the police or military had to be able to punish defaulters promptly and efficiently. Tax in kind required an enormous investment in infrastructure, including collection points, tithe barns, reliable roads, vehicles and animals, markets and harbours. As I argued in chapter 3, being taxed was the dominant aspect of the experience of imperial rule.

Monte Testaccio in Rome gives some idea of the scale of this extraction of surplus. This is a pottery dump from the first 250 years AD, lying outside the warehouses which held goods brought up the Tiber from the main port at Ostia. It consists of the remains of almost 25 million olive oil amphorae, most of them from the Spanish province of Baetica. This represents some 7,000,000 kg of olive oil a year (Rodríguez 1998: 197). The machinery of production, taxation, commerce and transport which created this resource was an imperial project of the highest order.

What effect does imperial control have on the settlement pattern of the province? The demand for surplus encourages intensive agriculture on fertile and well-watered land, often in the form of large estates working on an almost industrial scale. In colonial situations these can be worked by settlers from the imperial metropolis, who are generally given the most productive land. Important road junctions and administrative centres attract settlers, and often develop into new or enlarged settlements. By contrast, many people choose to live away from the cities or main roads, following the tradition of their family or community, or else because of their occupation, political beliefs or identity. There is often a tension in the settlement pattern between centralization and dispersal, between keeping to the main roads and good land, and deliberately spurning them.

As with all such landscape studies, we have to look beyond the cities, elite sites and major roads to what lies beyond them, so often represented by blank spaces on the map. For our case study in Roman Anatolia, we start with the roads, garrisons, accessible arable land and administrative centres, and then move away to what lies beyond them. Because of the way archaeology has been practised in Turkey over the last hundred years or so, most of our evidence for rural areas is limited to monuments and inscriptions, with occasional small sites mapped or described by extensive survey projects.

On the road in Roman Anatolia

The history of the vast and varied Anatolian peninsula during the Roman period is one of ongoing 'settlement' (Figure 4.1; S. Mitchell 1993). It began when Attalus III of Pergamon died in 133 BC, bequeathing his kingdom to Rome and so providing the core of what became the Roman province of Asia. Seventy years later Pompey defeated Mithridates of Pontus, and immediately set about creating city territories and incorporating the territory into the new province of 'Bithynia et Pontus'. This has become universally known in the English language literature as 'Pompey's settlement of the East'. Similarly, when Rome's client king Amyntas of Galatia was killed in action against the intractable Homonadeis in 25 BC, Augustus decided to annex his kingdom and create the new province of Galatia. And so it went on. As rebellions were subdued and client kings died, more territory was annexed and had to be 'settled'.

Settlement had military, judicial and administrative aspects. Even after new territories had been conquered or otherwise acquired, there were still groups who hung determinedly on to their autonomy. Cicero as governor of Cilicia in 51–50 BC, for example, had to campaign in the Amanus range in the east of his province, which he described as 'a mountain range full of enemies of Rome from time immemorial' (*Letters to Atticus* 5.20.3). A governor's other main responsibility was judicial, and consisted mainly of travelling round the country holding assizes. As much of the local administration as possible was carried out by the cities, including taxation, policing and public works. This was why Pompey's first task in Pontus was to divide it up into 11 city territories and create cities where there were none before. Once the system was in place, urban elites who benefited greatly in wealth and prestige from Roman rule could do the day-to-day administration. All the governor and his staff had to do was to check abuses in the law courts and make sure the territory was properly pacified.

Roads were crucial for all of this. The Roman General Wade was Manius Aquillius, who carried out the settlement of the new province of Asia after the death of Attalus III in 133 BC (Lintott 1993: 30–1; S. Mitchell 1999: 18–21). The focus of this activity was the building of a network of roads radiating out from the *caput viae* or 'head of the road' at Ephesos. Seven of his milestones are known, with inscriptions such as 'Manius Aquillius son of Manios, consul of the Romans, 223'. This example was found 50 km south-

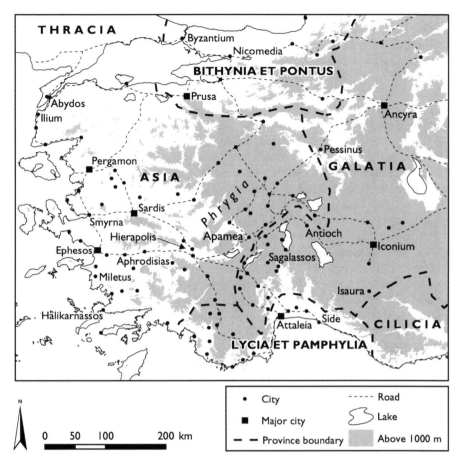

Figure 4.1 Map of western and central Anatolia in the first and second centuries AD.
Sources: Calder and Bean 1958; French 1988; S. Mitchell 1993: 120, 130.

west of Apamea, 223 Roman miles from Ephesos (French 1980: 707, 714). A
standard Roman highway in Anatolia was about 8 m wide, with paving stones
laid directly on the earth or rock. They sloped outwards from a central *spina*
or spine of slightly protruding uprights, with larger stones binding the edge
(French 1980: 704).

How much did these roads direct the experience of the people who travelled on them? As soon as travellers set foot on the great paving slabs, were
they swept up into an inescapable network of Roman control and domination, every mile marked by the name of a governor or emperor? Or did they
incorporate them into their own world view, or resist them in some way?

For those who constructed them, the experience of these roads was one of
bodily domination. The building of the 9,000 km or so of Roman highways in

Anatolia was far too expensive and labour-intensive for the Roman army to carry out, or for the Roman state to finance. Most of them were built by the cities whose territories they crossed. Even so, the costs were far too great for these communities to pay wages to the workers. The principal method was forced labour (S. Mitchell 1993: 126–7). Stephen Mitchell compares figures from the nineteenth century, when for the province of Erzerum 742 km of highway were built and maintained by the forced labour of just over 250,000 people. This came to more than 23 per cent of the province's population (S. Mitchell 1993: 127). An offhand and hopelessly unrealistic comment by a provincial governor from the second century AD covers a potential nightmare of forced labour and harsh conditions: 'There are plenty of people in the countryside, and many more in the town, and it seems certain that they will all gladly help with a scheme which will benefit them all' (Pliny, *Letters* 10.41).

Travel was clearly a constant activity and preoccupation among the population of Roman Anatolia. To take an example from popular culture, this is very evident in the dice oracles common throughout the south-west. These oracles give advice and prophecies based on the 56 combinations produced by five dice. In a typical example, that from Cremna in Pisidia, 28 of these responses are concerned with travel: whether the questioner should travel, or what is happening to a friend or relative away from the city (Horsley and Mitchell 2000: 22–38). This is hardly surprising, given the extent of long- and short-distance trade, the administration and law courts in regional centres, and the importance of periodic markets in the rural economy. Being on the road was a major part of many people's lives.

The roadside monument with which I began this chapter illustrates the problems of reconstructing people's experiences (Figure 4.2). My fictional muleteers are clearly illiterate; the man appropriated the inscription and used it to protect himself against the enemies he expected to meet on the road. Any literate members of the urban elite would have made a very different reading, assuming they could be bothered to stop and read it. The first 12 of the 17 lines are taken up with the titles of the Emperor Hadrian and a wish for his safety and well-being. The rest explains that the pillar was put up by the council and people of the Apollonians, and is dedicated to the 'boundary gods' (Christol and Drew-Bear 1987: 16). The monument, in other words, indicates the boundary between the territory of Apollonia and Apamea, which at this period was also the boundary between the provinces of Galatia and Asia.

Different groups are clearly going to have different attitudes to this monument, and we can only interpret it with a wide knowledge of its social context. To the pro-Roman aristocrats who built imperial temples and passed decrees honouring the emperor and his officials, this is one more profession of loyalty, and the road along which they are travelling is one of the practical benefits of Roman rule that the orators loved to extol. To peasant farmers who rarely visited the city and could read Greek with difficulty or not at all, it

Figure 4.2 The boundary stone of the Apollonians, on the road between Apollonia and Apamea. Source: Christol and Drew-Bear 1987: 15–16: plate 2 (with the permission of the Österreichische Akademie der Wissenschaften). Drawing: Lorraine McEwan.

looked more like a sanctuary dedication or gravestone, and so inspired some vague act of piety or prayer for protection, much needed amid all the dangers of travelling. To a road gang sent out by the aristocratic council of Apollonia, it was a welcome sight, marking the end of their stint and the point where their opposite numbers from Apamea took over.

Many people, particularly those travelling by horse, donkey or mule, quite deliberately chose to avoid the road, and walked along a dirt track at its side. To the wife of a British district commissioner in late nineteenth-century Cyprus, this was a sign of stupidity or ingratitude:

> The Engineers have made a capital causeway, which, however, is little used; the natives, it will hardly be conceived, actually preferring to go out of their way, and make a new road for themselves over corn-fields or uncultivated lands, as the case may be. But it takes a great deal both of time and patience to drill anything into a Cypriote brain.
>
> Scott-Stevenson 1880: 137

To anyone with more practical knowledge, the hard paving stones were unsuitable for lightly shod animals, and anyone riding or leading pack animals travelled along the edge of the road (S. Mitchell 1993: 134). Few rural Roman roads have been excavated, but a rare example from south of Paris revealed sandy tracks about 1.5 m wide on each side of the road metalling (Chevalier 1976: 93).

The worst aspect of the Roman road experience was living beside it. The official traffic was constant. Governors and their long retinues travelled from one assize town to the next. Procurators in charge of logistics and army supplies rushed backwards and forwards arranging grain shipments and clothing for the military. Lines of requisitioned wagons carried those shipments across the province. And then there were the troop movements: troops on campaign, troops moving to new quarters, troops being replaced by an incoming legion. The economy of the Roman administration and army depended on all of these officials and soldiers being fed and housed by the people who were unlucky enough to live along the road.

Most of our knowledge about this practice comes from the edicts of governors trying to stop the constant abuses. A particularly good example comes from Burdur, on the eastern edge of the territory of Sagalassos in Pisidia (S. Mitchell 1976). The stone is a grey marble slab framed with pilasters and a pediment, and publishes an edict of Sotidius Strabo, governor of Galatia in about AD 15. According to its inscription, the people of Sagalassos had to provide wagons and either mules or donkeys to provincial officials, military officers, and visiting Roman senators and knights. This applied between the cities of Cormasa and Conana, in other words while in the territory of Sagalassos (Figure 4.3). In an effort to stop the evident abuses of the system, a clear maximum was set for the numbers of wagons and mules to be supplied, depending on the rank of the official. Private persons transporting grain or anything else were specifically excluded from receiving free transport.

The long inscription is in Latin as well as Greek, and so is clearly aimed at Roman officials and the inhabitants of the various Roman colonies. It was not found in situ, but according to the text the same inscription was set up in

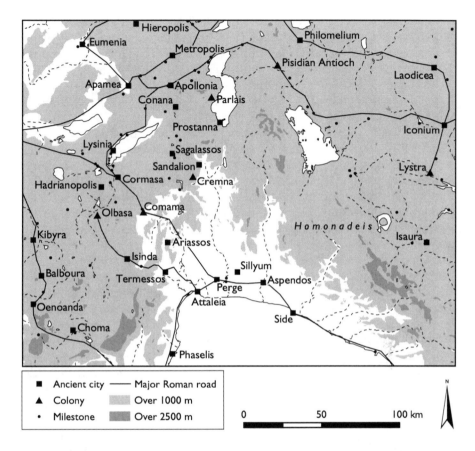

Figure 4.3 Map of Pisidia and Pamphylia. Sources: French 1988; S. Mitchell 1993;
Waelkens and Loots 2000.

'the individual towns and villages' of Sagalassos. The overt intention is that
local people are protected from abuses by full publication of the law, so that
both they and the travelling officials know the limits of what has to be provided. Even so, these large and imposing inscriptions in the centre of each
community are all too visible reminders of the obligations of being on the
colonizers' road.

The military were continually moving along the road, but they were also
permanently stationed on it. Every day's journey or so the traveller would
pass a garrison or gendarme-post, normally called *stationes*. As usual, we
know about them from the constant complaints and occasional attempts to
rectify abuses (Lintott 1993: 125–6; S. Mitchell 1993: 122–4; cf. Corbier
1983). These *stationarii* or rural gendarmes had a variety of functions, ranging
from patrolling the roads to collecting taxes in kind, to taking fines for the

violations of tombs, and in general maintaining law and order in the country-side. With relatively small and isolated detachments, the opportunities for extortion and abuse were legion. By the third and fourth centuries AD the paying of protection money to local soldiers had evolved into a system of military patronage, where, for a price, the soldiers would intercede for villagers and protect them from abuses by other soldiers or officials (S. Mitchell 1998: 60–2).

The road from Apollonia to Apamea passes the boundary stone on the crest, skirts down the side of a spur to the floor of the alluvial basin, and turns sharply north, squeezed between the mountainside and what were then marshes covering the basin floor. At the narrowest point, best placed to control the traffic and beside some excellent springs, was the garrison of Aulutrene (Christol and Drew-Bear 1987: 33–4). Some 27 squared blocks of local limestone show the outline of a structure about 20 m square, and early travellers described a building with three aisles separated by arches. This structure may actually have been Byzantine, but if so was certainly built on the remains of its second-century AD predecessor.

These remains are identified as the *castellum* of Aulutrene by an inscribed limestone altar removed from the site, 1.30 m high and dating to between AD 198 and 209 (Christol and Drew-Bear 1987: 34–42). The Latin inscription dedicates it to Jupiter Optimus Maximus and Juno, and professes the soldiers' loyalty to the imperial house. The garrison consisted of the commander Nonius Felix, a second-in-command and seven other legionaries from two different legions. This narrow corridor between marsh and mountain, then, is a characteristic node of Roman control, the arena for a variety of oppressions, intimidations, negotiations and evasions.

A major function of the main roads of Roman Anatolia was the extraction of surplus by means of taxation. As with most provincial Roman administrations, the system depended on delegating the collection of taxes to outsiders who could do the work, take the risks, and make a profit if they were able. In broad terms, villagers and city-dwellers alike paid tax via their cities. Members of the city's elite could take on the tax collection as a 'liturgy' or public duty. As they were liable for the amount owed, they could suffer spectacular losses (Corbier 1991: 231–2). More normally, taxation was tendered out for periods of five years to *publicani* or tax-farmers, who ran substantial and sophisticated companies with partners, directors and a range of local representatives (Lintott 1993: 86–91). With such an indirect system, opportunities for abuse were manifold.

Even in the first two centuries AD, when taxes across the Roman Empire were commonly collected in cash, it seems that many taxes in Asia Minor were collected in kind (S. Mitchell 1998: 63; cf. Hopkins 1980). With at least 80 per cent of the economy being firmly rural, there was simply not enough cash to send annual deliveries of it to Rome. The increasing military presence, particularly with Anatolia being the road to numerous campaigns in the east, meant that there was a huge demand for food, clothing and equipment, and above all for grain.

As I discussed in chapter 3, taxation in kind requires a huge investment in the machinery for delivery, storage and transport. Even the purchase of grain for the military required a similar system. Across Anatolia, in addition to the gendarmes' *stationes*, there was a network of *mansiones* on the main roads. These were collection points for the tithes, manned by the *frumentarii* or 'grain commissars', to become notorious in the third and fourth centuries AD as the empire's secret service (S. Mitchell 1993: 245–53; 1998: 60–1). Transport of such quantities of grain was too onerous and expensive for individual cities, tax companies or even legions. As with providing transport for officials and their revenues, it fell to villagers and townspeople to cart the army's grain along the roads that crossed their city's territory.

Travel on the roads was also marked by a series of tolls and dues imposed by cities and provincial administrations. Travellers had to pay duties on merchandise at city gates, tolls on bridges and main roads, transit dues at city boundaries, and customs dues at provincial boundaries (de Laet 1949: 273–81; Lintott 1993: 83–5). As with tax collection, *custodiae* or customs posts were run by societies, who usually appointed slaves as the collectors. The manager of the Apollonia office, a regional headquarters, was buried in a fine, though not quite finished, marble sarcophagus, apparently paid for by his staff (Pflaum 1975).

Long abuse by the customs companies led to the full publication of the imperial regulations in AD 62. They were recorded and displayed on a marble slab found re-used in the church of St John in Ephesos (Engelmann and Knibbe 1989). This slab was originally 3.15 × 1.47 m, with one side covered in letters between 1.0 and 1.5 cm high and the other set against a wall. As with the Apollonia boundary marker, this had a two-edged message. By publishing the regulations it helped to stop excessive demands and extortion by officials. Simultaneously, this great wall of writing was a concrete reminder of the complex web of regulations that enmeshed the inhabitants of the province.

Customs collectors clearly needed to control the traffic, so they could only let through those who had paid their dues plus whatever bribes might be demanded. Termessos in the south-west of Anatolia was one city that was particularly keen to control the traffic that climbed up to its mountainous site or passed through the valley below. In 68 BC the *Lex Antonia de Termessis* made it a free city, exempt from the demands of Roman tax collectors, and able to control its own territory and tax those passing through, with the exception of tax-farmers transporting taxation in kind (S. Mitchell 1994: 102).

Down below Termessos, a fortification wall with ten towers and a substantial gate crosses the narrowest part of the valley, which was the route of the main road going east from Attaleia (Winter 1966: 127–32). Although its original function in the Late Hellenistic period is most likely to have been defensive, it was the obvious place to collect customs dues from travellers in transit through the city's territory. Some 45 minutes' walk up the mountain-side, half-way towards the city itself, is another gate, blocking the narrow road between the mountainside above and the cliff below. It probably dates to the late second century AD, and is too isolated to have any military value. Its most likely function was a toll-gate, to collect dues from those who were entering the city proper (Winter 1966: 132–6).

As with other inevitabilities such as the weather or the growth of the crops or religious festivals, the experience of Roman rule came in cycles. The post-harvest tithes had the greatest impact, of course. But the other event which structured the impact of imperial control was the governor's assizes, those 'yearly visitations stirring up Asia' (Plutarch, *Moralia* 501F: Burton 1975; S. Mitchell 1999: 22–9). A variety of major and middle-ranking cities had assize status, and the governor and his entourage would travel to them in turn, trying cases and hearing petitions from the people of the region. This was where the symbols and realities of Roman power were displayed: the basilica in which the cases were heard, the governor's tribunal, his *fasces* or rods of office, and the governor himself in official dress.

Dio Chrysostom, writing in the early second century AD, gives an idea of the broader impact the assizes had, talking about the city of Apamea:

> The assizes are held here every other year, and a countless number of people gathers here, litigants, jurors, speakers, magistrates, servants, slaves, pimps, grooms, merchants, whores, craftsmen, so that retailers sell their wares at the highest prices, and nothing in the city goes idle, animals, horses, or women. Now that brings great prosperity, for where the largest number of persons congregates, that is necessarily where the most money is to be found, and the place naturally thrives.
>
> Dio Chrysostom, *Oration* 35.15–16, trans. Jones 1978: 67

Because of all this associated social and economic activity, assize centres became major nodes in the road network and a second rank in the settlement hierarchy, after provincial capitals such as Ephesos and Ancyra. They complemented the roads in giving material expression to the intermittent, reactive and very localized nature of Roman executive power in the provinces. People met with Roman authority in the public spaces of the cities, during the assizes, and above all on the road. This gave them the opportunity of finding their own spaces and times away from that authority: outside the city, between the assizes, and off the road.

Off the road in Roman Anatolia

The urban centres that dominate the discussions of Roman Anatolia are only one part, even a minor part, of the lives and experiences of the people of the time. Even when we add the highways, garrisons, road stations and other arenas of Roman power, there were many areas in the local landscape where these were irrelevant or peripheral. Central and western Anatolia had a strong tradition of rural communities, with nucleated villages and shared social institutions. The 'first man in the village' was a far more influential figure in most people's lives than the provincial governor, toll collector or gendarme (MacMullen 1988: 58–9).

One indicator of the strong rural initiative that continued to define communities and create identities consists of the local languages whose use persisted right through the imperial period. Many tribal groupings in more mountainous areas fought the Romans, continued a determinedly rural existence, and spoke languages incomprehensible to Roman ruler and Greek city-dweller alike (S. Mitchell 1993: 172–6). The Homonadeis in the Pisidian mountains, who killed the last Galatian king, Amyntas, are one such group; their neighbours, the Isaurians, are another. Pisidian, Lycaonian, Solymian and Lycian also continued to be spoken.

Many of these language-users chose to appropriate some aspects of Greek, particularly for the purposes of inscribing gravestones and dedications to their gods. Their selectiveness is shown in spelling and grammar – and, presumably, pronunciation – which would have made their 'Greek' almost as incomprehensible to a city-dweller as their native language. The range and strength of stereotypes expressed by the urban literate classes show how alien they considered these rural dwellers to be (Hopwood 1983: 179–80).

Because of the nature of our sources, agriculture and settlement tend to be the most representative and useful indicators of rural activity. Settlements have the added advantage that they are easily identifiable in the archaeological record. As in many colonized countries, the organization of agriculture in Anatolia shows a tension between large-scale estate-based production and much smaller-scale peasant farming.

The estates are well-documented in the literary and epigraphic evidence (S. Mitchell 1993: 149–58). Influential Italian settlers, local aristocrats and the Roman emperor himself built up large and semi-autonomous estates, which produced cash crops such as wheat, barley and wool. These were usually run by agents who were freed slaves, and the labour was supplied by the villages lying within the estate boundaries. Fertile land nearer the city, best-placed for feeding urban populations, was clearly more in demand than very distant land, and tended to be divided into smaller parcels than the more distant estates, and controlled by the urban elite.

Estates can be identified in the archaeological record by means of unexpectedly large quantities of elite goods, monumental architecture and large-scale agricultural processing machinery in relation to the size of the site. The Sagalassos project in northern Pisidia carried out an extensive, site-based survey between 1993 and 1996, mostly using local information to identify sites in the territory of the major Roman city of Sagalassos (Vanhaverbeke and Waelkens 2003). Of the 41 Roman-period sites over 10,000 m² discovered by the project, other than Sagalassos itself, some 23 stand out for the numbers of monumental tombs, ashlar architecture and large olive presses. These suggest the presence of a major landholder, controlling large-scale agricultural production and using the surplus to display his high status (Vanhaverbeke 2003: 244–6).

The other 18 large sites in the Sagalassos territory without high-status artefacts and remains are more likely to be settlements of peasant smallholders or, more likely, tenant farmers. Even the 28 small, special-purpose farmsteads discovered by the project were all on or near the best arable land and commonly had large-scale agricultural facilities such as olive and wine presses and grain mills, as well as substantial buildings with ashlar masonry and window glass. These are much more likely to be small estates or outposts of larger ones than to belong to individual smallholders.

A typical example is the one at Dikenli Tarla in the south-western part of the city's territory (Figure 4.4; Waelkens and Loots 2000: 113–114). This was located on a series of rich alluvial fans, now intensively cultivated with wheat. As well as various buildings of mortared rubble and large amounts of red slip pottery manufactured in Sagalassos, there are several monumental ashlar tombs, a carved sarcophagus and an inscribed funerary altar. This was clearly the estate of a relatively wealthy landholding family who produced substantial crops for sale presumably in Sagalassos, and buried its members in imposing tombs beside the estate.

We know from inscriptions that the commonest gift by rural landowners serving their cities as magistrates consisted of goods in kind, particular grain and oil, but also wine and occasionally the labour of their estate workers (Vanhaverbeke 2003: 260–1). These estates are very much linked into the urban centre and the ostentatious display of a pro-Roman elite, and need to be added to our 'arenas of Roman power', along with roads, cities and assizes.

What about the arenas of local power? Poorer agricultural land, or good land in small patches, was usually left out of the estates or the huge surveyed tracts of 'centuriation' so popular elsewhere in the Roman Empire. This is neatly demonstrated by the double system of settlement and agriculture in the north-west Peloponnese in Greece during the early imperial period (Rizakis 1997). The coastal plains were dominated by the Roman colonies of Patras and Dyme, with their associated villa-based estates, centuriated land, highways, and a few dependent villages scattered among them. On the plateaux between the rivers and higher up on the flanks of the mountains was a separate pattern of more autonomous villages with much longer histories and exploiting very local resources.

It is not just the poorer or remote agricultural land that was the domain of villagers who lived outside the direct influence of Roman authority. The *saltus* or 'waste' land was anything but waste. Forbes' ethnographic work in Greece reveals some of its innumerable products: a vast range of fruits and

Figure 4.4 Ashlar blocks from monumental tombs at Dikenli Tarla, with rich wheat fields behind. Source: Sagalassos Archaeological Research Project, Katholieke Universiteit Leuven.

vegetables, game, grazing, construction materials, fuel, resin, fodder, aromas and medicines (Forbes 1997). It can also acquire major cultural meanings, such as being the location of hermits or freedom-fighters, or as a symbol of authentic rural identity for city-dwelling hunters or for nationalist propaganda (Forbes 1996: 68–9). This was the enormously valuable land which had to be left out of the centuriated land and often escaped even the greediest estate-owner (Corbier 1991: 222).

Small villages of peasant farmers are well attested in Roman Anatolia (S. Mitchell 1993: 176–87). The most complete documentation comes in an inscription setting out the regulations for the 'Demostheneia' games at Oenoanda, endowed by C. Iulius Demosthenes in AD 124 (S. Mitchell 1990; Wörrle 1988). The games were opened by a procession and by a sacrifice of 27 bulls in the theatre. Of these, 13 were contributed by the various city officials, and 14 by the villages. There are about 32 villages in all, the bigger ones contributing a bull on their own, the smaller ones contributing bulls jointly in groups of up to three, and one group of 12 villages giving two bulls jointly. The name of each village is always followed by the term 'with its associated farmsteads' (S. Mitchell 1990: 186). The farmsteads are clearly attached to villages, and the villages to the city. The farmers and villagers presumably attended the games and joined the magistrates and city-dwellers in feasting on the sacrificed bulls, though that is nowhere stated (Corbier 1991: 229). If so, the games would act as an incorporating movement, counteracting the centrifugal or autonomous tendencies of the rural dwellers.

It is clear from other inscriptions that these rural communities had real pretensions towards semi-autonomy (S. Mitchell 1993: 148–9). Thanks to their own social hierarchies and often conservative morality they could normally handle their own law and order. Collective activities are recorded in inscriptions, such as prayers for the whole settlement and annual festivals or competitions. These are evidence for community identities quite separate from the systems of city bureaucracy and Roman imperial rule to which they technically belonged.

There are some characteristic examples in the territory of Oenoanda's northern neighbour, Balboura (Coulton 1998: 231–6). Before the second century BC the area did not have an urban tradition, so the foundation of Balboura itself and the land allotment that accompanied it was very much an external imposition. In the early imperial period the city saw most of the usual trappings of provincial Greco-Roman society: public entertainment in the theatre, a piped water supply, a monumental street through the civic centre, and statues and inscriptions put up by a status-hungry elite.

With a territory of some 700 square km and elevations ranging up to 2,600 m above sea level, there was plenty of opportunity for creating local identities very different from those of the urbanized elite. Typical villages consisted of 10–20 stone house complexes, often with press-weights and tanks for wine production. Villagers and city-dwellers alike continued the long-established Anatolian tradition of carving relief figures of deities on rock outcrops, in particular south-facing outcrops near springs (T.J. Smith 1997). Local divinities such as Kakasbos and an axe-wielding Triad began to be dressed in Greek clothing. A pair of warrior horsemen were given the new names of Castor and Polydeuces in Greek inscriptions, though most of their dedicators had non-Greek names. Figure 4.5 shows one example, where the horsemen and the woman have been given Greek dress and put in a schematic pedimented temple. This is not Hellenization or assimilation: local deities and meaningful associations with the landscape are as strong as ever, and a few elements of the urban culture are appropriate and re-interpreted according to local systems of meanings.

The social landscape supports even more local autonomy and identity as we move beyond the villages. About 1.5 km south of Balboura and 2000 m above sea level was a shepherds' encampment (Coulton 1991: 49). This lies on the side of a steep rocky hill, above a well-watered grassy basin holding the tents and hearths of their modern successors. The remains consist of a thin scatter of pottery and three small fields, bounded by rocky outcrops and, in one case, a rubble wall. More work on sites of this kind will give us a fuller picture of these landscapes, which in many ways could be totally indifferent to Roman rule. As we will see in chapter 7, imperial officials and city-dwellers often saw little difference between mountain shepherds and bandits.

Figure 4.5 Rock relief from Gölcük, in the territory of Roman Balboura, showing two horsemen and a draped and veiled woman (T. Smith 1997: D44: plate Ib). Photograph: J.J. Coulton.

And bandits there certainly were. Even on the roads just outside Rome they were a problem, judging by the tombstones of those who had been murdered by them (Shaw 1984: 10–12). One of the more successful outcomes of Quintus Cicero's governorship of Asia in 60 BC was the quelling of the notorious bandits of Mysia in the interior of north-west Anatolia (Cicero, *Letters to Quintus* 1.1.25). In contrast to city-dwellers dependent on the trappings of civilization, and peasant farmers tied to their land, the mobility of bandits and outlaws gave them freedom (Shaw 1984: 31). With extensive local knowledge and support networks in the villages, bandits and outlaws turned on its head the landscape of city-dwellers and bureaucrats. Roads became resources and targets, rather than means of communication, and the highlands were domesticated, in contrast to the dangerous wilderness of urban control and Roman rule.

In response to the threat to law and order and to their ordered regime, the cities ran rural police forces (Hopwood 1983; S. Mitchell 1993: 195–7). A member of the elite was appointed eirenarch or 'magistrate for the peace', and he organized and paid for it. The actual patrolling was done by officers termed *paraphylakes* or 'guardians', supported by 'pursuers'. Like the military, they lived off the villages they passed through or based themselves in. An inscription from Hierapolis limits their requisitions to firewood, fodder and lodging (S. Mitchell 1993: 195). The need to regulate it demonstrates that the considerable scope for extortion in these rural areas was enthusiastically exploited. On the other hand, pursuing bandits brought its own dangers, and there are many rock-cut reliefs and dedications by rural policemen to appropriate deities such as the Mountain Mother, Good Luck, Nemesis, Artemis the Hunter, and, best of all, the great bandit-hunter Herakles (S. Mitchell 1993: 196).

There is another, overlapping social landscape in the highlands of the interior, that of the tribal groups such as the Homonadeis and the Isaurians. Most of them were infamous for their resistance to Roman rule and rejection of urban civilization. This took place on a variety of levels, and included military, cultural, linguistic and also economic resistance:

> At this period the Cietae, a tribe subject to the Cappadocian prince Archelaus the younger, resisted compulsion to supply property-returns and taxes in Roman fashion by withdrawing to the heights of the Taurus mountains where, aided by the nature of the country, they held out against the prince's unwarlike troops.
>
> Tacitus *Annals* 6.41

As with all tax-evaders, the reason why we know about the Cietae's resistance is that they were unsuccessful. In AD 36 Marcus Trebellius, the Roman commander sent out to deal with them, built earthworks round the two hilltops that they fortified, killed all those who tried to break out, and forced the rest to surrender. For this reason the incident made its way into the historical record. The successful cases, by definition, did not.

Most ancient sources for these resisting groups are hostile, and often simply equate them with criminal bandits who seek only their personal advantage. Strabo, for example, describes the villages dependent on the cities of New and Old Isaura as 'settlements of robbers' (12.6.2). There is some major stereotyping going on here, and a binary opposition of two different landscapes. To Strabo, the farmers of the Pamphylian plain are obedient and 'peaceable', whereas the mountaineers to the north are 'trained in piracy' and 'governed by tyrants' (12.7.2–3). This environmental determinism also appears in modern discussions of the area. Mountainous topography is typically viewed as a physical barrier to external control, and allows its inhabitants to assert their autonomy. This would mean that the patterns of settlement and resistance in the Roman period are identical to those of the Ottoman period in the same area (Shaw 1990: 199, 262–5).

People give meanings to their landscape in highly complex and variable ways (chapter 2). To understand local identity in these mountainous areas, we need to look much more systematically at the social structure and patterns of activity in the landscape. Even Strabo undermines his own stereotype by admitting that the plains-dwelling Pamphylians are involved in 'the business of piracy', and that there is a 'very fertile' area along the top of the Taurus range with excellent vines, olives and abundant pasture (12.7.2–3).

One fruitful approach is to examine the archaeology of fortified settlements in the highlands. Before the onset of Roman rule, the social structure of the central Anatolian plateau was essentially tribal, mostly consisting of the three Galatian tribes which settled the area in the third century BC. Their society was based on an elite who controlled settled agricultural and pastoral regimes and competed in status by mutual feuds and raiding (Darbyshire *et al.* 2000: 93–4). The characteristic settlements of these groups consist of hilltop enclosures with solid and carefully built rubble fortification walls, often with prominent D-shaped bastions, and ranges of rectangular and sub-rectangular buildings within them (Darbyshire *et al.* 2000: 89–93).

Later leaders such as Amyntas, the last king of Galatia, clearly took on many aspects of Greek lifestyle and material culture. Forts such as Amyntas' Isaura used ashlar blocks, polygonal towers and drafted margins in the best Hellenistic tradition (Darbyshire *et al.* 2000: 88–9). The dating of the rubble-walled forts is still problematic, with their rough masonry and coarse pottery, but it seems clear that many of them continued in use during the Roman period. In his *Natural History*, published in AD 77, Pliny the Elder characterizes the Homonadeis as living in a city and '44 other fortresses lying hidden among rugged valleys' (*Natural History* 5.94.23). Even with Roman control of the roads and cities, entire communities and societies that lived 'off the road' could still create their own worlds.

Conclusion

The Roman settlement of Asia Minor was very evident in many parts of the landscape. Temples to the deified emperor dominated cityscapes and their hinterlands in cities such as Sagalassos and Pergamon. Colonies such as Cremna and Pisidian Antioch were controlled by a Latin-speaking elite, as were many of the most productive estates. The provincial governor drew a multitude of litigants, traders and hangers-on wherever he held his assizes. Urban elites vied with each other to proclaim their enthusiasm for the world empire and its divine ruler, and to show off the trappings of a Roman lifestyle. Meanwhile the gangs of labourers sweated over the construction of the beautifully engineered roads, and travellers submitted themselves to tolls, customs dues, harassment and extortion.

But most people still lived in rural settlements and farmsteads. Usually there was no reason to travel on a Roman road, unless you were unlucky enough to live on one. The world of these rural dwellers was one of good and bad harvests, village headmen, the rocky sanctuaries of obscure local deities, and the occasional visit of an avaricious rural policeman. The piecemeal and intermittent nature of Roman rule allowed substantial local activity, identity and autonomy. It also allowed choice. People could and did choose to go and live in the city or in an expanding roadside settlement, where they could benefit from the growth in trade, transport and construction and the many opportunities that those brought.

So the two muleteers on the road to Apamea had a choice. They could continue down the road and past the garrison at Aulutrene, hoping not to be fleeced by the soldiers on duty there. Or they could try to lead their heavily laden mules cross-country to Apamea – not an inviting prospect. Roman roads and Roman soldiers had become part of their world, along with the bandits, roadside inns, icy winds and everything else that the gods saw fit to bestow on travellers. But that world, and their decision, was still their own.

5

LIVING BETWEEN LINES

The colonial project is now well-explored terrain. Censuses, surveys, boundaries, grids, roads, representations, museums and all the other paraphernalia of colonialism have been mapped out and deconstructed by the critics. Instead of discovering and recording facts, we now know colonial projects *created* facts by constructing elaborate systems of classification and demarcation. These systems, from the right-angled field boundaries of Roman surveyors to the postage stamps of Indochina, have been mapped, surveyed and recolonized by the postcolonial critics.

And yet, like colonialism itself, most of these studies take the god's eye view. They look at the imposition of lines and categories in the abstract, and produce their own systems of 'enumerative modalities', 'totalizing classificatory grids', and 'mathesis and taxinomia' (Anderson 1991: 184; Cohn 1996: 8; Foucault 1970: 71). Can such abstractions address the experiences of real individuals living embodied lives surrounded by the materiality of artefacts, buildings and landscapes? What happens when a line on the map becomes a barrier in your landscape, and you are forced to tick one box on the census form rather than both or none?

For a fearful colonial administrator, a population map or census report felt safe and knowable, as opposed to the dark corners, tangled alleys and alien dialects of a village or 'native quarter'. It is all too tempting for the critic or historian to follow the same by-pass, rather than braving the contingencies of narrative, the ambiguities of material culture, and the subjectivities of trying to understand someone else's experience. Bernard Cohn discusses the Indians' epistemological spaces and meanings which the British had to translate or reconstitute before they could understand and control them (1996: 18–19). Can we explore these epistemological spaces, and real ones, before they were translated into colonial facts?

New readings of old documents are clearly insufficient, particularly as most of those documents are, precisely, colonial facts. There is no point in reproducing distribution maps and population tables when what we are interested in is how people refused to become dots and boxes. Even deconstruction focuses attention and importance on the colonial officials and products being deconstructed, rather than on the people who inhabited alternative worlds of meaning and materiality. One much-neglected approach is landscape archaeology. While no panacea, this is very much concerned with exactly these sorts of issues, such as local constructions of meaning, non-elite communities, and human activity in specific contexts.

In chapter 4 I examined the mechanics of 'settling' an empire, and its effect on the colonized. In this chapter I want to explore one specific aspect of that. If the colonial project was based on demarcation and classification, how did people incorporate these lines and categories into their own lives? Did they reject them, obey or exploit them? My aim, in other words, is to fill the gap between the experienced lives of embodied individuals and the numbers, boxes and polygons into which they were inserted.

As a case study I am taking the forest boundaries imposed by the British colonial government of Cyprus between the 1880s and the 1920s. The recent time period means that there is plenty of archaeological and architectural data, supported by rich documentary and oral historical evidence. I am also able to use data from the Troodos Archaeological and Environmental Survey Project (TAESP), one of whose aims is to examine such unmapped spaces (Given *et al.* 2002).

Because of their rich resources of materials and meanings, forests in the European colonies of the nineteenth and twentieth centuries became major social and political arenas. This was where the public agents of the state and the individual agencies of forest dwellers played out their urgent games of contest, cooperation, control and resistance. In Sivaramakrishnan's happy metaphor, the canopy of hegemony was both constrained and penetrated by the undergrowth of practice and resistance (1995: 8). Now, of course, those canopies have fallen to the postcolonial axe, and been clear-felled by the chainsaw of deconstruction.

Or have they?

Lines

A line, like a bang, creates a fresh distinction between one side and the other, what came before and what comes after (Needham 1967). For a colonial administrator faced by an unknowable morass of incomprehensible dialects, unwritten custom and alien logic, lines created neat packages of land ownership and local administration. They chopped up that unknowable morass into defined and labelled categories of people, languages, religions, soils, trees.

To take on some sort of material existence, a line must be represented, and this was the function of the all-important map. To a European mind, a map seems scientific and measured, and therefore true. Just by appearing on the map, the boundary lines created differences which became increasingly real, while its spots and dots differentiated the important bits, such as ports and resources, from the unimportant bits, represented as blank space (Sparke

1998: 323). This, then, was the represented world of the colonizers, not a 'model of' society, as society was infinitely too complex to be modelled or represented in its unknowable entirety, but a 'model for' society: the way it really ought to be (Cohn 1996: 4–5; Given 2002: 3–4). Like generals moving flags on a situation map or Hitler gloating over his models of Berlin, you can put your finger on a polygon and say, 'this is mine.'

These lines and boundaries had to be disseminated beyond the colonial Secretariat and Land Registry Office, and that was the job of the survey teams. They became ubiquitous throughout every colony: setting up their triangulation stations, binding the land with their 66-foot long 'chains', and interrogating peasants about their land-holdings. By the end of the seventeenth century, for example, Ireland was one of the best-mapped countries in the world. This was a direct expression of the English drive to impose their version of order and spatial hierarchy on the fluidity of Gaelic social structure and land-tenure (Delle 1999: 20–1; O'Sullivan 2001: 91). As the Ordnance Survey built on this work in the first half of the nineteenth century, the bright red coats of the military surveyors were an all-too-visible demonstration of the intrusiveness and ubiquity of this restructuring (A. Smith 1998: 72–3).

The role of the census in the colonial project was to inhabit the new polygons and boxes with the representations of a properly ordered and structured society. This required drawing social as well as spatial lines, by creating categories of religion, language, occupation and family size. The aim was total knowledge of the society, hence the enormous scale of the census operations. By the 1880s, the census of India required 500,000 workers (Cohn 1996: 8). This massive scale had the added advantage of incorporating large numbers of local people into the colonial project. Like the surveyors, the census takers played their role in the theatre of domination. When the Ottoman Census Master and his commission arrived in a Greek village, the entire population had to appear before them, headed by the priests and notables. This communal act of submission was repeated at an individual level when the name of every male over 13 was formally inscribed into the register (Kiel 1997: 317; cf. Gosden and Knowles 2001: 15–16).

Lines were imposed at the level of the settlement, not just to structure the way in which people lived but to produce an ordered representation of the way in which society was organized. In a city of the Raj, the lines between Europeans and Indians were obsessively mapped out. Social and spatial entities such as the civil lines, cantonment and native city were carefully divided and distinguished by their architecture, material culture, language and regulations (King 1976). Even more intrusively, 'model villages' for the colonized represented the colonizers' ideal of the society and physically forced people into it. This is particularly evident in the model villages designed by French administrators of Algeria in the middle of the nineteenth century, where families were slotted into four different types of identical containers depending on their place in a four-tier social hierarchy (T. Mitchell 1988: 45–8).

Resistance to these lines took place at a variety of different levels. Most straightforwardly, there were many who crossed lines, destroyed the markers, and either attacked or refused to cooperate with the census clerks and surveyors. The sixteenth-century Palestinian villager who rudely told an Ottoman census official to 'write down what you want' is one of innumerable examples (Singer 1994: 91). A model village might be called a 'geometric jail' by one of its residents (T. Mitchell 1988: 92), but it is still possible to make small alterations and decorations to demonstrate your own agency and create your own identity in the face of the uniformity imposed by the state (Meskell 1998a).

Other groups appropriated the tools of their colonizers. One possibility was to redraw or re-interpret colonial maps as part of a 'cartographic struggle' to reclaim your own landscape (Sparke 1998: 305; cf. Bender 1999). Nineteenth-century Irish nationalists did exactly this in grounding their identity on the ancient heritage represented by the maps made by the English Ordnance Survey (A. Smith 1998). Another example was Shawnadithit, a Beothuk Indian woman from nineteenth-century Newfoundland who learnt to draw European-style maps. Rather than leaving them as Cartesian, disembodied abstractions, however, she populated them with the people and stories of her own world (Sparke 1998).

Nomads were one group of people famous for ignoring lines and creating their own interpretations of the world regardless of colonial regulations. From the shepherds of Roman Italy and the bedouins of Ottoman Jordan to Irish tinkers and the shifting cultivators of India, nomads threatened the colonial sense of order at every level. Settled peasant cultivators could be counted, mapped, taxed and controlled. Nomads crossed boundaries and evaded officials, and so were stigmatized by officials as unproductive, lazy and criminal (Sivaramakrishnan 1995; O'Sullivan 2001: 87). Although to the colonial authorities they seemed unregulated, their systems of unwritten agreements, community obligations and local knowledge could be complex and sophisticated, more than a match for the census clerk or forest guard.

One of the most dramatic confrontations between colonial line-drawing and nomadic resistance followed the Italian invasion of the Cyrenaica in 1911 (D. Atkinson 2000). The greatly outnumbered Bedouins and Sanussi rejected the Italian model of formally recognized territory and a linear front. Instead, they exploited their mobility and local knowledge to develop 'nomadic strategies' of guerrilla warfare and raids far into what the Italians regarded as settled territory. The Italians responded in characteristically territorial and disciplinary fashion. The Egyptian border was defined and sealed by a barbed wire fence 282 km long, to block the supplies being sent in to support the resistance. The bedouin themselves were imprisoned in a series of rectilinear concentration camps 1 km square, bounded by barbed wire and controlled by corridors of surveillance.

My aim in this section was to map out the principles of colonial line-drawing and local resistance to it. Almost all of the sources that I have used have been historical, with some input from anthropology and architectural history. What about the archaeology? Clearly it is virtually impossible to discover the sites where census officials were mocked or forest guards assaulted. Even with material markers such as bandit hideouts, destroyed boundary cairns and illegal production sites, it is unlikely that archaeological survey will find enough securely identified and precisely dated examples to start analysing their distribution, as if they made up a map of settlement sites.

This is no reason for rejecting landscape archaeology as a means of addressing these questions. We can use the historical documents to create a broad and rather generalized map of the activities, and so incorporate them into our archaeological interpretations of the landscape. Police reports, land use maps and pottery scatters are all part of the analysis. The individual examples of boundary cairns or illegal pitch kilns that we do find may not form a representative sample, but they are still very much there in the landscape. Rather than just using them to 'illustrate' the documents, like pictures of precious vases or palaces in a coffee-table book, we can analyse the means of access to them, the view of and from the sites, their organization of space, and the whole landscape context of the dramas that were played out there. This is how we can reconstruct the experiences of the shepherds, nomads and villagers, to compensate for the disapproving officialdom of the police reports and the dehumanizing of the census boxes which make up most of our documentary sources.

Drawing the line

The arrival of the Forest Delimitation Commission in a village was not a welcome event. The British officials who headed it represented the government departments which penetrated most intimately into the lives of a forest community: the District Commissioner's Office and the Forest Department. Accompanied by Greek and Turkish representatives, translators as required, clerks and surveyors, it initiated on each occasion an intense period of protest, argument and negotiation. To the government, this was essential to protect the forests of Cyprus from the ravages of uncontrolled goat grazing and timber cutting. To the villagers, the land which they had been using for generations to earn their livelihoods was being taken away by an arbitrary and dictatorial government.

Thanks to some behind-the-scenes diplomacy at the Congress of Berlin, the British took over the administration of the island of Cyprus from the Ottomans in July 1878 (Figure 5.1). To their eyes, Cyprus was an oriental country. The state of its agriculture, economy, sanitation and forests demonstrated all too well the impact of its rulers' oriental despotism combined with the fatalism and indolence of its inhabitants. As for the Cypriots, initial optimism that taxes would be reduced and living conditions improved quickly

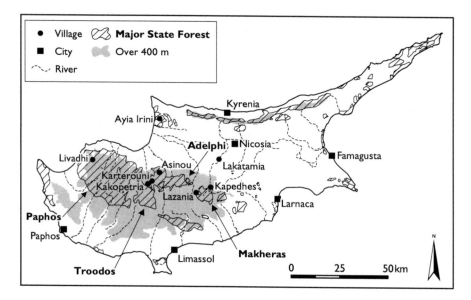

Figure 5.1 Map of Cyprus with Major State Forests.

turned to disappointment when they realized that the British were determined to continue most of the Ottoman taxes, actually enforce them, and add a host of regulations of their own (Katsiaounis 1996: 65–72).

In this environmentalist age it is easy to be persuaded by the first forestry reports to come out of the new British possession. The first two forest officers, A.E. Wild and Paul-Gabriel Madon, were aghast at the scenes of desolation and wastefulness that they found in the scrublands that had once been forest. The more respected of the travel writers who flocked to Cyprus in the early days of rule, particularly the explorer Samuel Baker, added to this picture of oriental misrule (S. Baker 1879: 327–46). All of these opinions and observations have been quoted approvingly by a long list of writers (e.g. Hutchins 1909: 11–13; Thirgood 1987: 77–85).

It is clear from these reports that in the last decades of Ottoman rule the more accessible parts of the major pine forests were not being allowed to regenerate naturally, and that the exploitation of timber was not being carried out on a sustainable basis. It is equally clear, however, that these 'barren wastes' were intensively managed and harvested for an astonishing variety of subsistence and trade products. Hamish Forbes has shown convincingly that in the Mediterranean context 'wasteland' is anything but waste, and plays a major role in the economy of local communities (Forbes 1996; 1997). The reports from Cyprus in the 1880s show that the forests and scrubland produced fuel, charcoal, grazing, fodder, medicines, pitch, aromas, and innu-

74

merable edible plants, as well as timber for construction, furniture, vehicles and numerous tools and items of household equipment. From an archaeological perspective, Julia Ellis Burnet's survey work in the Makheras and Adelphi forests similarly shows the extent and complexity of human activity in the forests during this period (Ellis Burnet n.d.: chapter 9).

The same applies to the working practices. The reports set up a stereotype of profligate and incompetent woodsmen with no thought for the future, and blamed them for the destruction of the forest. Exactly the same was argued by the Indian Forest Department (Sivaramakrishnan 1995: 7). By contrast, Samuel Baker breaks off from his catalogue of mindless destructions to note the extraordinary skill of Cypriot axemen (1879: 334–5). Coppice stools of Golden Oak and Arbutus are common in the higher altitudes of the Makheras Forest. They are much rarer in the Adelphi Forest, but this is a factor of later forest policies which removed this understorey in favour of the newly planted monoculture of Calabrian Pine (*Pinus brutia*) (Ellis Burnet n.d.). What is clear is that coppicing and careful management were far more widespread than is suggested by the continually quoted image of woodcutters felling a 150-year-old pine to make a single trough (Wild in 1879, quoted in Thirgood 1987: 81).

At another level, the forests were a rich source of agency, memory and identity. This was where children learnt to use an axe, to recognize and distinguish a huge range of edible plants, and where to find the best grazing in an unusually dry summer. Much-repaired goat folds, abandoned villages which could be used for occasional shelter, and little pockets of terraced hillslopes were all material reminders of the depth and closeness of their attachment to the forest landscape. Rocks, localities and even trees were given names, stories were told, and memories recounted. Visits on saints' days to the many ancient and remote mountain churches further sanctioned the sense of belonging that these village communities felt for their landscape.

And then the Forest Delimitation Commission arrived. The 1881 Forest Delimitation Law had declared all uncultivated land with trees, scrub or brushwood to be state forest. Felling timber, producing resin and above all goat grazing were forbidden within its limits, unless villagers went through the complex procedures of applying for a permit. So that those limits would be totally unarguable, the Commission had the task of defining the precise boundaries. This was done by mapping them and drawing them physically on the ground, first by a 'trace' or continuous dug line, and then by cairns. A notice was posted in English and Greek, or English and Turkish, and villagers had to lodge claims with the District Commissioner within six months (Thirgood 1987: 105–6, 113–15).

The villagers argued, of course. Archibald Law, barrister turned Assistant Commissioner turned Forest Officer, complained about his difficulties as President of the Forest Delimitation Commission in 1882. At just one village, Agia Irini north of Morphou, he had to investigate 130 separate claims, and recommended that villagers should not sign their claims: 'as the majority cannot write, they make blots and smudges as their "marks", all over the record' (SA1/2021/1880–3). His sense of order and demarcation is offended, but for a non-literate villager, as Sivaramakrishnan has pointed out, this bureaucratic process is tantamount to 'unilateral forfeiture' (1995: 14). Even if the village headman was literate and could translate and interpret, his co-villagers were very much in his power, and at the mercy of any feuds or disagreements that might fracture village society.

The physical markers of the forest boundary are of considerable archaeo-logical interest. Designed to be visible and dominating, they overturned people's experience of their own landscapes. Before the Delimitation Com-mission, goatherds took their goats to pasture and woodcutters harvested their coppices to supply the furniture makers. Now, following the same path up the hillside, they crossed a tangible, visible line, and automatically became forest offenders and fugitives from justice.

A.E. Dobbs, a professional forester and successor to Law as President of the Forest Delimitation Commission, was very concerned with the appear-ance and location of the cairns that marked these boundaries. They should be set at points of vantage, and wherever the boundary turned a corner (SA1/2045/1880–3). The ones being built in November 1883 were 60 cm in diameter but only protruded 23 cm above the ground (SA1/2087/1880–3). As time went on they were made larger and more monumental, set in lime concrete with identification numbers 7.5 cm high (SA1/334/1884). Trilin-gual notices were printed threatening a £5 fine or three months in prison for damaging them – clearly a regular occurrence (SA1/2220/1884). By the end of 1885 they were pyramidal in shape, 105 cm high and 122 cm wide, spaced every 400 m, and whitewashed with their numbers picked out in black (SA1/4471/1885).

Most of these monumental stone forest guards were replaced by concrete versions in the late 1930s and 1940s, mostly because the masonry and mortar ones were all too easily destroyed by protesting grazers and forest villagers (*ARFD* 1938: 5; 1947–8: 4). Some communities within the forests were entirely surrounded by forest boundaries. As a forest livelihood became impossible, many of these settlements were abandoned and acquired by the Forest Department, and in such cases the masonry cairns still survive.

Karterouni is one such enclave, lying between two spurs on the eastern side of the steep Kourdhali river valley (Figure 5.2). Four substantial stone and mud brick structures make up the core of the settlement, with two smaller outliers 100 m away. An impressive system of channelled streams, threshing floors and stone terraces up to 3 m high demonstrates its circum-scribed but highly intensive agricultural production. Botanical survey in and around the settlement showed at least 15 species of edible plants, including hawthorn and terebinth berries, fennel and caper, and emergency carbo-hydrates such as winter wild oats and asphodel. Just as importantly, the wild

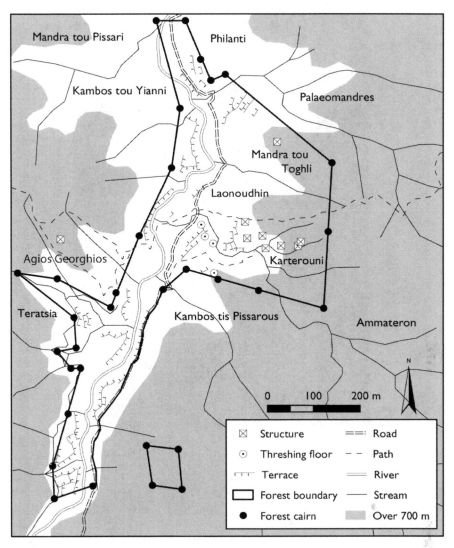

Figure 5.2 Map of Karterouni settlement, enclosed by forest boundaries. Adapted
from Department of Lands and Surveys, Republic of Cyprus, Cadastral
Map XXVII/14.

fodder resources are rich and various, with a wide range of nutritious
grasses, vetch, clover and assorted browse trees and shrubs available at different times of year, even in the dry summer.

The forest cairns which excluded the villagers from the grazing, timber
and fuel resources of the landscape around them are dominating in both
construction and appearance (Figure 5.3). They are usually square in plan,

Figure 5.3 Masonry and plaster forest cairn, with part of Karterouni settlement visible behind it. Height of cairn: 1.0 m. Photograph: Michael Given.

tapering to an irregular top, ranging from 90 to 150 cm high and typically 90 cm wide at the base. Large chunks of gabbro, some of them extending across the cairn's entire width, are bonded together with thick white plaster, and the whole cairn was covered with a creamy yellow whitewash. In a forest shaded by pines and darkened by a floor of cistus and pine needles, these white monuments are stark reminders of colonial intrusion.

To the south, the forest boundary comes within 100 m of the settlement, with the cairns placed along the top of the steep-sided spur overlooking it. It was not just while taking goats to pasture or fetching firewood that the inhabitants experienced the colonial demarcation of their landscape. Even during the daily activities of working in the terraced fields, processing the crops or sitting outside their houses, they could see the cairns towering above them from the ridgeline. Conversely, a forest guard patrolling the boundary could look over the entire settlement and its arable land. To the east the boundary also passes close to the settlement, but more room is allowed to the north to allow for a goat fold ('Mandra tou Toghli') and a small group of agricultural terraces. Along the valley bottom the boundaries press as closely in as they can on the fields along the floodplain of the river and its main tributary.

The government map on which Figure 5.2 is based, originally surveyed in 1925, shows a great contrast between the busyness of structures and field plots in the Karterouni enclave and the empty spaces of the Adelphi Forest outside. But the local memories embedded in the surrounding landscape are clear from the locality names which the map records within the state forest. Immediately north of Mandra tou Toghli is Palaeomandres, 'the old goat folds'. To the south is the 'Plain of Pissarou', where 'Pissarou' (feminine) is probably a name originally meaning maker of *pissos* or pitch. 'Goat-fold of Pissaros' (masculine) clearly combines two outlawed professions, while an actual 'Kiln of Hadji Yeorgiou' lies 1 km to the east. As well as names, the map records a group of five 'Sheep Folds (In Ruins)' 1.2 km to the south-east of the settlement. To a government map, sheep folds within the forest are by definition 'In Ruins'.

On a prominent spur immediately across the valley from Karterouni is the ruined church of Agios Georghios (Saint George). Local memory has not just preserved the name but re-incorporated the ruins into later landscapes: a cult involving the deposition of re-used bottles, presumably for oil, was clearly active during the twentieth century. Immediately to the west of the church are the rubble piles and pottery of a rather longer abandoned settlement, coinciding precisely with an astonishingly luxuriant stand of asphodel. Other stories and memories clearly lie behind other forest locality names around Karterouni, such as 'Pits of Saint John', 'Check dam' and 'Carob'. Once the forest boundary had been drawn, these became memories of a different type. The line created a distinction in place between forest and community, but also a distinction in time between a 'free' past where goatherds and woodcutters roamed at will and a present where activities were controlled and circumscribed by forest guards and whitewashed boundary cairns.

Meanwhile the Forest Department kept a tally of how much land it had delimited in this way. It announced 126 square miles in 1884, 230 in 1885, 516 in 1891, and finally 700 in 1909, making up 19.5 per cent of the entire island (SA1/1271/1884; Thirgood 1987: 113). Maps were produced 'showing the progress of the Forest Delimitation of Cyprus' (e.g. Gole 1996: 19, Figure 19). This went hand in hand with all the other aspects of the colonial project. Every ten years from 1881, the census reduced people and communities to a series of boxes and categories, while Kitchener's 1885 map of Cyprus demonstrated total knowledge of the island at a scale of one inch to a mile (Given 2002). If people had been as easy to manage as trees, Cyprus would have been the perfect colony.

Crossing the line

On 11 January 1935 Nicolis Stavrinos of the village of Lazania passed between the forest cairns and entered the Makheras Forest. With him were his 57 goats, which he was taking to pasture at the Mouttari tou Papavassili locality. His fellow-villager Lazaris Michael was in the same locality on the same day with another 30 goats. Meanwhile on the northern edges of the forest three men from Kapedhes were harvesting Golden Oak for tool-making and fuel, while a fourth man from Lakatamia was grazing 50 goats and 60 sheep.

These were the ones who got caught. It had been a busy day for the four forest guards based at Kionia Forest Station, covering the whole Makheras Forest. Nicolis Stavrinos' case came to court on 5 June of that year, and he was fined 12 shillings. All of these 'forest offences' and their punishments were duly inscribed into the Makheras Forest 'Confiscation and Prosecution Register'.

Clearly, there were many more who got away with it. The forest cairns round the Makheras Forest marked out a perimeter of 73 km, and much of this area consisted of steep slopes, thick undergrowth, impassable gorges and few forest tracks. There was a limit to how much of this ground four forest guards could patrol. In chapter 2 I argued that a large part of people's identity and world view derives from their habitual practices. Before the 1880s, most forest villagers were by practice and profession woodcutters and goatherds. After the imposition of the forest boundaries, the same practices made them habitual law-breakers and opponents of the colonial government.

Resistance to the forest laws took a wide variety of forms, and saw considerable development from the casual disregard of the 1880s to the political protests of the 1920s. When poorer Cypriots realized that the British were actually going to enforce the multifarious Ottoman taxes, their initial resistance consisted mainly of reluctance to part with their meagre surpluses and means of subsistence. They refused to pay tithes, and persisted in grazing their goats and taking fuel from the forest. Their resentment was also expressed in attacks on tithe collectors and petty acts of vandalism and banditry. This became particularly widespread after the drought and agricultural crisis of 1887–8 (Katsiaounis 1996: 143–9).

These acts of everyday resistance grew so widespread that the British became worried about their crime statistics, which just 15 years after the occupation showed an enormous increase. William Smith, the Chief Justice, put his finger on the problem in his *Annual Report* for 1892–3:

> The substantial increase in the number of offences reported during this year has therefore occurred in 'other offences', under which are grouped together offences against the Revenue laws, Forest laws, the laws known as the Field Watchmen laws, the Quarantine laws, breaches of municipal ordinances, &c. . . . As the area of the

delimited forest is extended from year to year the number of offences against the provisions of the Forest laws increases.

quoted in Katsiaounis 1996: 143–4

By imposing a complex web of bureaucratic procedures on every aspect of everyday life, the colonial project has essentially produced its own resistance.

There were always ways round procedures and regulations. The chair-makers of Kakopetria relied on Arbutus and Golden Oak for their substantial craft industry. In 1880 the government conceded the legitimacy of this, but only allowed them to continue their trade with a permit, for which it charged a complex scale of dues and imposed nine separate conditions. The trees had to be cut level with the ground, only between 1 October and 1 March, and only in places approved by the Forest Officer. To control this, all chairs from approved wood were stamped with the government mark (SA1/2153/1880–3). The Forest Officer marked one of the bars of each chair, so the chair-maker promptly removed the bar and re-used it in other chairs made from untaxed wood. The government took 15 years to catch up with this, and characteristically responded by imposing further procedures, instructing its forest officials to stamp all four legs of each chair with the government mark (SA1/1333/1895).

More powerful institutions could appropriate the government's own tactics of legal argument and intensive communication. This particularly applied to the monasteries, many of which were major land and livestock owners. After most of their privileges under the Ottomans had been removed by the British, they were all too ready to protest against any further threat to their wealth and authority. From 1885, for example, Makheras monastery carried out a protracted argument with the government over the position of the forest boundaries and its grazing rights within the forest. The 700-year-old monastery demanded exclusive and guaranteed grazing rights within the forest which had taken its name. In June 1886 the Abbot's secretary argued that the forest had been the monastery's pasture land 'ab antiquo', as was proved by a golden bull granted by the Byzantine emperor Manuel Comnenus (1143–80), and by the presence of its goatfolds and an old church (SA1/380/1886; SA1/2289/1886).

Compromise was reached only after the monastery threatened to take the government to court. The forest boundaries were imposed across most of the monastery's grazing areas, but the monastery was given a permit each year to graze a certain number of goats, initially 600 and later 750. Parts of the forest were kept in rotation as reserves to allow regeneration. Like many villagers, however, the monastery regarded its permit as licence to graze where and as much as it liked. The same thing happened in India, where forest communities happily paid the government tax, but then assumed that this gave them free rights to the entire forest (Guha and Gadgil 1989: 158–9). As the Principal Forest Officer, Archibald Law, pointed out in 1889, it hardly helped the government's case that the Forest Guard lived at the monastery itself, thus allowing the monks to control the guard rather than vice-versa (SA1/710/1889). The colonized had appropriated the act of surveillance.

As more and more goatherds and forest villagers were prosecuted for crossing imaginary lines and breaking petty regulations, they became politicized, and began to use forest offences as a means of protest. The climax was the ultimate forest weapon: arson.

Even before the British occupation in 1878, arson was recognized as a means of protest. A report by the French forester de Montrichard in 1874 urged against any stricter regulation of fuel collecting, because the population was too poor to pay and enforcement would have led to hatred and fire-setting (Thirgood 1987: 86). As resentment against the British colonial Forest Department grew, it became clear that more and more forest fires were being set deliberately by goatherds who had been excluded from the forest (Thirgood 1987: 122–5; cf. Guha and Gadgil 1989: 167–8). This came to a climax in the 'Goat Wars' of the 1920s.

The firestorm of protest that passed over the forests in the 1920s was the culmination of several political, economic and social factors. More and more land was becoming either private property or state forest, leaving very little opportunity to landless goatherds. During the First World War, the Forest Department had concentrated entirely on timber felling for the war effort in Egypt and Palestine, allowing the goatherds to graze unchecked. Considerable resentment followed the government's attempts to recover this lost ground. This was also the first major period of Greek Cypriot demonstration in favour of enosis, union with Greece, and thanks to increasingly wide education almost all levels of society were familiar with this ideology.

These tensions were exacerbated by the harsh line taken by the Forest Department, and particularly by the Principal Forest Officer from 1921 to 1936, Dr Arthur Unwin. Unlike most of his predecessors, Unwin was a fully trained and professional forester, and he was responsible for the rehabilitation of the forests after the ravages of the First World War. His obsession with goat-grazing, however, was notorious, and comes out clearly in the special pleading and contradictions of his 1928 book *Goat-grazing and Forestry in Cyprus*. When he warns of the huge dangers of rapidly expanding pastoralism, for example, it is 'a most lucrative business' (1928: 17). When he argues that its abolition will be no economic loss, all that it amounts to is that 'a few gaunt goats produce some dirty milk' (117).

Even Sir Ronald Storrs, Governor from 1926 to 1932, wrote publicly that Unwin 'loved his trees like human beings, only a good deal more' (1943: 486). The local press was considerably less circumspect in its comments, and in its private correspondence the government was severely critical of the Principal Forest Officer's high-handedness in dealing with goatherds and forest communities (SA1/1164/1914). As for the goatherds and villagers, they quite literally demonized him: mothers threatened naughty children that they would give them, not to the devil, but to Dr Unwin (Thirgood 1987: 352).

One of the worst forest fires to hit the island was started by the goatherds of the village of Livadhi in the Paphos forest in March 1924. It burnt for a week and destroyed 9 square miles of forest (*ARFD* 1924: 38). The year as a whole saw a total of 66 fires, most of them caused by arson. They destroyed some 18 square miles of forest and £100,000 of timber (Thirgood 1987: 146). Quite apart from the financial losses, these attacks marked what was all too clearly a disastrous failure of government policy.

The various government reports show a clear concern with the social causes of this protest. Some, such as the Commissioner of Paphos talking about Livadhi village in 1924, are relatively sympathetic: 'It will be well to remember that these people have never known anything but goats and the forest, and that their ancestry and traditions speak to them of nothing else' (SA1/278/1924: Red 26). Others, such as Unwin himself, are less so:

> Livadhi is a very backward village, whose inhabitants are comparable only with the Vroisiades for ignorance, cunning and lawlessness. They are practically all shepherds, and live in a dirty, undeveloped little village in a beautiful and well stocked part of the forest. They have very large numbers of goats, totalling, as far as I know nearly 2,000 which they graze over an enormous area of the forest . . . They possess no permits, so that they break the law continually in this way. They also steal timber, fuel etc. from the forest as they require it for their own use or for sale.
>
> SA1/278/1924: Red 10

Unwin's contrast between dirty village and beautiful forest is particularly characteristic, and it is no coincidence that Livadhi was the first village targeted by the Forest Department for wholesale removal to a new site outside the forest. Deconstruction of these alienating texts, however, will hardly bring us much closer to the experiences and world views of these clearly highly independent villagers. Perhaps landscape archaeology can help.

Asinou

At first sight the Asinou Valley in the northern Troodos mountains is remote, isolated and agriculturally marginal (Figure 5.4). This is exactly the sort of location that Arthur Unwin would happily have cleared of its people and goats to make room for the trees. For most of its course within the Troodos mountains the Asinou river has incised a deep gorge, hemmed in by the steep mountainsides and has little or no floodplain. There is one stretch, only a kilometre long, where a lower gradient and a series of tributaries from the south have allowed a few alluvial terraces and relatively deep-soiled colluvial

Figure 5.4 Asinou settlement from the south-east, with a goat fold in the middle ground. Photograph: Chris Parks.

slopes. This was the focus of an agricultural, pastoral and forest community in the early years of British colonial rule.

The only exception to Asinou's apparent remoteness and marginality is the twelfth-century church of Panagia Phorviotissa. This UNESCO World Heritage monument is famous for its Byzantine frescoes, and is the target of numerous tourist coaches and Cypriot baptism parties. This is a recent phenomenon, however. The first road was not constructed until the 1930s, and the monastery founded with the church was abandoned in the eighteenth century (Klirides 1968: 83–4). Even the census officials of the Ottoman and British empires ignored or were unaware of it. The Venetians recorded 45 free peasant householders in 1565, but the community does not appear in the Ottoman village list of 1831–2 or the British census of 1881 (Grivaud 1998: 469; Theocharides and Andreev 1996; Census 1882).

Apart from the art historians who have studied and published the frescoes of the church, archaeologists have given the Asinou Valley the same treatment as the rest of the mountain areas of Cyprus: total neglect. When the Troodos Archaeological and Environmental Survey Project (TAESP) started work in the region in 2000, one of its aims was to focus on this valley, to see if that neglect was justified. After three seasons of intensive survey and oral history interviews, it is clear that the landscape of the Asinou Valley and the

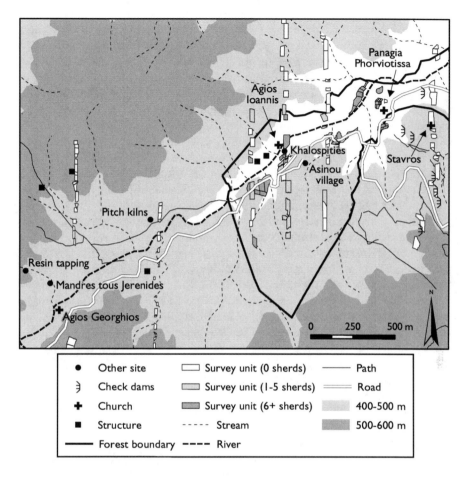

Figure 5.5 Map of the Asinou Valley. Source of archaeological data: Troodos
Archaeological and Environmental Survey Project.

mountains around it has been vibrant with memory, activity and meaning for
at least five centuries (Given *et al.* 2002: 32–4).

The church of Panagia Phorviotissa lies on a low spur at the downstream
end of the more open section of the valley, clearly visible from all around
(Figure 5.5). Its founder, Nicephorus, built it on the site of his estate in
1105/6, but quickly turned it into a monastery and became its first abbot
till his death in 1115 (Stylianou and Stylianou 1985: 117). Further up the
spur, 150 m from the church, TAESP mapped a series of three substantial
structures dating probably to the seventeenth and eighteenth centuries,
and resistivity survey showed traces of a fourth structure some 15 m long.
Between these structures are two huge, hollow olive trees probably dating to

the sixteenth century. It seems very likely that these structures were part of the monastery complex.

Intensive survey in the almond grove below the church on its west and north produced dense concentrations of pottery, particularly notable for the fifteenth- and sixteenth-century fine wares. Most of the rest of the material, though difficult to date any more closely than Medieval to Modern, consisted of heavy, chunky sherds from the storage, processing and serving vessels used by a small agricultural community. The material round the probable monastery is similar in date and function, but without the glazed wares.

A more recently abandoned village lies 550 m to the south-west of the church, on a high spur above the river. This settlement, usually referred to as Asinou, consists of an integrated group of some eight dwellings, with a complex history of infill, reuse and recycling of different structural elements. Two goat folds and two threshing floors suggest the small scale of its economy, though botanical survey produced some 13 species of edible wild plants. Fat Hen and Amaranth, both rich in carbohydrates and proteins, were particularly abundant.

As well as seven intensive survey units immediately adjacent to the church and another five round the probable monastery, TAESP's Team Central carried out seven transects of survey units crossing the valley from north to south, and a series of 19 units along the alluvial terraces of the valley bottom. One of the most striking finds was a major concentration of pottery in the valley bottom below the Asinou settlement at the locality with the suggestive name of Khalospities or 'ruined houses'. Just two survey units produced the impressive total of 554 sherds. Apart from nine sherds from the fourteenth or fifteenth centuries, the bulk of this material dated to the nineteenth and twentieth century. Particularly striking was the wide range of vessel types and functions: glazed bowls, frying pans, juglets, water jugs, storage jars, and two fragments of vats used to receive grape juice during the pressing. Geomorphological mapping showed that this material was very much *in situ*, rather than slipping down the hill from the settlement above.

Intensive survey reveals much more about the landscape than the discovery of 'sites' such as Khalospities and the Asinou settlement. The seven transects provided cross-sections of the valley along 5 km of its length, and both they and the 19 survey units on the alluvial terraces showed a widespread, if never very dense, scatter across the cultivable areas of the valley. The main surprise was the substantial Roman component, particularly across the valley from the church of Panagia Phorviotissa, and in a building complex 4 km up the valley from the church. Many of the steep gullies to the east of the church had been dammed with short stretches of wall. Some of these form part of erosion control measures carried out by the Forestry Department in the mid-twentieth centuries. Others are clearly older than that, and were intended to catch the eroding sediment and create tiny fields for a couple of fruit trees or a small patch of barley. Judging by their distribution within the valley as a whole and their proximity to paths leading directly to Asinou, these were probably cultivated by the monks and other members of the community associated with the monastery.

Most of the pottery from across the valley could only be dated very broadly to the Medieval, Ottoman or Modern periods, though much of what could be dated more precisely was of the same date as the material at Khalospities and the Asinou settlement. The whole valley clearly thrived during the nineteenth and first half of the twentieth century, with a varied economy and widespread cultivation on the alluvial terraces and pockets of colluvial soils.

What is equally clear from the survey transects is that unlike the earlier Ottoman pottery and structures, this relatively recent activity stops abruptly on the forest boundary. There are technical problems which might have influenced this apparent pattern, not least the difficulty in spotting potsherds when the ground is covered in pine needles. We controlled this by systematically cleaning circles within each survey unit, and the pattern does indeed seem real. The scale and intensity of activity within the forest, as expressed in the densities of pottery, are much lower than outside the forest. To some extent this was enforced by the forest boundary of the 1880s, clearly visible in the modern concrete cairns and the occasional tumbles of stones from their predecessors. It also works the other way, though. Because of the fierce negotiation of the villagers, the forest boundaries were drawn along the edges of the areas they cultivated.

The lack of pottery on the steep, forested hillslopes does not mean a total lack of human activity after the 1880s. This is where the systematic and therefore unbiased transects are complemented by more 'purposive' survey, such as checking up sites marked on the cadastral maps, talking to local villagers and foresters, and following old paths to see where they lead. At this broader scale, the mountains round the Asinou Valley were alive with all sorts of different activities from the sixteenth to the early twentieth centuries (Figure 5.5).

The forest settlements tend to be the easiest to find, as many were marked by the colonial surveyors. The oldest that we know about is Aspri, 4 km south of Asinou and 960 m in elevation. According to the Venetian census of 1565, this settlement had six free peasant householders (Grivaud 1998: 470). In 2003 TAESP mapped a row of very tumbled structures along a ridge line, a substantial church with nave, narthex and one aisle, and a scatter of mostly utilitarian pottery.

A more recent settlement is Mandra tous Jerenides, mapped by TAESP in 2002. From the pottery built into its walls and the style and condition of its masonry, it is clear that it belongs to the same nineteenth- and early twentieth-century date as Asinou and Khalospities. Both its locality name and the cadastral plan suggest that it is a collection of goat folds, and Pater Kyriakos, the priest from Nikitari village, remembers this as being the winter settlement of the shepherds of Spilia village to the north.

Two of the four structures are substantially built with cut stones carefully chinked with stones and sherds. All four of them consist of linear ranges of two or three rooms, rather than single rooms in a large enclosure or complex of enclosures, which is the more normal form of a goat fold. A bread oven 2 m in diameter similarly suggests a broader and more substantial economic basis than might be expected for a temporary base for a few shepherds. Immediately across the river gorge to the east is a similar though more ruinous settlement, with a ruined church remembered as being dedicated to Agios Georghios (Saint George).

There are other ruined churches in the Asinou area, whose locations and names still form very strong memories in the landscape. On a hill dominating the narrow entrance to the valley in the north-east lie the ruins of a rectangular structure about 8 × 4 m, with an apse at the eastern end. This is the church of Stavros or 'Holy Cross', a typical dedication for a hilltop church. An imposing ashlar wall exposed in the river bank immediately opposite the dense pottery scatter at Khalospities is remembered as the church of Agios Ioannis (Saint John). To a goatherd or forest villager looking round the mountains, the landscape was as much a network of religious and personal significance as it was a source of livelihood.

A more unusual set of structures lies 700 m to the north of Mandra tous Jerenides, on either side of a gully among the Calabrian pines (Figure 5.6). On each side of the gully is a circular structure built roughly out of local diabase, one with a diameter of 2.5 m, the other 3.5 m. The larger structure is better preserved and has an internal diameter of 1.8 m. Their condition implies that they were in use in the last two or three centuries, but other than that they are almost impossible to date. Their function, however, is easier to identify. Their size, form and location make it clear that these are pitch kilns. From the classical period to the early decades of British rule, resin in its raw form and pitch, the result of the distillation of resin, were used for a wide variety of purposes, from coating the insides of water jars to producing dyes and medicines. Resin was harvested by cutting out a vertical strip of bark some 80 or 90 cm long near the base of a pine tree, and allowing the resin to seep out and collect in a jar at the bottom of the strip. This could be converted to pitch in a small kiln or pit, but more normally pitch was produced directly by burning branches and offcuts slowly in a sealed kiln made of stone and mud. The liquid pitch would then trickle out into a receptacle or pit at the side, where it was set alight to flare off the wood oils. In a later version, it dripped through a perforated iron plate into a bucket below the main chamber of the kiln (S.W. Baker 1879: 335; Hutchins 1909: 81; Thirgood 1987: 118).

The initial British strategy for the resin industry was to encourage and develop it, and numerous samples were sent off to Kew Gardens for analysis (SA1/1731/1880–3; SA1/1735/1880–3). It soon became apparent, however, that the market was saturated because of over-production throughout the

Figure 5.6 Circular pitch kiln in the Asinou Valley. The scalebar is 1 m. Photograph: Chris Parks.

Mediterranean (Thirgood 1987: 98). At the same time the reports were coming in about the state of the Cypriot forests, and resin-burners quickly joined the woodcutters and goatherds in the Forest Department's demonology. Reports bemoaned the devastation caused by the 'merciless hacking' and wastefulness of resin-burners, and were particularly worried that it was done in 'out-of-the-way places' and at night, so was very hard to detect (S.W. Baker 1879: 208; SA1/1955/1880–3). Apart from some small-scale production licensed by the Forest Department in the Paphos Forest, resin tapping and pitch production were banned outright (Thirgood 1987: 118).

Just 150 m northwest of the settlement at Mandres tous Jerenides is a stand of five Calabrian pines which are some 100 to 150 years old, clearly much older than those round them. Each of these pines has a resin tapping scar on its uphill, western side, typically about 90 cm long and 10–20 cm wide. They were cut with adzes striking downwards, and two of them also show areas of charring. The growth of bark over the resin scars and the age of the trees make it very likely that these were done after resin harvesting was banned by the British.

The cadastral plan records two 'lime kilns' to the south and south-east of the settlement, but in this igneous area it is much more likely that they are pitch kilns. Three more pitch kilns are known from other parts of the Adelphi Forest (Ellis Burnet n.d.: chapter 9). While it is very hard to date these kilns

precisely enough to say whether they were in use before or after resin production was banned, it is very clear that they played an important role in the local
forest economy. We also know from the prosecutions that illegal pitch production was a significant problem for the authorities (SA1/1966/1880–3). It
seems more than likely that the 'shepherds of Spilia' and whoever else lived at
Mandres tous Jerenides supplemented their income by tapping and burning
the resin from their forest.

Memory is a powerful tool for creating meaning in the landscape, and as
our interviews in the area showed it is still very much alive. Panayiotis Alexandrou Loppas, for example, spends his summers in the mountaintop fire
lookout post of Kakos Anemos ('Evil Wind'), situated at 761 m with a pan-
oramic view overlooking the Asinou Valley and its surrounding mountains
(interviewed by the author, 16 and 22 July 2001, and by Marios Hadjianastasis,
12 August 2003). Panayiotis was born 'under a pine tree' at Karterouni in the
1930s, one of eight children of parents who were both goatherds. Much of
his early life was spent moving round the forest with his father and their
goats, staying in shelters constructed of pine branches covered in cistus. The
ruined Medieval houses at Aspri, he told us, made particularly good shelters.

In 1941 Panayiotis and his family moved to Asinou village, which with
some 50 residents was quite a shock to the boy brought up in the forest. The
Forestry Department offered his father money to stop being a goatherd and
leave Asinou, but he refused, because he would have no house, no flocks.
They closed off the forest with cairns, said Panayiotis, pointing from his
Kakos Anemos eyrie down to the Asinou enclave way below us. His father
and the other six or seven goatherds in the same position grazed their flocks,
went to court, paid their fines, and continued to graze their flocks. On one
occasion in the 1940s, his father was fined 34 times in one month:

> My father's argument when he went to the court was: 'Your honour,
> the month has 31 days, how come I got fined 34 days?'. The judge
> said, 'I don't know that, the employee who fined you must come to
> testify'. And the employee went to the court and said 'Your honour,
> I fined him four days more because I found him in the morning and
> told him to leave. He didn't leave and I found him again in the after-
> noon in a new plantation where we had planted young pine trees, in
> the area where there had been a fire and were no pine trees and we
> did a reforestation and Mr. Alexandros went and put them [the
> goats] in and they ate them.'

The judge decided that all the goats belonging to Panayiotis' father should be
sold off, to make him quit his job. The village headman supported his fellow-
villager rather than the government, and wrote in the report that Panayiotis'
father had 47 goats, rather than the 800 he actually had, and they were duly
sent to auction. With no competition from the rest of the villagers, Panayiotis'

mother bought the 47 goats back from the government, and the family continued to graze their goats in the Asinou forest.

The local knowledge of Panayiotis and many of the other villagers we interviewed is superb, and invaluable to archaeologists hungry for evidence of past human activity in a forest landscape difficult to survey. Ruined churches, settlements, charcoal-burners' platforms, resin kilns, paths, threshing floors and shelters are all parts of the landscape that Panayiotis sees when he scours the forests with his binoculars looking for forest fires. The memories often swing from nostalgia for fresh, home-made food and a simple way of life to distress at remembered poverty, as well as resentment towards the authorities who tried to cut them off from their already meagre livelihood. What is clear from such rich memories and the wealth of archaeological evidence is that the forest was an arena of intense and dynamic human activity, full of meaning and memory, even after the colonial Forest Department imprisoned it inside cairns.

Conclusion

Even at the time, the Forest Department was criticized for its unworkable policies and the harshness with which it enforced them. Samuel Baker commented on the futility of making laws which stopped people from cutting down trees on their own property, but had no means of enforcement (1879: 331–2). After the nightmare decade of the 1920s, a formal investigation into the activities of the Forest Department found that it was 'overworked, overextended and over-centralized', with its work 'characterized by excessive detail' (Thirgood 1987: 150). The same applied to the Indian Forest Act of 1878, which became a model for several other colonies, including Cyprus. Many Raj officials outside the Forest Department criticized the act as tantamount to an act of confiscation, which would just produce protest and discontent (Guha and Gadgil 1989: 145).

In many respects the colonial project carried the seeds of its own resistance. The forest boundaries drawn by the Delimitation Commission in the 1880s were impossible to enforce, particularly considering the pittance given to the Forest Department by the government (Thirgood 1987: 110). So all this excessive line-drawing was self-defeating: it just politicized the rural poor. What had been fuel-collecting and goat-grazing became first a forest offence and then an act of political protest.

The economic and social value of a healthy forest is unarguable, and in many respects the forest-dwellers of Cyprus were suffering the same as their fellows across the world at the hands of modernization. But it was to take the more thoughtful and long-term policies of a later generation of forest officials to bring together the needs of people and trees. Today the forests of Cyprus are thriving, and the Forest Department has a forward-thinking policy of focusing on their environmental value, their role in improving the quality of life for the people of Cyprus, and their use for sustainable green tourism. That was what the colonial line-drawers were trying to do, to some extent. In the long term, in principle, for society as a whole, the forests had to be protected. But this was a colonial vision of an orderly, balanced society, with people and nature in some sort of utopian harmony with each other. To the goatherds, the cairns of the newly imposed forest boundary cut across their habitual routes and activities. Rather than obeying or ignoring them, they incorporated them into their own new vision of society: one of colonial demarcation and deliberate, politicized resistance.

6

THE DOMINATED BODY

Imperialist regimes survive on the exploitation of their subjects. By taxation and forced labour they extract surplus food and work from the population and redistribute it as they wish. This is not just an economic phenomenon. Through the physical actions of paying taxes and working in labour gangs, people experience imperial rule in their bodies.

To many who live in developed countries today, taxation is abstract and impersonal, a number on a payslip which might well seem excessive and annoying but is rarely demeaning or humiliating. When the tax is paid to an actual representative of the state or empire it becomes a bodily experience, just like forced labour or political persecution. When it is paid in kind, the confiscation of your hard-won food is all the more direct. You and your family have laboured over that heap of grain on the threshing floor for an entire agricultural year, and now a self-important official comes to measure and manipulate it and take a third of it away. Under the eyes of your family and community, all you can do is watch the assault on the fruits of all your hard work. Taxation is the public dispossession of earnings, autonomy and dignity.

Because taxation was used as a means of control and domination, it tended to accumulate a battery of officials, titles, uniforms and occasions, supported by an elaborate material culture of measures, receipts, seals and official storage buildings (chapter 3). The visit of the tax collector or his harbinger, the census official, became a formal ceremony, where members of the community were called out to witness the power and knowledge of the state and their own inferiority and humiliation (Gosden and Knowles 2001: 15–16; Wolf 1966: 51–3). In return, the taxpayer is given a receipt: a piece of paper or broken potsherd with writing on it. To an illiterate peasant family, that is a material demonstration of the state's control and penetration into their lives.

The ceremonial of taxation, of course, helped to legitimize it. Invocations of a deity and the display of religious symbols made taxation seem divinely ordained, as natural as the agricultural cycle of which it was an integral part. In spite of their oppression, people could be drawn into the pageantry of the occasion and so incorporated into the state. Nicholas Biddle, a 20-year-old American from a prominent Philadelphia family, noted this paradox when he watched the local Ottoman governor visiting the central Greek village of Livadia in 1806:

> Tho' bleeding under the scourge they were tickled with the pomp of their oppressor, and came out in the burning sun & waited on the grass 3 or 4 hours his coming. He came at last. Preceded & followed by a herd of savage cavalry & infantry, a band of music consisting of a quantity of kettledrums & a flute or two, he received the elders of the town who kissed his hand, & he then went on to his lodgings.
>
> McNeal 1993: 102

The governor's followers, some 200–300 of them, all had to be given food and accommodation for three days. This 'hospitality', a common means of supporting travelling officials, was not just expensive but highly intrusive (chapter 4). By welcoming your tax collectors and oppressors into your home, you give up your private space and even the opportunity for telling stories of resistance and ridicule.

Forced labour is far more important to a colonizing power than just providing a work force. People are incorporated into the colonial project and given new identities as subjects, while the product of that labour, particularly monumental architecture, symbolizes their acquiescence. Labour is a form of habitual daily practice, through which people act out relationships and construct identities (Silliman 2001b). Through labour the colonizers can try to impose religious ideals, state loyalty, strict discipline, or just plain punishment. For the Franciscans running plantations in late eighteenth- and early nineteenth-century California, for example, Indian labour was considered a 'morally enriching disciplinary activity that figured prominently in the Indians' conversion from savagery to civilization' (Hackel 1998: 122). This was carried out by strict daily routines which dovetailed work and prayer. In all such cases, the labourers might adopt or transform these loyalties and identities, or find new ones among themselves.

Monumental architecture provides particularly interesting examples of forced labour, because of its explicitly representative or symbolic role. By definition such architecture is bigger than it needs to be, and so demonstrates the ability to control labour (Trigger 1990: 125). The finished product with its impressive size, representational sculpture and symbols of power is only one aspect of the wider project. Rather than confining our analysis to a building's 'aesthetic' or 'artistic' aspects, it is important to examine the historical and material context of its production, which often shows radically different experiences and meanings than those evoked by the final structure (Jaskot 2000: 2, 5). Even when finished, it can carry very different associations from those intended by the elite who commissioned it. The labourers, for example, can reject its representational role and see it as a monument to their own achievements (Hutson 2002: 65–6).

In this chapter I will examine three different experiences of imperial rule. The highly elaborate taxation system of Roman Egypt shows intense control not just of people's income but of their labour and movement. This can be best seen in the monumental granaries and gates that characterized the cities of the Fayum Oasis. I will then investigate the experience of building monumental architecture, using two contrasting case studies: the Nuremberg and Berlin building projects of Nazi Germany; and the pyramids at Giza in Old Kingdom Egypt.

From threshing floor to grain ship

The streets of Karanis seemed entirely made of earth and sand: packed earth underfoot, scattered with donkey and camel droppings; mud plaster on the facades of the blank-walled houses; and sand blowing everywhere, through the gates that closed off different sections of the streets, and over the little walls and steps that tried unsuccessfully to keep it out of the houses. A little caravan of some five donkeys was plodding down one of the streets leading into the village from the east, heavily laden with sacks of grain and urged along by what was clearly a single, large family. The street met another one at right angles and the family paused, eyed by the soldiers guarding the imposing double entrance of the barracks building on their left. Across the street in front of them was the two-storey facade of a dovecot, noisy with the clapping of wings and throaty calls of the pigeons. Behind the dovecot they could just see the towers of their goal, the main state granary of Karanis.

The family waited in the busy street, getting in the way of passers-by, while the father stepped over the wooden threshold of a doorway round the corner to the right of the dovecot. His ten-year-old daughter peeked after him, and saw a crowded courtyard dominated by a circular grain mill in the centre, every available space taken up by storage bins, an oven and a kneading trough. Here a miller and baker were working, presumably making bread for the granary staff. The acrid smell of pigeon dung combined with the warm aroma of freshly ground wheat. Her father was first ignored, then shouted at. She stepped back quickly, and a minute later her father reappeared and hurriedly led them round to the side of the huge complex.

The courtyard was only 3 m wide, but it stretched all the way along the granary's northern side. The wall on the granary side was lined with 13 animal feeding troughs built out of mud brick. The whole place was seething with donkeys, camels, farmers and their families. After much pushing, shoving and shouting, their sacks of wheat were safely unloaded and heaped in one corner, and the donkeys were clustered round one of the troughs, eating hungrily the fodder that the family had brought for them. The father had disappeared into the granary, worried about whether he should report to the Grain-Receiver, or the Grain-Measurer, or one of the secretaries or assistants or granary guards, or even to the Sitologos himself. The only thing that was sure was that he would have to bribe them, and that it would be more than he could afford.

The girl decided to go exploring. At the far end of the courtyard a doorway beside a big storage jar led up a step and through the 60 cm-thick granary wall. The room inside seemed empty apart from two trap doors in the floor, leading down into huge vaulted storage chambers underneath. In the next room she had a choice: the door in front of her led to a narrow staircase, crowded with people carrying full sacks up and empty ones down, shouting and barging into each other. She turned right instead, where a doorway led out into a courtyard. There were arches all round her as she stood in the middle, trying not to get in the way of all the farmers carrying in their sacks of grain. In the floor under each arch was a pair of trap doors, leading into underground vaults like the ones she had seen before. The men were running into the arches and through the narrow doorways that they sheltered. Above them ran a balcony and another series of doorways, and above that she could hear people on the roof, where there must be a third storey of grain stores.

She turned, and had a sudden vision of the god Harpocrates. But this was not the friendly Harpocrates, the Horus-child who carried a pot or a duck and brought fertility to their crops and animals. This one was seated on a great throne, carrying the lotus flowers on which he was born at the beginning of time. He was flanked by a fearsome sphinx who wielded a black dagger in each paw and had cobras entwined around its legs and a jackal and a dog growing from its neck. He was clearly more interested in the protection of the granary and its officials than in the crops of families like her own.

It was a long wait until the officials were ready for them, but carrying the sacks of grain through the shouting, frenzied crowds seemed to take even longer. A secretary had shown them the vault where they were to deposit their grain: through the two entrance rooms, up the dark metre-wide staircase, round the narrow balcony with just a 65 cm-high parapet to stop them falling into the courtyard below, and then along a dark passageway and into the vault at the end. The plastered walls were covered with a black wash, and the slit window at the top seemed to give little light and no air. The doorway led onto a wall 30 cm wide, with separate storage compartments on each side. They walked carefully along the wall and poured the grain out of the sacks into the compartment at the end. As they poured the light dust floated upwards, dancing in the narrow beam of light, and clung to their sweating arms and bodies and penetrated their eyes and lungs and clothing.

The family that led a line of unladen donkeys out of Karanis that evening was silent, weary and caked in wheat dust, after labouring all day to give up a substantial proportion of their crop. The father was doing accounts in his head, adding the various bribes, fees and the hire of the donkeys to the actual tax. He clutched a broken fragment of water jar to his chest as if it were gold, which in a way it was. On it the secretary had written out his receipt, and the Grain-Receiver had countersigned it. This was his weapon against false accusations and attempted extortions, proof that he had paid his grain tax in full.

* * *

About a third of the grain needed for the vast population of Rome came from the province of Egypt. The collection, processing and transport of the 135,000 tons that this came to was a huge, complex and highly intrusive operation. Other Egyptian crops such as wine, oil and vegetables were not needed for Rome, so they were taxed in cash. All males from the age of 14 to 60 also paid the poll tax, and there were numerous other taxes and dues on produce, the use of facilities, and transporting goods. All in all, there were well over 100 different taxes and duties (Lewis 1983: 159–76). The machinery of Roman taxation, law and government penetrated into every village and household; it was 'ubiquitous and inescapable' (Hobson 1993: 197).

Before about AD 200, almost all of this taxation was administered not by Roman officials or by tax-farmers but by local people with a certain level of property, who were compelled to carry out various official duties without salary for between one and three years (Lewis 1983: 177–84; Sharp 1999: 225–6). These liturgies, as they were called, ranged from being *sitologoi* (village tax collectors) and grain transporters to inspectors of the Nile flood and guards of the threshing floors. If they failed in their duties, their property could be confiscated by the state in lieu.

There were, of course, abuses of the system, and extortion and fraud were endemic at all levels among soldiers and officials. This is particularly clear from the numerous and evidently unsuccessful edicts of prefects and emperors trying to suppress them (Brunt 1975: 125, 139). Tax collectors often employed bodyguards or took soldiers as escorts, and breaking into debtors' homes was commonplace. The numerous petitions preserved in the papyri are very often concerned with the 'violence' and 'insolence' of tax collectors (Hobson 1993: 201). Here is a characteristic example from a Karanis farmer in AD 193. He and his brother have delivered nine out of ten *artabas* of grain tax that they owe (the *artaba* varied, but was usually about 39 litres):

> Now, on account of the one remaining artaba the grain-tax collectors Peteësios son of Tkelō and Sarapion son of Maron, and their clerk Ptolemaios as well as their assistant Ammonios, broke into my house whilst I was out in the field, and tore off my mother's cloak and threw her to the ground. As a result she is bedridden and is unable to [move about].
>
> quoted in Lewis 1983: 162

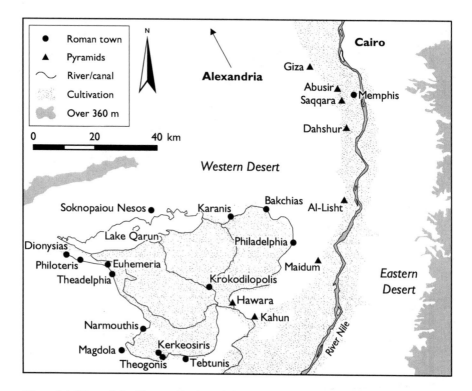

Figure 6.1 Map of the Fayum Oasis and the adjacent part of the Nile Valley. The cultivation, canals and course of the Nile shown are modern.

One of the richest agricultural areas of Roman Egypt was the Fayum Oasis, thanks to its elaborate network of Nile-fed canals (Figure 6.1; Rathbone 1996). Because of the thousands of papyrus documents that survive from its towns and villages, it is also one of the best-known. From villages such as Karanis, excavated by the University of Michigan from 1928 to 1935, we have astonishingly well-preserved structures and a wealth of detailed information about specific individuals, families and relationships. Much of this documentation is, unsurprisingly, concerned with the day-to-day mechanics of taxation. Karanis reached its peak in the second century AD, with a population in the 170s of between 2,200 and 2,500 (Boak 1955: 160).

The first stage of a grain of wheat's long journey to the table of the urban proletariat of Rome takes it from the field to the village threshing floor. Owners or tenants of private land had to take their harvested crop themselves; tenants on public land could use government donkeys – for a fee (S.L. Wallace 1938: 33–4; Rowlandson 1996: 225–6). It was threshed, winnowed and measured under the eyes of a range of liturgical officials, who variously inspected the grain for purity and cleanliness, oversaw the measuring, and guarded the piles of measured grain on the threshing floor (S.L. Wallace 1938: 34).

The next stage of the wheat's journey was to the granary, and again it is clear from leases and other documents that this had to be done entirely at the tenant's expense (Rowlandson 1996: 226). Small-scale farmers used their own families as free labour. My narrative at the beginning of this section tries to evoke something of the bodily experience of taking your grain to a state granary. It is based on the University of Michigan's excavations of building C65 at Karanis (Husselman 1952: 62–3; 1979: 58–62), papyrological evidence for the role of such granaries (Lewis 1983: 166–7; S.L. Wallace 1938: 35–8), and iconographic studies of Harpocrates as he appears in this building and elsewhere (Dunand 1979: 73–85; Frankfurter 1998: 40, 119–20; Husselman 1979: 61–2).

Ten large granaries were excavated at Karanis, plus several smaller examples and numerous grain stores that were parts of private houses (Husselman 1952: 58). Granary C65 was built in the second half of the second century AD, with later alterations. Enough remains of its top floor for all three storeys to be reconstructed, with their impressive total height of 10–11 m (Figures 6.2, 6.3). Because of its size, its position opposite the barracks, and the papyri found there it is the best candidate for being the official village granary which received the grain tax, though there may well have been several such granaries sharing that role (Husselman 1952: 69–70).

The receipts which farmers were given for their grain were written on readily available materials, usually a potsherd or a scrap of papyrus. Here is an example of a papyrus receipt from Oxyrhynchus, a town in the Nile Valley 110 km south of Karanis, dated by the emperors' reigns to 180 AD. The last sentence, which I have put in italics, is written in a different hand:

> There have been measured into the public granary, of wheat from the crop of the past 19th year of Aurelius Antoninus and Commodus Caesars our lords, through the grain collectors for the western toparchy, to the credit of Sarapion son of Charisios, of Episemos' Place, 4 artabas of wheat (= wht. art. 4). *I, Diogenes, grain collector, have signed [certifying] the 4 artabas of wheat.*
>
> quoted in Lewis 1983: 124

From the state granaries in the villages the grain then had to be transported to the nearest harbour on a major irrigation canal or on the Nile itself. Camels and donkeys were the main animals used, the camel being able to carry two to three times as much as a donkey. Like everything else, driving the animals was a compulsory liturgic service (Lewis 1983: 167).

It is clear that considerable amounts of time and energy were being invested at major Nile ports such as Memphis in guarding and controlling the tax grain and other products that passed through. The importance of the

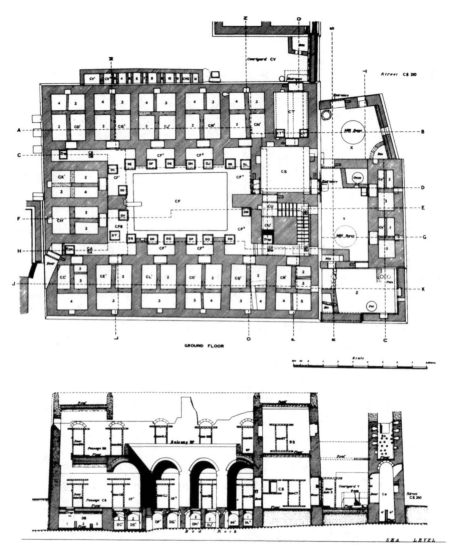

Figures 6.2 and 6.3 Plan of and section through Granary C65 at Karanis. The scale is in metres. Source: Kelsey Museum Archives.

port at Memphis had increased greatly during the Ptolemaic period with the expansion of agriculture in the Fayum. As well as receiving the tax grain and other goods overland from the north-eastern Fayum (Figure 6.1), it had a large income from shipbuilding, trade, and especially from tolls on passing Nile traffic (Thompson 1988: 59–61). There are customs house receipts from the second and third centuries AD showing that the Memphis harbour tax was paid by shipments from the Fayum cities of Dionysias, Soknopaiou

Nesos, Karanis, Bakchias, Philadelphia and Philopator/Theogonis (Thompson 1988: 297). In Ptolemaic Memphis there was a central guard post, which also acted as toll point and public record office, and further guard posts on the Nile to the north and south of the city. These were presumably still in use in the Roman period, and there are certainly records of a military garrison in the city (Thompson 1988: 62, 269–70).

At ports such as Memphis the tax grain was loaded onto north-bound ships, in return for a detailed receipt. The cargo was accompanied by a sealed and labelled sample of the grain in a small pot or leather wallet, so that the granary officials at the far end could check that the wheat had not been adulterated by the skipper and crew with dirt or barley (Rickman 1971: 189–90). The laden ships journeyed down the Nile, along the Rosetta branch and then by canal to Lake Mareotis immediately south of Alexandria.

The central state granaries for all the Egyptian grain to be exported were situated at Alexandria's Lake Mareotis harbour, on the southern edge of the city. The archaeologists of Napoleon's expedition to Egypt in 1798 noted some stone piers there, probably Byzantine, but apart from that nothing is known archaeologically about the site (Rodziewicz 1998: 101). According to Strabo, who spent several years in Egypt in the late first century BC, the goods coming in from the south were so numerous that 'the harbour on the lake was in fact richer than that on the sea' (Strabo 17.1.7). There are also numerous references in the papyri and inscriptions to a senior official termed the 'Procurator of Neapolis' who was in charge of the state granaries, clearly referring to the same place (Rickman 1971: 303–6; Sharp 1999: 233).

Once the grain had been received, accounted for, and checked for purity, it was transported by canal across the city to the main western harbour on the Mediterranean, where the grain fleet was waiting to transport it to Rome. By the fourth century AD, when Egypt was providing Constantinople with about 220,000 tons of grain a year, this required some 647 grain ships of average size, or 32 ships leaving Alexandria every week during the sailing season (Haas 1997: 42). This was a massive and very visible extraction of the labour and resources of the province's villagers and farmers.

Gates, trade routes and bandits

Control and surveillance of people's movement was a major part of the machinery of government in Roman Egypt, particularly where taxes and duties were being imposed. We have already seen the barracks opposite the state granary at Karanis, and the Ptolemaic guard posts on the Nile north and south of Memphis. Another striking example of the control of major land and water routes comes from the harbour of Taposiris Magna, on the north side of Lake Mareotis' western arm (Rodziewicz 1998: 102–3). A breakwater 3 km long runs parallel to the northern shore, with a peninsula on the west and another breakwater on the east enclosing the vast harbour. What is really striking is that a third wall runs from the main breakwater right across to the southern shore of the lake, which at this point is 2 km wide. This means that any shipping passing along Lake Mareotis had to pass through the harbour of Taposiris Magna. Similarly, the land route passing along the spit of land between the lake and the sea to the north is cut off at the same point by a wall running right across it.

The same concern with control of people's movements can be seen at a smaller scale in the architecture and layout of the Ptolemaic and Roman towns of the Fayum (see Figure 6.1 for a map). Tebtunis lies on the desert edge in the south, an important position on the route to the Nile Valley and the south. Right on the southern edge of the town was a large enclosure measuring 28 × 32 m, with a four-roomed building, several ovens, and a massive 5 m-high square tower (Gallazzi 1994: 28). Judging by the papyri and coins found there, this was a guard post of the Desert Guards during the second and first centuries BC, providing a desert watchtower and control post where traders paid their customs duties.

Bakchias has a similar position on the north-eastern edge of the Fayum Oasis, controlling the all-important overland route to Memphis and the Nile Valley to the north. On the north-eastern edge of the town was an impressive double gate in a massive mud brick wall, reinforced at the corners with pillars, with a paved passage running through it and a channel 1.6 m long for a sliding bar to lock the gate (Piacentini 1994: 46–51; 1996: 60). A room adjacent to the passageway contained a burnt patch with fragments of animal bones and a storage jar full of grain; this was presumably a kitchen for customs officers or guards. A road runs south from the gate across an open square, but then has to skirt round a large thick-walled structure which may have been a garrison and guard tower (Pernigotti 1999: 26; Piacentini 1994: 53). Roman period papyri from the town record the taxes paid by merchants and caravans passing 'through the gate of Bakchias' on their way between the western oases and Memphis (Piacentini 1994: 67).

Soknopaiou Nesos lies in the north of the Fayum on the northern shore of Late Moeris, the predecessor of the modern Lake Qarun (Figure 6.1). Thanks to this position, it controlled the caravan route going into the western desert. The huge numbers of papyrus customs receipts found there demonstrate the importance of this in a village whose resources otherwise consisted of minimal arable land, fishing in the lake, and pilgrimage (Bernand 1975: 125). On the edge of the desert outside the town there are a series of spring mounds topped with mud brick structures and Ptolemaic or Roman pottery, which were probably watchtowers guarding desert routes or irrigation systems (Caton-Thompson and Gardner 1934: 153).

The town itself is dominated by the temple of Soknopaios, the crocodile god, with substantial walls round the sanctuary and a long *dromos* or ceremonial way leading up to it. An interpretative problem faced by the excavators is that the sanctuary walls are considerably thicker than the city walls, which are barely strong enough to be of any use for defensive purposes. No traces of them were found in the southern part of the town, though they might have been made up of a continuous line of houses. It seems more likely that the perimeter walls were intended to keep the wind and sand out, and above all to control access to the town, forcing merchants and others to pass through recognized gates and guard posts (Davoli 1997: 52–3).

It is hardly surprising that the state was careful to control merchant traffic, and to extract dues and tolls wherever it passed through essential nodes such as desert-edge towns and ports on major canals and the Nile (de Laet 1949: 313–17). The obsession with controlling people's passage and movement was much wider than this. There were gates in town streets dividing one quarter from another, such as a gate 100 m south of Granary C65 in Karanis, on the town's major north–south street (Husselman 1979: 12). Acoris similarly had two monumental gates within the town, the north one perhaps giving entrance to an acropolis or military area, the south one providing a monumental entry into the sanctuary of the temple (Lesquier 1911: 115–21).

Even within sanctuaries and temples, successive entrances and pylons gave a sense of penetrating further and further into the presence of the deity, while some classes of people were excluded. This is most dramatically seen in the ancient monumental temples such as the Luxor Temple, where a ceremonial way, three vast gateways leading into broad and high halls, and some 170 columns intervened between the visitor and the inner Roman-period shrine. At all levels, anyone walking or riding through a Roman Egyptian town was seen and controlled, and at the many architectural barriers was either denied or allowed passage.

What about the resistance? The province of Egypt was famous for being 'gossipy and ingenious in devising insults for its rulers', as the Roman writer Seneca put it in the mid-first century AD (*To Helvia on Consolation* 19.6). The *Acts of the Pagan Martyrs* revelled in its narratives of Greek Alexandrians defying and mocking the Roman Emperor to his face, while a series of Egyptian apocalyptic texts prophesied the gory downfall of the Roman Empire (Lewis 1983: 198–9, 205–6). There were also outright rebellions, most famously by the Bucoli or 'herdsmen' who defeated a Roman army and even threatened Alexandria from their hideouts in the swamps of the Nile delta in 172–3 AD. This gave rise to a series of stories, myths, and even a Greek novel (Lewis 1983: 205; Winkler 1980). As always, the narratives are as important a source of resistance and pride as the actions themselves.

For a peasant farmer ground down by excessive taxation, poor harvests and brutal tax collectors, there was always one way out: flight. Again and again the rulers of Egypt expressed their concern about what they termed *anachoresis* or 'going up', the flight of cultivators from their fields, causing an immediate reduction in tax revenue. As the emperor Domitian put it, 'If the farmers are snatched away, the lands will remain uncultivated' (Lewis 1983: 174). In 147/8 AD a total of 120 liturgists in Oxyrynchus did not have the resources to fulfil their duties and ran away, leaving their property to be confiscated (Bowman 1996: 69). The situation was so bad in the Fayum in the 50s AD that the village of Philadelphia suffered severe depopulation, with 152 fugitives from taxation (Lewis 1983: 164). Their taxes were normally spread round the remaining taxpayers, with occasional amnesties to entice people back, especially for the census every 14 years. In the 160s AD so many villages were semi-abandoned that all taxes of fugitive villagers were suspended, in the hope of tempting them back home (Lewis 1993; Sharp 1999: 232).

A few of these fugitives gravitated to the big cities, especially Alexandria, but most ended up in the swamps of the Delta or in the hills along the edges of the Nile Valley, hence the term *anachoresis*. They automatically became outlaws, and survived by raiding villages for food. Banditry became endemic in the entire country (Lewis 1983: 203–5; 1993: 101–2). Lake Mareotis south of Alexandria was particularly attractive because of the many hiding places in the marshes and the rich traffic coming past on its way to the southern harbour of Alexandria (Haas 1997: 37).

Hideouts are by definition hard to find, particularly 2,000 years later. One very convenient location, however, would have been in the many ancient tombs that lined the cliffs and slopes of the desert edge, many of them already looted. We know that several New Kingdom tombs at the workers' village of Deir el-Medina were remodelled in the Late Roman period for habitation (Montserrat and Meskell 1997: 186). Similar tombs would have provided ideal hideouts and bases for the thousands of bandits and fugitives from the villages of the Nile Valley, Fayum and Delta.

Even without fleeing, there were always ways of hiding income from the tax collectors. This is closely tied to architectural materials and means of construction. Mud brick was the universal building material in these towns, with stone reserved for the monumental facades of temples or gateways. As the desert sand blows in and the mud brick and plaster is scoured away, the floors and rooms fill up, and a new building layer must be constructed at a higher level. This gives the characteristic *kom* or tell, the artificial mound of an ancient Near Eastern city, and explains the multiple building levels of towns such as Karanis.

Because a house is normally built on top of the ruins of another house, there are numerous foundation spaces and opportunities for underground storage and hidden cellars. The houses of Acoris, for example, tended to use the walls of their predecessors as foundations, which gave not just an unchanging plan but easily constructed cellars (Lesquier 1911: 127). Some of these were clearly intended to be hidden. A cellar under a storeroom in a Roman villa in Quseir Al-Qadim was perhaps used by a merchant to hide his more valuable goods (Meyer 1982). A coin hoard deposited in Bakchias after AD 165 was hidden beneath the mud brick floor of a storeroom (Grenfell *et al.* 1900: 40, 65).

More intriguingly, in a large building in Narmouthis in the Fayum, perhaps the headquarters for the village officials, a storeroom in the furthest corner from the entrance could only be entered by means of triangular steps from the roof above. One of the mud bricks making up these steps concealed a storage jar set horizontally inside the step, only revealed by removing the mud brick (Bresciani 1967: 46). Could an employee or servant be pilfering and hiding valuables? Unfortunately by the time the excavators found it the jar was completely empty.

Labour and architecture in Nazi Germany

Berlin was to become 'Germania', the new world capital, and the plans and models that Hitler commissioned from Albert Speer in 1937 had to show an appropriate grandeur. The central avenue was to be 5 km long, with a triumphal arch at the southern end 50 times the size of the Arc de Triomphe in Paris. The Domed Hall would allow Hitler to address 180,000 people inside it, and just the lantern at the top of it would be bigger than the dome of St Peter's in Rome. Even the model of the new Berlin was 30 m long (Fest 1999: 69–81; Speer 1978).

Why did Nazi public architecture have to be so immense? What did buildings such as this mean to the people who built and used them? A building is not just a pattern of materials, shapes and decorations. It provides the arena for a range of specific activities and experiences during the construction of it just as much as after it is finished and in use. When the structures are as immense as Hitler and Speer's projects in Berlin and Nuremberg, or the Giza pyramids in Fourth-Dynasty Egypt, then their actual construction takes on an enormously important social and political role.

The Nazi building programmes in Berlin and Nuremberg can be seen at a variety of levels. Public buildings were intended to be representational: they had to give an image of the state, and a big structure meant a great state. 'If they are to have a lasting significance and value, they must conform to the largeness of scale prevalent in the other spheres of national life,' declared Hitler in a speech in 1935 (Lane 1985: 189). This explains the competitiveness that appears in Speer's writing about his structures: everything had to be bigger than its counterparts abroad: the Arc de Triomphe, Grand Central Station, St Peter's, St Paul's, the Empire State Building, Khufu's pyramid (Scobie 1990: 91).

Style was also seen as carrying political meaning. Because of the disparate nature of Nazi political command, there was no official architectural policy, and different ministers and patrons favoured different styles (Lane 1985: 9, 186). Hitler and Speer preferred a pared-down classicism with an emphasis on geometry and rhythm rather than decoration. This gave them the opportunity for dominating facades, axial symmetry and a hierarchical organization of spaces. The associations with the cultural and political grandeur of ancient

Greece and Rome demonstrated Germany's role as the heir of their Aryan greatness (Jaskot 2000: 57; Scobie 1990).

The materials, however, should be German, not international. This meant stone, not concrete or iron, and in particular good German granite. According to Speer's 'theory of ruin value', the remains of his stone buildings would demonstrate Germany's greatness in 2,000 years' time, just as Roman ruins did today (Scobie 1990: 93–6). By developing stone as the monumental building economy's main material, they would also not conflict with the iron and steel needs of the rapidly growing armaments industry (Jaskot 2000: 58–9). As we will see, this provided a major economic opportunity which the SS were quick to seize.

Most of Speer's largest designs were specifically of stadiums and arenas for Nazi ceremonial, a specialism that he termed 'assembly-architecture' (Scobie 1990: 69). This is seen most clearly in his complex for the annual Nazi Party rallies at Nuremberg. His earliest structure there was the Zeppelinfeld, an almost square stadium for 90,000 marchers in the centre and 134,000 spectators round the four sides (Lane 1985: 193; Scobie 1990: 85–7). The classical rhythms of the yellowish-white travertine colonnades were interspersed with Nazi flags, and broken by the massive central podium on the east side with the Führer's pulpit, a recurring theme in Nazi public architecture.

In 1934 Speer designed not just the structure of the Zeppelinfeld but the ceremonial that took place within it (Fest 1999: 50–1; Speer 1970: 58–9). His famous 'cathedral of light' extended the colonnade 8 or 10 km into the night sky, with 130 searchlights shining vertically upwards. Blocks of officials, soldiers and cadets formed structures and avenues across the main square, with marching groups directing every spectator's eye towards Hitler in the pulpit on the front of the central podium. As Leni Riefenstahl's film of this event shows so graphically, Nazi propagandists understood that architecture is not made of bricks or stones but of people, light, sound, experience, emotion.

There is another side to monumental architecture such as this which rarely appears in the artistic or even the historical analyses. What effect did the massive construction projects have on the labourers, the society, and the associations that the finished building would carry? Albert Speer's first major success in working for Hitler was not so much as an architect but as an organizer. In January 1938 he was told to design a new monumental Reich Chancellery, and that it had to be finished in a year's time (Speer 1970: 102–3; 1978: 22). The massive building with its 420 rooms and 20 million bricks was built in nine months. A total of 4,500 workers laboured in two shifts, with several thousand more producing the components. Speer had no building schedule; he relied on his own 'brilliant improvisational genius' (Fest 1999: 103). It was this genius that carried him from being architect to becoming Minister of Armaments in February 1942. By 1944 he was responsible for the organization and control of 28 million workers (Sereny 1995: 332).

A building site can be seen as a microcosm of the state. It has a clear social hierarchy, there must be total discipline and control, and there is a very obvious goal to be successfully achieved. According to the 'Führer-principle', Hitler brought together all powers and identities of the state and the German people to be unified in himself. This meant that the 4,500 workers constructing his official headquarters were constructing the state itself. After the completion of the building they were all invited to tour it, and were then addressed by Hitler:

> Whenever I receive anyone in the Chancellery, it is not the private individual Adolf Hitler who receives him, but the Leader of the German nation—and therefore it is not I who receive him, but Germany through me. For that reason I want these rooms to be in keeping with their high mission. Every individual has contributed to a structure that will outlast the centuries and will speak to posterity of our times. This is the first architectural creation of the new, great German Reich!
>
> quoted in Speer 1970: 114

Hitler's personal liking for visiting building sites and examining architectural models was partly due to his own architectural aspirations and interests (Fest 1999: 52, 68, 75). But the role of construction in the literal and metaphorical rebuilding of the German state went much further than that. The famous autobahn building programme begun in winter 1933 had the specific purpose of providing both employment and self-respect for the German people, who were still suffering the political and economic consequences of the Treaty of Versailles, war reparations and the economic collapse of 1929. This was fully exploited in the official propaganda (Overy 1994: 82–7; Zeller 1999: 220). At a different level, the 'Beauty of Labour' office which Speer took over in 1934 had a mission to improve hygienic and aesthetic conditions in factories and workplaces (Fest 1999: 45). Monumental building projects gave the Nazi state the opportunity to combine the representation of German greatness with National Socialist ideals of the glory of labour and the importance of discipline and hierarchy.

Not all labour was intended to incorporate its labourers into the Nazi state. Some was intended specifically to destroy them. This 'destructive construction' (Jaskot 2000: 138) began with the first concentration camps in 1934, and accelerated in the years immediately before and during the war. The SS who ran the camps were not interested in efficiency: the most important purpose of labour was to brutalize, dehumanize and kill (Allen 1998). After 1938 the supply of Jewish and East European prisoners seemed endless, and SS managers and camp commandants saw no contradiction between extermination through labour and the need for high productivity. As labour needs became ever more urgent during the war, skilled workers were separated out and treated better. Even so, unskilled workers were still given deliberately primitive technology and endured punishing conditions. The construction of the V2 rocket facilities killed more workers than its products killed the enemy.

The SS were quick to see the economic opportunities given by Hitler's obsession with monumental architecture. In 1938 they set up the Deutsche Erd- und Steinwerke ('German Earth and Stone Works') to take advantage of this niche. The use of forced labour in their concentration camps gave them an immediate advantage over their rivals, as did their political links with Nazi leaders. When they decided to build two new concentration camps in 1940, for example, they first asked Albert Speer what sort of stone he needed for his Nuremberg and Berlin projects. At his suggestion, they built Natzweiler in south-west Germany to quarry red granite for Speer's massive German stadium in Nuremberg, and Gross-Rosen in the south-east for its blue-grey granite (Jaskot 2000: 70).

The concentration camp of Mauthausen in north-west Austria was begun in 1938 and exploited the abundant fine-grained blue-grey granite in the area. This was originally intended for the monumental reconstruction of the nearby city of Linz, designated as a 'Führer-city', though that never passed beyond the planning stages. Unlike Hitler and Speer, Himmler favoured a medieval 'Germanic' style for his SS buildings. The two most visible sides of Mauthausen were defended with a granite curtain wall complete with turrets and completely unnecessary sight-holes, and a monumental entrance flanked by towers. Electrified barbed wire sufficed for the other two sides (Jaskot 2000: 134).

Of all the work details inflicted on the prisoners, the Wienergraben quarry immediately west of the camp was the worst. As usual, the technology was deliberately primitive. During the construction of the camp prisoners had to carry blocks of granite often weighing 50 kg on their back, up the 186 steps which led out of the quarry. All structures acquire meaning from the experiences of the people who used them, and these steps have become known as the Todesstiege, or 'steps of death' (Figure 6.4). This was where prisoners collapsed under the weight of the granite and the blows of the kapos and guards, and where Jews were driven up and then pushed off the top onto the quarry floor deep below (Razola and Constante 1969: 69–71). The Spanish republican Sebastián Mena was one of the prisoners carrying blocks up to the camp for paving the streets and building the fortification wall:

> So we were continually suspended between life and death, from the quarry to the camp. This distance was about a kilometre; we covered it every day ten or twelve times, and as we had each time to climb or descend the steps of the quarry . . . you could say that our Calvary consisted of 24 times 186 steps. For the Nazis, a block of granite had more value than a human life.
>
> quoted in Razola and Constante 1969: 76

Figure 6.4 Prisoners carrying blocks of granite up the 'steps of death' in the quarry at Mauthausen concentration camp, north-west Austria, in 1942. Source: United States Holocaust Memorial Museum, courtesy of Archiv der KZ-Gedenstaette Mauthausen.

Even in these conditions there was resistance, and a determined clinging to pride and self-respect. For the Spanish republican and communist prisoners this meant, above all else, solidarity. They began an 'offensive' in the quarry, expressed by stealing vegetables from the quarry commander's garden, insulting the kapos, and carrying out small acts of sabotage. They made sure that their weaker comrades were given blocks to carry which were the same size as the rest but less dense and so lighter, and that they were on the inside of the column, furthest from the sticks and fists of the kapos. A group of Jews who knew they would be killed marched towards the sub-machine gun in the quarry watchtower singing *L'Internationale* (Razola and Constante 1969: 65–74).

What are the meanings, associations and memories of a building which has been constructed from these blocks? 'We had to push wheelbarrows of sand for a distance of a kilometre, and carry big stones on our backs, always under blows, of course, and often the stones were stained with blood' (Razola and Constante 1969: 68). A building holds within itself not just materials, patterns and organization, but the labour and experience of the people who constructed it. The monumental architecture of Nuremberg and Berlin was built of these bloodied stones.

Labour and architecture in Old Kingdom Egypt

The pyramids of the Fourth-Dynasty pharaohs at Giza are famous for their statistics. Their 5 million cubic metres of stone were quarried, transported and put in place within some 80 years, between Khufu's accession in 2551 BC and Menkaura's death in 2472 BC. By the time the various temples, satellite and queens' pyramids, causeways and officials' tombs are added, the total comes to 9 million cubic metres. To give some human meaning to that figure, a cubic metre of limestone weighs about 2.5 tons, and is the typical size of a core block in Khufu's pyramid. Using a sledge on a built and lubricated runway, a worker can drag between a third and half a ton on the flat. So just to transport the blocks from the quarries to the pyramids we are talking about some 10 or 15 million individual trips.

Out of curiosity, it is worth comparing these statistics with Speer's monumental buildings (Table 6.1). To Hitler, there was no question: 'Even the pyramids will pale against the masses of concrete and stone colossi which I am erecting' (Fest 1999: 59). The massive German Stadium at Nuremberg with seating for 400,000 spectators seems larger than Khufu's pyramid in terms of volume, which was certainly what Speer claimed (1970: 68), but much of this was open space. In terms of sheer volume of stone moved, and therefore labour exploited, the Pharaohs win the day. Only the impossibly vast Domed Hall in Berlin would have seriously dwarfed the pyramids.

What impact did these massive labour needs have on Fourth-Dynasty Egypt? Were workers incorporated into the state by their labour, or were they alienated and destroyed? First of all, it is clear that the technology they used was far from being deliberately primitive. Middle Kingdom reliefs show giant statues being pulled on a sledge along tracks, which are being lubricated just in front of the sledge. The remains of such tracks have been found, again from

Table 6.1 Comparison of monumental architecture in Old Kingdom Egypt and
Nazi Germany.

	Volume (m³)	Stone (m³)	Height (m)	Base (m)
Khufu's pyramid	2,583,000	2,583,000	147	230 × 230
Khafra's pyramid	2,211,000	2,211,000	144	215 × 215
Menkaura's pyramid	235,000	235,000	65	105 × 103
Reich Chancellery	360,000			420 × 55
German Stadium	9,000,000	350,000	109	662 × 553
Domed Hall (not built)	21,024,000		265	380 × 380

Sources: Fest 1999: 57–9; Jaskot 2000: 60; Lehner 1997: 17; Scobie 1990: 78, 99; Speer 1970: 68, 153–4;
1978: 22.

the Middle Kingdom, but modern experiments have shown that using these
methods one worker can pull up to about half a ton or 500 kg on the flat
(Lehner 1997: 202–3). Compare this with the inmates of Mauthausen carrying 50-kg blocks on their backs. The massive ramps, which constituted some
two-thirds the volume of the pyramids themselves, were clearly constructed
to minimize the gradient and maximize the convenience to the quarries and
the port (Figure 6.5). Given the restricted space available on the Giza plateau,
the only way to achieve this was to have the ramps spiralling round the growing pyramids (Lehner 1985: 128–32; 1997: 215–17). Compare this with the
186 'steps of death'.

Two thousand years after the construction of the pyramids, the Greek
travel writer and historian Herodotus was told by the Egyptian priests that the
work for Khufu's pyramid 'went on in three-monthly shifts, a hundred thousand men in a shift' (Herodotus 2.124). The number seems wildly excessive. If
100,000 workers were the total employed, rather than being the number in
each shift, this would give four separate shifts of 25,000 men, each shift lasting three months. If the volume of stone in the pyramid is extrapolated to the
amount of labour required to quarry, transport and place it, then 25,000
labourers working continuously would have been enough to build the pyramid within Khufu's reign (Lehner 1997: 224).

We know something about the organization of these workers from the
inscriptions and masons' marks on many of the blocks, particularly from
Khufu's and Menkaura's pyramids (Eyre 1987: 11–12; Lehner 1997: 225;
Roth 1991: 119–22). The entire workforce was split into two separate gangs,
whose names were always derived from the pharaoh's name. For Menkaura's
pyramid they were called the 'Companions of Menkaura' and the 'Drunkards
of Menkaura', and seemed to have been responsible for the south and north
sides of the pyramid respectively. Each of these was split into five groups
usually known by their later Greek name of *phyle* or tribe. They had standardized names derived, like our 'watches', from parts of a ship. These were further
divided into ten 'divisions' or 'tens', each of which constituted 20 workers.

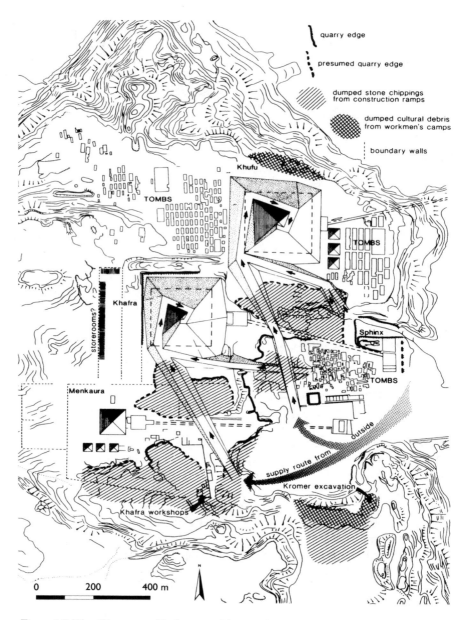

Figure 6.5 The Giza pyramid plateau, with quarries, construction debris and suggested positions of the construction ramps. Source: Kemp 1989: 131, reproduced with the permission of Routledge.

On the second course of large core blocks in Menkaura's pyramid are texts written in red ink, with signs about 30 cm high. They were clearly written before the blocks were laid in place, and each one spelt out the name of the gang, phyle and division (Roth 1991: 127). By the succession of phyle names it is clear that they worked in sequential shifts: this is how the rotation mentioned by Herodotus worked, rather than the workforce changing wholesale every three months. In later dynasties this became the standard way of providing regular labour for temple duties and agricultural production. Service was compulsory: a prison register from the Middle Kingdom records the execution of a woman who ran away without performing her state service. Her family had been held hostage until her capture (Kemp 1989: 129).

The organization and administration of this workforce was clearly a massive undertaking in itself. Tomb inscriptions from the Fourth Dynasty record an important official post of 'Overseer of Royal Works and Workforces', and it is clear that organizing the workforce was a major part of this official's job (Strudwick 1985: 218, 243–4). Even the quarry expeditions for non-local stone were huge operations. As always, later periods are better documented, and the expedition led by the herald Ameni to the quarries of Wadi Hammamat in 1933 BC is particularly informative (Mueller 1975: 256). Under his command he had 17,000 unskilled workers, 400 skilled quarrymen, stone cutters and rowers, and 1,000 guards. They were managed by 80 assorted officials, and the service personnel included 30 hunters, 60 sandal-makers, 20 brewers, 20 millers, 20 bakers and 50 butlers.

There are many examples of elaborate calculations of how much bread and beer a workforce such as this required. These make it clear that the state was concerned with feeding its workers properly, as well as controlling the administration that did the feeding (Kemp 1989: 117–28). Herodotus was shown an inscription recording the amount spent on radishes, onions and leeks for the workers (2.125). The pharaohs clearly did not expect their workers to survive – or die – on starvation wages. Recent excavations on the edge of the flood plain below Menkaura's pyramid have revealed some of the facilities for feeding the labourers who built it (Hawass and Lehner 1997: 34–5; Lehner 1997: 236–7). Two parallel rooms 6.2 m long were clearly bakeries, with vats for mixing dough, large bread pots, and the baking pits where the pots were buried in ash. These would have mass-produced a heavy, starchy bread for feeding large numbers of workers. Adjacent was another structure which included a series of troughs and benches with the remains of the gills, fins and bones of catfish and schal embedded in the floor. Local Nile fish was clearly an important source of protein for the workforce.

Did these workers identify themselves in any way with the enormous project they were engaged in, and with the pharaoh who initiated it and was to be buried inside the pyramid they were building? The phyle system clearly consisted of meaningful social units, unlike the barrack blocks or different work details referred to by the Mauthausen inmates. By naming all the gangs after the pharaoh, they were directly associated with him, and the positioning of the different gang and phyle names on opposite sides of the central chambers suggests a sense of rivalry between the groups of workers. By carrying out their phyle service for perhaps one month in ten (Kemp 1989: 113), working on the pyramid became an inevitable and natural part of the year.

Being formally given clothes by the state was another reminder of the source of their employment and the purpose of their shared labour. In the Sixth Dynasty the commandant at the limestone quarries of Tura protested at his work crews being sent away to receive their clothing from the vizier in person, particularly when the clothes could easily have been brought by a courier who was coming over anyway on the stone barge. 'It is a single day only that should be wasted for this battalion when it is clothed' (Gardiner 1927: 78). To the central government, however, this was an opportunity to show them who they were really working for. As with Hitler addressing the builders of his new Chancellery, this was a visible and public demonstration to the workers that by their labour they had been incorporated into the state.

Just 50 m to the south-west of the Giza bakeries and fish-processing plant is a large cemetery for workers and artisans, dating to the Fourth and Fifth Dynasties (Hawass 1997). The 43 tombs in the upper part of the cemetery are larger and more elaborate. The tombs are rock-cut or have stone facades, and their grave goods are relatively expensive. According to their inscriptions, these belonged to people with titles such as 'Overseer of the side of the pyramid', 'Director of the draftsmen', 'Overseer of masonry', and 'Director of workers'.

In the lower part of the cemetery are about 600 graves, which seem to belong to labourers. They are much poorer, usually built out of nothing more than mud brick or stone rubble. Many of the men had died at the age of 30 or 35, and many women below 30. This is notably lower than the aristocrats buried in the monumental mastaba cemetery by Khufu's pyramid. Arthritis was common, and there were many fractures, particularly of arm and lower leg bones. Most of these had healed completely, so they had presumably been properly splinted and cared for. There were two successful amputations.

What is most interesting about this artisans' and labourers' cemetery is the way in which many of those buried there seem to identify themselves with their work. Ptah-shepsesu in the upper cemetery had pieces of granite, basalt and diorite used in the pyramids incorporated into the walls of his tomb. Other tombs used similar fragments from the mountains of quarry waste, trimmings and ramp material that the project generated. Inty-shedu, a boat carpenter, was buried with a group of five statues, just like the five statues in the pyramid temples of Khafre and Menkaura. In the lower cemetery one tomb seems to have a miniature ramp leading up and round its dome, like a pyramid under construction. Others are miniature mastabas with tiny courtyards, copying the officials' tombs that were being constructed round the pyramids.

This is clearly very much the opposite of alienation between the work force and the project. People are calling themselves by the king's name, proudly stating their role in the construction of his tomb, and incorporating the material, appearance and layout of his tomb into their own. The construction of the great pyramids of the Third and Fourth Dynasties came at exactly the time when the Egyptian state was reinventing itself as a vast administrative and controlling structure (Baines 1988; Kemp 1989: 136; Mendelssohn 1971: 216). People were incorporated into this structure by the pyramids themselves. New systems of supply, labour and organization were developed, and after several generations of annual pyramid-building, people were used to regular labour, discipline and organization. Above all, by identifying themselves with the building of the pyramid, they had identified themselves with the building of the state.

Conclusion

The experience of imperial rule or any other form of centralized control is clearly felt at a deeply personal level. Taxation and forced labour extract two of the most important constituents of people's lives: food and energy. In Roman Egypt villagers did not just watch their grain being removed from their fields and towns: they had to carry it themselves. Any movement of people or goods was carefully watched and controlled by a series of gates, watchtowers and guard posts. The machinery of taxation and customs penetrated into almost every aspect of people's life and experience.

Forced labour is an even more direct, bodily experience of imperial rule. The state appropriates time and energy which could have been spent on subsistence or family and community activities. The building site is the ideal arena for the state or empire to impose ideological structures and new loyalties, or to inflict punishment and humiliation. The Giza pyramids and Hitler's autobahns did more of the first, while the concentration camps focused on the second. In each case the raw materials have become human experiences: bloodied stones, sweaty grain, a limestone block with a work-gang's name.

7

THE PATRON SAINT OF TAX
EVADERS

There are many stories about Saint Mamas, the Cypriot patron saint of tax evaders. Here is one of them, the version told in the village of Yerolakkos in the mid-twentieth century (Klirides 1951: 107–8).

The shepherds of Saint Mamas in Morphou refused to pay their taxes to the king. So the king sent his tax collectors to arrest them and bring them to Nicosia. The shepherds were terrified, and called out to Saint Mamas to save them. At once the saint appeared to them riding on his lion, and told them that he would go to the king in their place, as he was their shepherd and they were his flock. The tax collectors were terrified, and ran back to Nicosia to tell the king, who promptly ordered that the city gates should be shut to keep out the saint.

Meanwhile Saint Mamas took the road towards Nicosia, riding his lion and flanked by his companions Saint George and Saint Dimitrios. In the village of Philia they made their first stop. And in the place where they stopped the villagers built a church and dedicated it to Saint Mamas. In the village of Yerolakkos they made their second stop. They rested a little outside the village and drank water from a small spring that was there.

And at the moment when they set out for Nicosia, the lion roared. It roared so powerfully that the earth was shaken all the way to Nicosia, and the city gates were flung open and crashed against the walls. The king was terrified, and at once sent his messengers to Saint Mamas. They told him that his shepherds were excused their taxes, and that the king would never demand taxes from them ever again. And in the place where the lion roared, the villagers of Yerolakkos built a church and dedicated it to the saint.

What a charter for not paying your taxes! The tax evader is justified by religion and protected by a saint, and this hidden transcript allows people to express their independence and pride in the face of imperial exploitation. The story is also embedded in the landscape, retold whenever people visit these churches, pass along the road from Morphou to Nicosia, or kiss the icons of the saint which were so popular in Cyprus from the thirteenth century (Figure 7.1).

There are many forms of tax evasion. For a small community taxed largely

Figure 7.1 Late thirteenth-century icon of Saint Mamas, from the church of Saint
Mamas Kouremenos in Pano Amiantos. Source: Sophocleous 1994:
no. 27, courtesy of Sophocles Sophocleous.

in kind, the easiest form was secret food production. By growing and processing your crops away from the view of the tax collector, you can enjoy the
entire proceeds of the harvest, rather than the two-thirds or half left by the
tithe gatherer or tax farmer. As well as the direct material benefit, there is the
pride in thumbing your nose at the tax collector and the state – in relative

safety. As a type of everyday resistance, this is even better than pilfering or vandalism (chapter 2). Tax evasion can easily been seen as keeping what is your own, and so is morally justifiable and can be sanctioned by the likes of Saint Mamas.

If political and military histories are written by those who win, then the histories of tax evasion are only written about those who get caught. Because of this, archival sources tend to be biased against the tax evaders, and can say nothing about the unknown numbers of people who got away with it. There are also archaeological problems. Tax evasion is by definition secretive, and therefore hard to find in the material record. Finding the material evidence of secret production and crop processing, for example, requires intensive survey in the highlands, not just site-spotting in fertile lowland plains. This sort of analysis also needs to be sensitive to the stories, memories and associations that are expressed in the landscape.

In this chapter I will examine the archaeological evidence for secret cultivation, processing and storage, and look more widely at some narratives and experiences of tax evasion. Cyprus during the sixteenth to nineteenth centuries provides a wealth of archaeological, documentary and oral historical data, as well as the striking figure of Saint Mamas. First we need to look more closely at the mechanics of secret cultivation, and the ways in which it becomes embedded in the landscape as narrative.

Secrets and stories

The census official and land surveyor were the main agents of the state's penetration into people's lives (chapter 5). Historical sources from a wide range of periods and regions show that there were always people who successfully hid their land from the state's attempt to catalogue the resources of its subjects. In Egypt in the mid-nineteenth century AD, for example, people managed to keep their land out of the tax registers, and community solidarity resisted the government's rewards for revealing such concealed land (Cuno 1992: 194). It was just as important to conceal your sons from the census, to avoid them being conscripted into the army and to reduce the poll tax you had to pay (Cuno 1999: 325). There was a long history of such resilience to imperial rule in Egypt. In the Roman period, the census was carried out every 14 years, and farmers quickly learnt that if a field was uncultivated in the year of the census, they could cultivate it without tax for the next 13 years (Corbier 1991: 227).

There is widespread historical evidence for the concern of states and landowners over secret production. Villagers in Ottoman Crete deliberately used small-scale, inefficient equipment for pressing olives rather than the village olive mills, specifically to avoid paying mill dues (Brumfield 2000: 69). Sharecroppers on the imperial estates of Roman Tunisia kept their beehives on estate land, but moved them to secret locations just before the honey was ready (Kehoe 1988: 99). The Dean of a late twelfth-century English abbey built a windmill without his Abbot's consent because, as he said, 'free benefit of the wind ought not to be denied to any man'. The Abbot was furious, complaining that 'the burgesses will throng to your mill and grind their corn there to their heart's content', and the Dean quickly demolished his own mill (Jocelin of Brakelond 1949: 59–60). The control of processing facilities was paramount in extracting surplus from cultivators.

A striking archaeological example of secret cultivation comes from the Jalase area in north-western Estonia. During the Medieval period, most fields were situated round the villages and cultivated intensively on a permanent basis, either as strips or as broader, usually irregular blocks. There is a contemporary and very different type of field, located in the forests up to 3.5 km from the settlement. These were typically some 200 m across, and were cultivated on a shifting pattern using the slash-and-burn technique, accompanied by major stone clearance. One such forest field had an area of 3 ha and a total of 66 clearance cairns, with charcoal under an excavated cairn dating to the fourteenth to sixteenth centuries AD. These fields were difficult to find and shifted on a regular basis, and would have been almost impossible to police. Historical sources record confiscations and fines for hiding the production on such forest fields, which clearly formed a substantial 'hidden economy' (Lang 1993–4: 69–71; 2002).

Storage can take on an important social and symbolic role, as well as just preserving food over the winter (chapter 3). This particularly applies to secret storage areas, which also become repositories of pride and identity. This was the point of the 'root cellars' which African-American slaves in eighteenth-century plantations maintained under the floors of their houses. Excavations at plantations such as Thomas Jefferson's Monticello in Virginia have shown that many or most slave quarters had rectangular pits under their floors, usually lined with brick or wood and ranging in size from 0.7 × 1.1 m to 1.5 × 2.2 m (Kelso 1986). The Monticello root cellars had a surprising consistency of artefacts: tools, locks, pottery, buttons, and butchered animal bones. It is clear from historical sources that slaves were pilfering food and utensils from their masters and hiding the giveaway debris, as well as keeping secret a range of valued possessions (Kelso 1986: 13–16; Morgan 1998: 115–17). Along with the privacy of individual dwellings and a range of autonomous practices and customs, this secret storage played an important role in maintaining slaves' sense of identity and pride.

On a broader scale, mountainous areas are ideal for secret cultivation and the avoidance of state exploitation. Their broken-up topography and difficult access, mean that officials would need extensive local knowledge to find particular communities or cultivation areas. As late as the 1970s, the inhabitants of the rugged peninsula of Methana in southern Greece were still resisting full incorporation into the nation state. This involved carrying out their own subsistence and risk-buffering strategies at a local level, and until recently surplus grain and other foods were stored in hidden stone-lined storerooms in the mountains above the villages (Forbes 1989: 96; Mee and Forbes 1997: 109).

In all of these cases, merely avoiding the tax collector or bailiff is not enough. To maintain identity and self-respect, you must make it into a story. This is the point of the hidden transcript, which does not even need a real event behind it in order to have effect. Social arenas such as the coffee house in the Ottoman Empire allowed people to talk and tell stories outside the control of the state or the mosque, and so were ideal for the creation and passing on of such stories and statements of pride (Baram 2000: 151).

Other stories focus on the actual machinery of food production and surplus extraction. On Corfu before the Second World War, for example, the deliberately inefficient and outmoded olive presses were torture instruments for the peasants, who were ordered to 'throw themselves' at the poles and strike them with their right thigh in order to move them. The vats of olive oil from these presses, therefore, represented the sweat and blood which had been squeezed out of the peasants by the landowner (cf. chapter 6). So what could make a better story than when the landowner paid an unexpected visit and 'accidentally' fell into the vat (Sordinas 1971: 14, 26)?

Unwritten villages

Like any new imperial power, one of the first tasks facing the Ottomans after their capture of Cyprus in August 1571 was to document the population, income and settlements of the island. This *mufassal defter* or 'detailed register' was carried out by a commissioner and a scribe, who investigated old records and travelled round the country questioning village elders about families, land ownership, and agricultural production over the last three years. They finished their work in October 1572, and the resulting register was used as the basis for the new taxation regime, which in most respects was considerably more lenient than that of the preceding Venetians (İnalcık 1973: 122–3; Jennings 1986).

What seems to be a perfect representation of the island and its population, however, is not as unambiguous and complete as it claims. The surveyors give no estimate of the accuracy or thoroughness of their work (Jennings 1986: 176). A summary of the preceding Venetian tax regulations carried out also in 1572, mainly to make pointed contrasts with the fairer new regime, has a substantial number of mistakes and omissions (Arbel and Veinstein 1986). Even if the census was complete and the taxation regime carefully constructed on that basis, changing populations and the actual practices of officials and villagers made tax collection a highly variable affair.

In spite of its claims to bureaucratic thoroughness, it is clear that the Ottoman Empire during its rule over Cyprus had a major problem with knowledge. One characteristic comment comes from a Spanish nobleman who travelled in Cyprus in 1806 under the pseudonym of Ali Bey:

The government has never succeeded in learning how many Greeks there are in the island. They own to a total of thirty-two thousand souls: but well informed persons raise this number to a hundred thousand. Last year a commissioner was sent to make an exact enumeration of the Greek families, but he was 'got at', loaded with gold, and went away – his task unfulfilled.

quoted in Cobham 1908: 396

The Ottoman Empire's policy of entrusting taxation to intermediaries required local groups who had the resources and local knowledge to carry out the actual collection. The taxation of Greek Cypriots was initially managed by a Greek Cypriot official appointed by the sultan and known as the 'dragoman'. As the church became increasingly powerful, it took on more and more of this role, and offered a measure of protection to its flock by being able to appeal to the sultan over the heads of the short-term governors (Sant Cassia 1986: 6–9). It became fiercely protective of its power, influence and sources of income. It was very likely the church, for example, which 'got at' the census commissioner mentioned by Ali Bey.

The most publicly expressed forms of resistance to Ottoman control of Cyprus were specifically aimed at what was seen as oppressive taxation. These 'tax rebellions' generally included Greek and Turkish Cypriots together, and occurred when protest through legal channels such as appeals by the church had failed (Kitromilides 1982; Malkides 2001). One such rebellion took place in 1764, during the festival of Saint Dimitrios which drew many villagers into Nicosia (Hill 1952: 80–4; Kitromilides 1982). The governor, Chil Osman, had charged double the normal poll tax for Christians in order to recoup the huge bribes he had spent on his appointment, as well as increasing a range of other taxes. While a delegation of bishops was in the palace appealing to have the taxes reduced, the floor suddenly collapsed beneath them. No one was killed, but the Venetian consul reported that the pillars supporting the floor had actually been sawn through in what was apparently a deliberate attempt to murder the bishops.

Three months later the governor was killed by a mob of Greek and Turkish Cypriots. The Islamic authorities on the island declared his oppressive actions an act of rebellion, so that any violence would not be seen as direct criticism of the sultan. This has the same convenient logic as the myth of the tsar-deliverer, redefining violence as righteous protest against an unlawful and disloyal official rather than rebellion against the tsar or sultan (Scott 1990: 97). The resistance was given formal legitimacy, and the rioting Cypriots saw themselves as justified.

Other forms of resistance to taxation are less easily found in the historical record. Church correspondence and other off-hand references show that protests were also directed at the church in its role of tax gatherer. This happened in 1780, for example, when a group of forest villagers attacked,

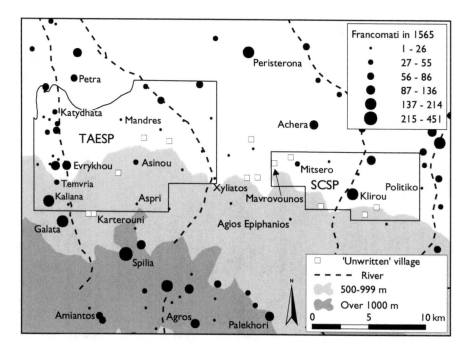

Figure 7.2 Northern Troodos mountains, Cyprus: settlements with numbers of
francomati (free peasant farmers) in 1565, with sixteenth- to nineteenth-
century 'unwritten' settlements unrecorded in 1565 or 1881 but known
from the archaeological record. Source of historical data: Grivaud 1998.

vandalized and plundered the vineyards of Kykko Monastery (Sant Cassia
1986: 13). Fuller documentation at the beginning of British rule in 1878
showed that the poor practised a wide range of acts of everyday resistance,
including vandalism, the 'forest crimes' discussed in chapter 5, attacking state
officials, and refusing to pay moneylenders, tithe collectors and the clergy
(Katsiaounis 1996: 8–9, 242).

There are other ways of discovering resistance in the landscape. If knowledge of the location and resources of taxpayers was so important, did some
communities manage to escape the census official and tax collector entirely?
As we will see in chapter 8, an estate manager in northern Scotland discovered to his astonishment in the 1810s that there were 408 families living
in remote parts of his estate without paying rent (Loch 1820: 81). Such
hidden communities are by no means unusual in many societies.

According to various histories of the Ottoman Empire in Greece, there
were a number of so-called *agrapha* or 'unwritten' villages in the Pindus mountains which were so remote that they were not included in the Ottoman tax
registers (Clogg 1986: 21). To some extent this is nationalist mythology from

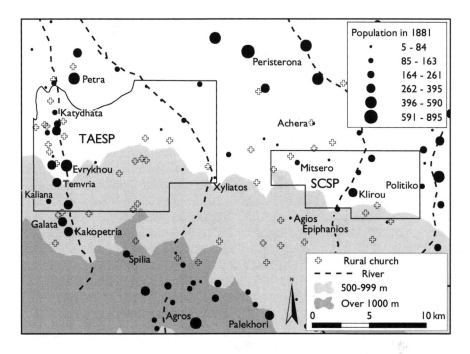

Figure 7.3 Northern Troodos mountains, Cyprus: settlements with population
figures from the British census of 1881, with sixteenth- to nineteenth-
century rural churches. Source of historical data: Census 1882.

the nineteenth and twentieth centuries, emphasizing Ottoman oppression and
celebrating Greek resistance (Kiel 1996). This is interesting and important in
itself. But even so, the idea of an 'unwritten village' cannot be dismissed on
the basis of official state documentation alone. So what do settlement patterns
in the mountainous parts of Cyprus tell us about resistance to imperial rule?

Figures 7.2 and 7.3 show the results of two censuses in the northern Troodos mountains of Cyprus, one just before the period of Ottoman rule and
one just after. The Venetian *pratico* of 1565 was intended to record all adult
male *francomati* (free peasant farmers, as opposed to *paroici* or serfs), along
with some extra categories such as boys and priests. This was intended very
specifically for the imposition of military taxes to finish the Famagusta and
Nicosia fortifications and pay for the peasant militias created seven years previously (Grivaud 1998: 77–8, 445–72). The British census of 1881, taken
three years after their occupation of the island, recorded the inhabitants and
houses of each town, village, estate and monastery, with separate categories
for males and females, and buildings which were inhabited and uninhabited
(Census 1882).

123

Clearly the two maps record different things, with the first showing free adult peasant farmers and the second the total population. When a circle on one map is the same size as a circle on the other, this does not necessarily mean that they have the same population. What they do show, however, is the general relationship between large and small settlements, the patterns in their locations, and how those have changed over time. At both periods the largest river valleys were clearly productive and densely settled, particularly the Solea Valley in the west. Gaudry commented in 1855 that this valley was particularly fertile because of the silt brought down by the annual floods, especially after the abandonment of the Venetian system of irrigation channels, and that it produced the best cotton in Cyprus (1855: 96–7, 159–60).

The topographical zone which was apparently much less settled and exploited in both periods consists of the steep-sided and deeply incised valleys of the diabase zone between 500 and 1,000 m above sea level, excluding the Solea Valley. Below that is a series of small villages in the foothills, especially in 1881, with a few such as Agios Theodoros Soleas and Xyliatos lying in deep river valleys which cut into the mountains. We will return to this zone later in the chapter, in connection with illicit agriculture. Above 1,000 m there is again a substantial scatter of villages, which continues up to about 1,300 m. These mostly lie on the gabbro ridge top, which is much more amenable to settlement and cultivation than the massive ridges and valleys of the diabase below.

A striking difference between the two maps is the substantial size of some of the mountain villages in 1565, compared with those of the river valleys, foothills and even plains. Galata (which includes the census figures for Kakopetria) and Kaliana in the Solea Valley lie on a major route into the mountains, and the valley is still wide enough for substantial agricultural production. These population figures are matched by Galata and Kakopetria's seven churches, one built in the eleventh century and the rest in the sixteenth. Spilia with its 386 *francomati* is the biggest village on the map, even though it lies on a steep mountainside with poor access to major communications routes and minimal agricultural land, requiring labour-intensive terracing.

The density of settlement in the highlands is usually attributed to the Greek Cypriot population's desire for security from their new Ottoman masters (Drury 1972: 166; İnalcık 1973: 125; Malkides 2001: 158; Sant Cassia 1986: 26). This interpretation is part of a wider mythology of Ottoman oppression, linked to the 'unwritten' mountain villages discussed above. The 1565 census figures, taken six years before Ottoman rule, and the numerous Byzantine churches dating back to the tenth century, show that mountain settlement in Cyprus has a much longer pedigree than the Ottoman period.

What the archaeology shows for both of these censuses is that there were many settlements and other rural activities not accounted for by the commissioners and census officials. Systematic survey by the Sydney Cyprus Survey

Project (SCSP) and the Troodos Archaeological and Environmental Survey Project (TAESP) has so far produced 12 unrecorded settlements from the sixteenth to nineteenth centuries (Figure 7.2; Given and Knapp 2003; Given *et al.* 2002). These show several different characters. Manastirka in the SCSP area was clearly based round a monastery. Mandres and the two settlements of Palloura and Siphilos, 3 km east of Xyliatos, were occupied seasonally by mountain villagers coming down to the plains in summer to grow cereals. This caused complications for census official and tithe collector alike.

Asinou is a particularly striking example. It is recorded in the 1565 census with 45 *francomati*, but then does not appear in village lists from 1735 and 1831, or in the British census of 1881 (Census 1882; Grivaud 1998: 200, 469; Theocharides and Andreev 1996). As we saw in chapter 5, archaeological survey of the valley shows rich evidence for settlement, agriculture, pastoralism and forest exploitation all through this period, with a clear peak in the late nineteenth century. The sharp-eyed explorer Samuel Baker spotted the same thing in 1879:

> I have, whilst shooting in the wild tracts of scrub-covered hills and mountains, frequently emerged upon clearings of considerable extent, where the natives have captured a fertile plot and cleared it for cultivation, far away from the eyes of all authorities.
>
> S.W. Baker 1879: 123

This is archaeology's other contribution to the study of unwritten villages and untaxed villagers. Continuous and intensive survey shows that human activity and settlement was not confined to the obvious 'villages' which were visited by the officials and made into bureaucratic entities. The range of activities in the Asinou Valley is one example (chapter 5). Another is the pastoral hinterland round the fourteenth to seventeenth-century village of Mavrovounos (Given and Knapp 2003: 104–7). The village itself is recorded in three village lists from about 1550, but for some reason escapes the 1565 census (Grivaud 1998: 462). Judging by the surrounding landscape, cereal and olive production was minimal and the village's economy was primarily pastoral. This is confirmed by the artefacts found amid the rubble piles, which contain a striking numbers of *galeftiria*, the characteristic wide-spouted milking vessels.

There are three goat folds in Mavrovounos' mountainous hinterland. One of them is certainly contemporary with the main settlement, with a 47 × 40 m enclosure, the remains of two structures, some agricultural terraces, and a considerable quantity of sgraffito pottery. While this complex is well-positioned to serve the largely pastoral economy of Mavrovounos, there is clearly more going on than a shepherds' camp. Its inhabitants were also carrying out small-scale agriculture, they could exploit the numerous edible resources of the surrounding forest, and they were permanent enough to bring substantial amounts of sgraffito tableware over some two centuries.

Figure 7.4 Threshing in Athienou, central Cyprus, in the late nineteenth century.
Source: Ohnefalsch-Richter and Ohnefalsch-Richter 1994: no. 65a,
reproduced with the permission of the Laiki Group Cultural Centre.

This tiny settlement certainly does not appear in any censuses or village lists. Its inhabitants may have been registered as part of Mavrovounos, or they may not have been registered at all. What is clear from this one area is that settlement and production, seen as human activities, were infinitely wider and more complex than the dots and numbers produced by the census officials.

Threshing and resistance

Once cereals have been harvested, the grains need to be separated from the chaff and straw in a process termed threshing. Before the advent of mechanical methods, this was usually done in the Mediterranean by means of an animal-drawn threshing sledge (Figure 7.4). This typically consists of two planks forming a board measuring about 2.0 × 0.8 m, studded underneath with up to 300 blades of chipped chert or flint. This is pulled across the harvested crop, spread out on a threshing floor, and the combination of rolling and cutting by the stone blades breaks up the ears and chops the straw into the appropriate length for animal fodder. The crop can then be winnowed and sieved to separate the grain from the chaff and straw (Ataman 1999; Gurova 2001).

In Cyprus such threshing sledges are first known from a set of estate

126

accounts in 1318 (Richard 1947: 150), and considerable work has been done on the analysis of the blades and the ethnography and oral history of their use (e.g. Ionas 2000; Kardulias and Yerkes 1996; McCartney 1993). They gradually fell into disuse after the Second World War, but many of the threshing floors survive, with surfaces of packed earth or else paved with stone slabs (Whittaker 1999).

A characteristic threshing floor from Mitsero is almost circular, with a diameter ranging from 14.6 to 15.7 m, built up with a retaining wall on its downslope side (Figure 3.1; Given and Knapp 2003: 113). It was paved with 31 lines of stones radiating out from two limestone slabs in the centre, with the spaces in-between the lines then filled in with river stones, smaller slabs, and at one point with two large cakes of copper slag from the neighbouring Roman slag heap. This forms a beautifully even and slightly dished surface, which is highly decorative. Each of the paved threshing floors has a different pattern. Some have radiating lines of stones, some parallel, and the centres are variously marked with slabs, slag cakes, or are not marked at all. According to local information, each one was privately owned by specific families, hence their consistent size but individual decoration.

The importance of such threshing floors to the families processing their grain on them is clear from the stories told about them and the religious and symbolic practices that were associated with them. A farmer from the village of Pakhna interviewed in 1968 remembered placing on the heap of threshed grain a wooden cross, an olive branch, and a large black stone – this last expresses the wish that the grain be as heavy as the stone (Ionas 2000: 337). The prophet Elijah could be called upon to provide the all-important wind for the winnowing (Ionas 2001: 391–2). Andriani Kosta Loïzou of the village of Mitsero remembered the 'wonderful sight' of everyone working together on their threshing floors, each family helping the other out, and then afterwards the feast of fresh bread, cheese and wine on the threshing floor to reward the helpers (interviewed by the author, 3 July 1999). The threshing floor became an arena for the celebration of harvest, income, family and community.

A less happy memory, which informants in Mitsero never volunteered, was the tithe being extracted from that same threshing floor (chapter 3). This was where families saw their grain being measured by the tithe collector and his assistant, and up to a third or a half of it being removed. Unless, of course, they decided to keep what God and their own hard labour had given them . . .

Threshing provides an ideal opportunity for the investigation of secret cultivation and processing. The tools and above all the threshing floors are easily identifiable in the archaeological record, and the floors were carefully mapped by later colonial land surveyors. Figure 7.5 shows the distribution of threshing floors in the northern Troodos, compared to the villages recorded in the 1881 census. The principle sources for the threshing floors are the cadastral maps

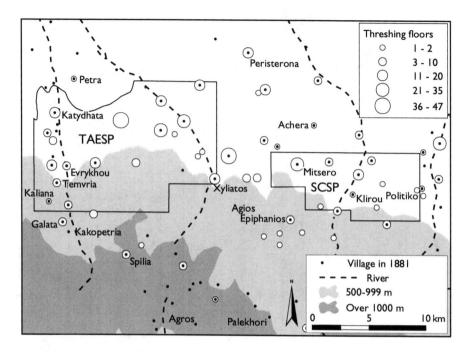

Figure 7.5 Northern Troodos mountains, Cyprus: villages recorded in the 1881 census, and distribution of threshing floors.

at a scale of 1:5000 and village maps at 1:1250. These were drawn up in the 1920s and revised in the 1980s, with even abandoned threshing floors still being marked. In a few cases, particularly in the plains to the north, threshing floors had been built on by the 1980s and therefore do not appear on the later versions of the maps. Within the two survey areas, and to some extent in the regions between and to the south of them, this information is supplemented by intensive survey, purposive investigation, and the examination of aerial photographs taken in the 1960s.

The general pattern is clear, and can be confirmed by visiting any village in Cyprus where threshing floors survive, or by talking to the older inhabitants. Threshing floors were situated round the edge of the village, rather than in the open countryside near people's fields. This fitted well with the nucleated settlement pattern where people lived in central villages and commuted to their usually dispersed landholdings. It was also laid down by the Ottoman *mejelle*, the codification of Islamic common law commissioned by the Ottoman government in 1869. According to this, the *mer'a* of a village was defined as the area where someone with a loud voice can be heard from houses at the edge of the village, and is set aside specifically for grazing, threshing floors, and wood-cutting (Mejelle 1901: 191). The maps on which

Figure 7.6 Threshing floors in three terraces outside Katydhata village, Cyprus, with the early twentieth-century copper mine of Skouriotissa behind. Photograph: Chris Parks.

Figure 7.5 is based and investigations in the villages within the two survey areas show that the threshing floors were usually clustered together on the more exposed edge of the village, to get the best wind for winnowing. They were usually within 100 m of the village, and never more than 200 m.

The advantage of this to the tithe collectors is clear. The whole community's income is spread out in one accessible and clearly visible area, and can be easily controlled (Figure 7.6; cf. Figure 1.1). The Ottoman government delegated tithe collection to the *mukhtar* or village headman, who had extensive local knowledge and was therefore harder for his co-villagers to avoid. The British, by contrast, were obsessed with taxing the individual rather than the community, and brought in tithe collectors from other villages who were supposed to have no local contacts or loyalties – and therefore no local knowledge. The spate of government correspondence after 1878 as the British tried to come to terms with the Ottoman system makes their concern with control very clear. The Ottomans contented themselves with large demands and a relatively low success rate. The British felt compelled to collect every grain that they were entitled to (Katsiaounis 1996: 71).

One problem that the new tithe collectors faced was when villagers, usually women, went to the threshing floors at night, sieved their grain, and took it to the storage jars and pits in their homes before it had been measured by the tithe collectors. The response to this was to have the *koldji*, or tithe collector's assistant, spend the night on the threshing floors (SA1/3938/1885). This is the situation behind my narrative in chapter 2 of the two women sieving their grain by moonlight.

The other means of evading control and supervision, of course, was to do the threshing away from the village, where tithe collectors did not come. The intriguing thing about Figure 7.5 is the exceptions to the general pattern of threshing floors being clustered round the villages. Some of these have other explanations. Mandres and Agios Georghios Kafkallou in the TAESP survey area, along with the two smaller clusters of threshing floors east of Xyliatos, are seasonal settlements. Farmers from a range of mountain villages, poorly endowed with arable land, came down in the sowing and harvesting seasons to grow and process their cereals (Given 2000: 217–19). Their threshing floors were still clustered round these settlements, though with farmers from different areas they upset the state's neat system of each village being a discrete unit of production.

Karterouni and Asinou, as we have seen, were 'unwritten villages', in that they were not recorded in the 1881 census. To what extent and for how long this enabled them to produce food without being taxed is not clear, but the small terraces and pockets of arable land that were available could only have supplemented their subsistence, rather than provide a substantial surplus. They had plenty of motivation for not giving up a fifth of their meagre cereal crop. A further explanation applies to the single threshing floors on the outskirts of Orounta and Politiko. These belong to monasteries, and have the characteristic large sizes of a communal threshing floor (up to 50 m in diameter) rather than a family floor (typically 12–15 m).

The other isolated threshing floors are not so easily explained. There are three between Agios Georghios Kafkallou and Vyzakia, one just north of Lazania, and an impressive six round Agios Epiphanios. Two of these are associated with substantial buildings, and may have been the successors of the large estates which carried out major cash crop production during the Ottoman period, or perhaps smaller estates owned by monasteries. The rest, particularly those round Agios Epiphanios, are genuinely difficult of access, requiring extensive local knowledge and considerable persistence to find. One of these is conveniently close to a now ruined church of Saint Mamas.

The single threshing floor to the north of Lazania is just 500 m from the village, perhaps worryingly close to be the location of secret cultivation and processing. It lies in a prominent saddle, and most of the terraces it is associated with are totally invisible from the village. From the threshing floor itself it is easy to look down on the roofs of the village houses, and see anyone coming up the steep hill. From the village, by contrast, the whole saddle is invisible from the narrow alleyways and even from the slightly wider courtyard of the church. Assuming reasonable community solidarity, more likely in the British period than when the village headman was in charge of the tithe collection, this location would allow secret and untaxed cultivation and crop processing (cf. Dar 1986: 192). The careful control of visibility has appropriated and overturned the surveillance of the tithe collector, and the experience of working on the threshing floor has become one of pride, autonomy and deliberate resistance.

Heroes and histories

Susan Alcock draws a helpful distinction between memories in Hellenistic and Roman Crete (2002: chapter 3). Different Hellenistic powers made treaties with individual Cretan states, and stimulated an intense and often violent rivalry between them. Rural sanctuaries on the margins of city territories helped maintain the borders, and people celebrated local memories by building shrines or making dedications in ruined Minoan palaces or the tombs of ancient local heroes. Under the Romans, by contrast, the island became a unified part of a larger province which included Cyrenaica in North Africa. The local heroes died out, and were replaced by pan-Cretan myths such as the story of King Minos and Crete's contribution to the Trojan war. These helped to unify the island and incorporate it into the wider Roman Empire. Only a few continuing cave-cults chose to ignore this globalization of cult and memory.

In many respects a similar pattern can be seen in Ottoman and British colonial Cyprus. After the partial suppression of the Orthodox church under the Lusignans and Venetians, the Ottomans allowed freedom of religious practice and gave the church a considerable amount of autonomy, including the right to collect taxes for the authorities and for itself. A wealth of local stories and traditions grew up, with narratives of saints, kings and warriors embedded into the landscape as churches, paths and natural places. A wide variety of population groups inspired an equally wide range of memories (Alcock 2002: 152). Greek Orthodox, Turkish Muslims, Armenians, Maronites, and various combinations and hybrid versions of these groups all had their own stories, memories and landscapes.

After 1878, two separate trends began to replace this rich variety with single, dominant ideologies. One was the British imperial pageant of loyalty to the crown, with activities such as Empire Days and boy scout movements. This looked to England's earlier occupation of the island by Richard the Lionheart in 1191. The other was its direct opponent, the Greek nationalism propagated in the Greek Cypriot schools and newspapers, which remembered and celebrated Cyprus' classical and Hellenic past (Given 1997).

Many narratives and memories from the Ottoman period celebrated local knowledge and pride, and in spite of attempts to replace and homogenize them they survived into the British colonial period and beyond. In many cases they functioned as hidden transcripts, expressing the individuality and autonomy of particular communities in the face of imperial oppression or exploitation. A German ethnographer in the 1880s noticed a Judas effigy being burnt on a pyre as part of the Easter celebrations after the resurrection liturgy. Instead of dressing him as a Jew, as was usually done, this Judas was clearly an English official, complete with top hat and cane (Ohnefalsch-Richter 1994: 79). This theatre of resistance is reminiscent of the re-enactment of the Ramayana in the Ganges Valley village of Senapur in the mid-twentieth century (Cohn 1961: 243). One of the unsuccessful competitors for Sita's hand was the Rajah of Manchester, wearing a badly-fitting white suit and pith helmet, and speaking a railway-station gibberish version of English. During the heightened awareness and emotions of the religious festival, the imperial rulers of the present are identified with the losers of the past.

Historical sources for Cyprus suggest a wide range of media for such stories and hidden transcripts, particularly from the better-documented nineteenth century. Ballad-singers recounted a variety of romances, murder stories and the news of contemporary events, while *karagiozi* shadow puppeteers presented their roguish trickster hero as an alternative to the models handed down by church, school and state (Katsiaounis 1996: 94, 161).

Bandit exploits were another fruitful topic for stories and ballads, particularly the 'social bandits' who confined themselves to robbing the rich and presented themselves as the protectors of the poor (Hobsbawm 1985). Such bandits had various origins. Some had been traditionally lawless mountain shepherds, others came from the powerful group of semi-independent estate overseers and watchmen, while others were peasants made landless by the substantial agricultural estates of the Ottoman period (Sant Cassia 1993: 776–8). Social banditry was particularly common after the poor harvests and widespread hunger of 1887, and was an important expression of the breakdown of the world of the rural poor (Katsiaounis 1996: 149–58).

The bandits' defiance of state representatives such as the police and the tax collector made them ideal folk heroes. Here is a characteristic example, the celebration of the oldest of the three Hassanpoulia brothers by the folk poet Christos Jabouras in 1892. The brothers were known as *poulia* or 'birds' because of their skill in escaping the police:

> He did what he did and at once blinded them,
> he pounded his feet on the ground and they lost him . . .
> the police ran after him without seeing him
> not knowing where they really went
> and as you gather they were scared to hell
> may God spare you from such a fright!

quoted in Katsiaounis 1996: 154

Another important source for the hidden transcripts of the past consists of oral history, whether gathered by past travellers and ethnographers or by contemporary researchers. Archaeological survey teams working in the landscape inevitably meet people and are told the local history of the area. The

Figure 7.7 The modern chapel of Saint Mamas, Klirou. The abandoned
settlement is on the small, overgrown ridge to the right. Photograph:
Karen Ulrich.

value of this is that such stories can be combined with archaeological data
and put into their proper landscape context. From the informants themselves, it quickly becomes clear how important a part of the story that
landscape is.

At the end of August, 1997, the Sydney Cyprus Survey Project's Team Central was working 2.5 km south-east of the village of Klirou, in a locality
named Agios Mamas after a rural chapel dedicated to the saint (Figure 7.7). A
set of rubble piles and a scatter of mainly coarse pottery from the sixteenth to
nineteenth centuries suggested a small settlement, and the narrow but deep-
soiled valley had clearly been created out of the surrounding eroded hills by
means of an impressive set of check dams to capture the soil (Given and
Knapp 2003: 153–7). There are no such settlements recorded in the censuses
of 1565 or 1881, and with its discrete location and the protection of Saint
Mamas himself, this is an ideal location for an 'unwritten village' carrying out
secret cultivation.

As we recorded the rubble piles and check dams, and carried out block
survey in the fields, it became clear that there were major preparations going
on at the church. It turned out that 2 September was the feast day of the
saint, and our whole team was invited to the liturgy. This took place in the
afternoon of the eve of the saint's day. The sixteenth-century icon, now kept

in the main village church in Klirou, was put in a stand on the back of a pick-up, and solemnly driven out at the head of a great procession of cars and pick-ups. Carrying his lamb and riding his lion, Saint Mamas was once again on the road, just as when he travelled into Nicosia to see the king and gain freedom from taxes for his people.

The chapel itself is modern, and we were told by the priest that it had been built a couple of years earlier, on the site of a ruined church of Saint Mamas marked on the cadastral map. The colonial land ownership map from the 1920s has clearly been appropriated and transformed into an important vehicle of local memory and identity (cf. Bender 1999). The icon originally came from the old church, so it too carries the memory, though as archaeologists we were disappointed to find that the actual ruins had been bulldozed into oblivion.

We took the opportunity of so many people being gathered in the landscape where we were working, both for the festival and for its preparation beforehand, to ask about the history of the settlement and its fields. There were once two villages, we were told, this one named Agios Mamas after the saint, and another one called Agia Irini or Agia Marina, some 300 m to the south-west at the head of the valley. Agios Mamas with its check dams and human-made fields depended on agriculture, and Agia Irini on goats and olives, and they also grew became rich from the local gold mines. They shared three threshing floors, just to the south of the church.

The headmen of the two villages were brothers and great rivals, and decided to have a contest to show which of the two villages was wealthier. They took it in turns to pile up their gold on one of the threshing floors, and the oxen pulled the threshing sledge round and round as if threshing grain. The heap of gold where the sledge kept going the longest before its blades struck the paving stones would be the winner. Such was the wealth of the winning village that the sledge managed to go round the floor three times before its blades cut down through the gold and reached the paving stones. We were not told which village had won: the point of the story was their wealth, not their hierarchy.

In terms of its surface archaeology, the 'village' of Agia Irini consisted of a line of rubble 50 m long and a desultory scatter of coarse pottery and tile from the Medieval to Modern periods. We recorded Archaic to Classical copper production 600 m to the west, but there is no evidence for gold mining in the area other than industrial-scale production at Mitsero in the 1930s. These stories and experiences are important for other reasons. They clearly put heavy emphasis on the church as the focus of memory for Saint Mamas. The remembered wealth and pride of the two communities is very striking, even though they only have a small catchment of good arable land, with wild resources which are useful but by no means exceptional. The official version of Ottoman history encouraged by church, school and state is one of grinding oppression and over-taxation. But that is forgotten amidst the memories of independence and pride, and how they had so much gold they could thresh it as if it were wheat.

The saint

The official version of the life of Saint Mamas dates to the thirteenth century, and makes no mention of his record of tax evasion (Klirides 1951: 125–37). He was born in Gangra, now Çankırı in central Anatolia, in AD 260. When his parents were imprisoned for their Christianity and died in prison, Mamas was brought up by a rich woman. At the age of 15 he was persecuted, whipped, and thrown into the sea weighed down with lead, but he survived and hid in a cave near Caesarea, drinking deer milk to stay alive. The wild animals came to love him, and he would ride a lion down to the city to visit the poor and heal the sick.

On one of these visits to Caesarea, he was captured by the cruel governor Alexander. This tyrant put him in a furnace, but an angel quenched the flames. He was put in prison without food, but the angel came and fed him. Then the tyrant threw him to the wild beasts, but they refused to touch him, and his lion came roaring into the theatre and tore the faithless to pieces. Another wild lion was set on him, but it grovelled before his feet. The faithless stoned him, but their eyes darkened and they stoned each other. Finally a man with a trident disembowelled him. Mamas took his entrails in his hand, and went outside the city and sat on a stone. A voice from heaven asked him what he wanted, and he asked for good on every animal and creature, health and blessing on everyone's animals and crops, and no plague for those who honoured the Lord's martyr.

So died the great martyr Mamas, relates his thirteenth-century *Life*, on 2 September AD 275. Because of his love for animals and wild places, he became the protector of shepherds, and his cult quickly spread throughout the Byzantine world. A suburb of Constantinople was named after him in the fifth century, and a sixth-century blessing pendant made of lead from Caesarea shows him riding his lion (Stylianou and Stylianou 1985: 251–3). His cult may have arrived in Cyprus as early as the eighth century, but it was only in the thirteenth and fourteenth centuries that his worship became widespread. The marble sarcophagus with his remains miraculously floated over the sea to the bay of Morphou, and the successive churches built in Morphou to house it became the centre of his cult on the island. By the twentieth century there were at least 66 churches dedicated to him (Klirides 1951: 96–9).

Many stories were told in Cyprus about Saint Mamas, and it was here that he took on his new role as patron saint of tax evaders. Medieval versions tended to focus on his arrival by coffin in the bay of Morphou, and its journey from the coast to its current position in Morphou town, where it decided to stop. In the Ottoman period, it is the story of his refusal to pay taxes that is the most widespread. Here is a characteristic retelling of it by Alexander Drummond, British Consul at Aleppo, who heard it during a visit to Morphou in 1745.

> When alive, he either could not or would not pay his kharaj, or poll-money, and the collectors were always restrained, by the operation of some praeternatural power upon their bodies and spirits, from using him in the same manner in which they treated others, who were deficient in their payments. The prince, being informed of this extraordinary circumstance, ordered him to be hunted out from the hollow rocks, caves, and gloomy woods in which he always lived, and brought into his presence; and Saint George and Saint Demetrius, hearing of his being taken, followed, overtook, and accompanied him in his captivity. During his journey to court, seeing a lion rush out of a thicket and seize a lamb, to the terror and astonishment of his guards, he ordered the beast to quit his prey, and his command was instantly obeyed by the lion, who fawned and wagged his tail, in token of submission. The good man, being tired with walking, took the lamb in his arms, and mounting the wild beast, rode forwards to court, to the amazement of all who saw him. He presented himself in this equipage to the king, who, being apprized of these circumstances, accepted the lamb, generously remitted the kharaj he owed, and gave orders that the Saint should live without paying any tax for the future: thus favoured he came hither and built a little church, in which at his death his body was deposited. This is one way of telling his story, which is varied by every papa whom you consult on the subject.
>
> quoted in Cobham 1908: 297

The sense of landscape, the picture of the ferocious lion wagging its tail, the look on the king's face when he sees Saint Mamas on his lion, all provide a wonderfully rich and vivid hidden transcript to justify a hard-pressed peasant's secret cultivation, or at least provide moral compensation after the visit of the tithe collector. The last sentence is particularly telling. The saint and his story is firmly rooted in the local landscape, and so every priest or villager has a differently, uniquely relevant, version.

The landscape's presence in the story is so strong that the converse is equally true: the story is embedded in the landscape. The Yerolakkos version of the story that I told at the beginning of this chapter was experienced by any traveller who passed 'the church where the lion roared'. By walking in procession to one of these churches, kissing his icon, or joining the liturgy on the saint's feast day, you incorporate yourself into the saint's story and share his defiance of the authorities.

There are many associations of natural places in the landscape with Saint

Mamas (cf. Bradley 2000). In the churchyard of Saint Mamas at Kato Amiandos, a rock was seen as the 'stool' of the saint. The inhabitants of Agios Mamas village in the Limassol district explained some red marks on the white rocks as the footsteps of the saint and the place where he laid his staff (Klirides 1951: 104–7). Such stories are common in Orthodox hagiography, of course. The importance of these 'natural places' is that their stories and associations provide the social and moral context in which local inhabitants live and work. Being natural, or apparently innocent like a church, outsiders and officials cannot know their deep-seated and often subversive associations.

It is not just rocks and churches that can carry such stories. Even the humble potsherd, apparently ignored by everyone other than archaeologists, can be full of meaning. The fifteenth-century Cypriot historian Leontios Makhairas lists the principal local saints and summarizes their legends:

> Also St. Mamas at Morphou, who came over from Alaya, and in his lifetime he used to catch lions and milk them, and made cheese and fed the poor. And the Turks ran after him, and he tripped, and the vessel of milk was broken and the milk was spilled, and the place where the milk fell can be seen in the village of Alaya to this day.
>
> Makhairas 1.33

To any Cypriot reader or listener, the 'vessel of milk' was a *galeftiri*, with a large opening for milking into and a broad tubular spout for pouring out of, but sufficiently closed to make it easy to carry without spilling (Ionas 1998: 42). This was what the Sydney Cyprus Survey Project found in considerable quantities at the fifteenth- to sixteenth-century pastoral village of Mavrovounos, described earlier in this chapter. Further to the west, the priest of Xyliatos told us of a locality called 'Galeftiri of Saint Mamas' (Dimosthenis Milidhoni, interviewed by Marios Hadjianastasis, 24 July 2002). To a pastoral community, Saint Mamas was their protector and shepherd. He was brought up on deer milk, milked his lionesses to nourish the poor, protected his lambs from danger, and saved his shepherds from the ravages of the tax collector. Even a scatter of sherds can tell the story of a saint.

8

LANDSCAPES OF RESISTANCE

Loch nan Trì-Eileanan Beag is not easy to find. The 'loch of three little islands' is only 100 m long, and it is deeply hidden between two dykes of gneiss bedrock (Figure 8.1). If you know where you are going, it is only half an hour's walk from the crofting township of Wester Alligin, on the shore of Loch Torridon in the north-western highlands of Scotland. If you do not, it is easy to get lost amidst the identical craggy dykes, all running from north-west to south-east, all with burns and boggy grass between them. Suddenly, as you stand on top of the sheer face of one of these dykes, you see the loch with its water-lilies and its three islands, two of them little more than mounds of peat and moss. Tucked in below the cliff face are the remains of a bothy. It is only 6.5 × 3.5 m, a rectangular structure roughly but solidly built out of red sandstone blocks. A tiny peaty burn runs along its eastern side and heads down the last 20 m to the loch.

This is what the 'gaugers' or excisemen found during a search in the later nineteenth century. The bothy was in working order then, and showed signs of recent use. By combing the area they found the expected evidence: the worm from an illicit whisky still, hidden among the rocks. The real prize only came when one of them waded out to the biggest of the three islands: a fine copper still, buried in the moss and carefully covered with heather.

This story appears in the memoirs of a retired exciseman and in a guide to historical walks in the area by a local historian (I. Macdonald 1914: 85–6; M. MacDonald 1996: 30–4). Such stories are very much alive throughout the north-western highlands, where illicit distilling continued much later than elsewhere in Scotland. Most of them have happier endings, from the distillers' perspective at least. They show a clear pride and delight in the way they fooled the gaugers and prepared, transported and drank the 'water of life' under their very noses.

The idea of a 'landscape of resistance' usually conjures up a picture of inaccessible mountains with impenetrable forts and invisible guerrilla hide-outs. Such landscapes have of course been common throughout history, and outlawed gangs and freedom fighters have often become integral parts of the

Figure 8.1 Loch nan Trì-Eileanan Beag. Photograph: Michael Given.

social fabric, even without overthrowing the political regime. Yet this is a very narrow view of resistance, and excludes all those who maintained their own pride and identity by means of routine and everyday practices (chapter 2).

During the eighteenth and nineteenth centuries, the people of the highlands of Scotland experienced a massive disruption of their lives. Pushed by debt and encouraged by the ideology of improvement, landlords evicted their tenants from the farming townships of the interior to make room for vast commercial sheep farms. Houses were burnt before the eyes of their occupants, elderly people and the sick flung indiscriminately out into the rain, and whole communities were forced into new lives on the coast, or else to emigrate outright.

So where was the resistance? Until the Crofters' War of the 1880s, it seems that there was surprisingly little outright resistance. There were a few cases of intimidating and assaulting the factors' agents or the removal party, and very occasionally organized rioting and campaigns, most notably in the 'Year of the Sheep' in 1792 (Richards 2000: 86–104). But these occasions were very few, and most contemporary commentators and eyewitnesses describe the people's reactions as a depressed and fatalistic acquiescence. The highlanders, it seems, were as timid and passive as the sheep which replaced them.

In this chapter I wish to examine the issue of resistance to the highland clearances, and see if people did in fact manage to maintain their pride, self-respect and identity in the face of the horrors of eviction and cultural dislocation. The distilling of illicit whisky was a widespread everyday practice which flourished during the time of the clearances. How can this and similar practices turn a wasteland of eviction and passive despair into an active and dynamic landscape of resistance?

Rhythms of rural life

It is easy to see life in the highlands of Scotland before the clearances as a timeless rural idyll, with chiefs and their clansmen inhabiting the mist-clad hills in perfect harmony, broken only by the occasional battle or cattle raid to prove their manhood. When we remove the filter of nineteenth-century romantic highlandism, the image becomes less rosy but much more dynamic (Devine 1994: 32–53; Dodgshon 1998). The old chiefdom society had been based on chiefly display and competition, with real or supposed kinship groups providing the food and fighting men to support the chiefs' feasts and feuds. In return the clansmen received an unwritten hereditary right to arable and pastoral land in the farming townships, and drew their surname and identity from their chief.

This had always been a fluid system, with kinship groups being absorbed by different clans and some chiefs expanding their territories and clansmen at the expense of others. But commercialism and the rise of state power began to infiltrate the margins of the highlands as early as the fifteenth and sixteenth centuries. This was the long process which culminated in the agricultural improvement and clearances of the late eighteenth and nine-teenth centuries, neatly encapsulated by Robert Dodgshon as the transition 'from chiefs to landlords' (1998). A society based on mutuality, hospitality and social space was gradually reoriented towards cash, profit and commer-cial space.

The characteristic settlement form of this changing society, before the radi-cal transformations of the clearances, was the nucleated farming township

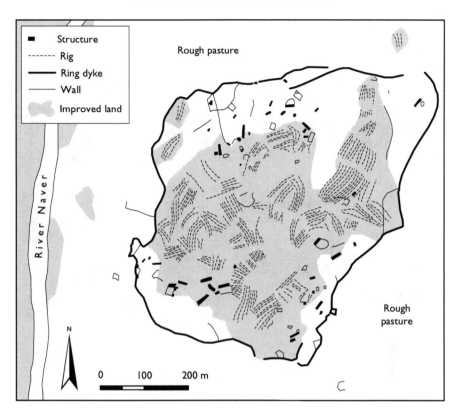

Figure 8.2 Plan of the pre-clearance settlement of Rosal in Sutherland. Source: Fairhurst 1967–8: 138 (redrawn with the permission of the Society of Antiquaries of Scotland).

(Dalglish 2003: 81–90; Dodgshon 1993). Such townships typically lay in valley bottoms along the base of the hillslope, with easy access to arable land, woodland and upland grazing. They were typically amorphous in plan, made up of clusters of houses with associated barns and grain-drying kilns, with enclosures for cattle, vegetable gardens and haystacks. This can be clearly seen in the plan of Rosal, a farming settlement in Strathnaver cleared by the Sutherland estate between 1814 and 1818 (Figure 8.2). Some 40 houses and 30 outbuildings are grouped into three distinct clusters, with about 20 enclosures of various sizes, most of them probably stackyards. The seven grain-drying kilns were built into natural hillocks and formed parts of small dedicated kiln-houses (Fairhurst 1967–8: 143–4).

Inside the rectangular or subrectangular houses there were few divisions to mark different activities. Domestic space was common to everyone, and often focused on a central hearth (Dalglish 2003: 101). The Rosal houses are

Figure 8.3 Long house at Rosal, with part of the byre in the foreground and the living end beyond it. In the background are the rigs contouring round the hillside. Source: Fairhurst 1967–8: plate 13a (reproduced with the permission of the Society of Antiquaries of Scotland).

typically 30 m long and 4 m wide, with a doorway in the middle of the long side allowing the visitor to turn one way into the dwelling area and the other into the cattle byre. The excavated long house had no apparent division between byre and living areas, but there was a separate room at the far end, apparently added at a late stage in the life of the building (Figure 8.3; Fairhurst 1967–8: 143–8). In many areas stone-built houses were often associated either with a chief's more lavish lifestyle or with the new 'improvement' farming of the eighteenth century (Dodgshon 1993: 422–4; Stewart 2003: 93–5). Most houses were built of perishable materials, such as saplings woven between poles and insulated with turf, and soot-encrusted thatch was regularly stripped for manure. Often it was the crucks, the substantial timber knees which supported the roof, which were the most valuable part of the house.

In a township situated in a valley bottom, the upper limit of its arable land was marked by an earth or stone 'head dyke'. As populations increased during the eighteenth century, this arable land was often extended upwards and a new dyke built (e.g. Boyle 2003: 22). Rosal lies in an arable 'island' within rough pasture, and so is enclosed on all sides by a ring dyke (Fairhurst 1967–8: 156). About two-thirds of the land inside the dyke was cultivated, mostly still visible in the rigs and furrows formed by the plough (Figure 8.2).

Eighteenth-century commentators with their improvement ideology ridicule the 'archaic' and 'laborious' cultivation methods and tools of these town-ships: the caschrom, a large spade with powerful leverage; lazy-beds, where in the thin soils of the Hebrides earth and seaweed manure were piled up in narrow raised strips; and various labour-intensive means of manuring, har-rowing, harvesting and threshing. As Dodgshon persuasively argues, such methods are highly appropriate in a marginal environment and conditions of high population pressure, such as prevailed in the eighteenth-century western Highlands. It was more important to use plentiful labour to increase produc-tion from a small area than to maximize labour efficiency (Dodgshon 1992).

Beyond the head dyke or ring dyke lay the rough grazing, and other resources such as peat for burning, turf and timber for building, and a rich variety of wild plants and animals for food, dye, medicine and a myriad of other uses. Non-arable land was no more a 'wasteland' here than it was in the Mediterranean (Forbes 1997). The cattle grazing was undoubtedly of great-est economic importance. Each summer the communal herders appointed by the township took the cattle up to the shielings, the upland pastures marked by clusters of shieling huts which provided their shelter (J. Atkinson 2000: 154–7; Bil 1990). As well as providing rich upland grazing, this kept the cattle away from the crops down on the valley floor, which were fertilized by the same cattle's winter dung.

This summary of pre-clearance rural economy and society in the Scottish highlands is descriptive, and therefore rather static. What about the experi-ence of individuals engaged in these activities? Can we reconstruct the actual rhythms of rural life, which were so abruptly broken by the clearances?

These landscapes of townships, cultivation, head dykes and shielings struc-tured the lives of their occupants. This is one half of the people–landscape dynamic. The other half is that people's everyday travels, activities and rela-tionships were sedimented into the paths, houses and rigs and furrows of the landscape, along with their knowledge and memories (J. Atkinson 2000: 157–8; Lelong 2000: 219). This is no romantic identity with the spirit of the land-scape; it is a matter of real, personal action in very specific material contexts. With small, crowded houses and long outdoor labour, most of people's time was spent outdoors on the rigs, moors and mountains (Symonds 2000: 202). Daily activities were carried out by social groups such as families and commu-nities; in fact it was those activities and their architectural and environmental setting which constituted the families and communities. This was the basis of highland clanship, no less than the much-discussed ideology of kinship (Dalglish 2003: 157–8).

And so there was the seasonal passage of the cattle and their herders from the township to the shielings, marking the beginning and end of the growing and pasturing season. There was the daily walk during the ploughing from the house to the cattle yard, and from there to the rig which had been allotted to you this year. There was another walk which took you on a path around the rigs and through the head dyke, and from there a track carried you zig-zagging up the hill to the peat cuttings. Once there, the long stone-built stands stacked up with drying peat were expressions of past family labour and future family warmth (Boyle 2003: 26–8).

At Rosal, the sedimentation of repeated activity and knowledge into the landscape can be seen most dramatically in the rigs and furrows of the ploughing (Figures 8.2, 8.3; Fairhurst 1967–8: 157). They cover well over half the area enclosed by the ring dyke, running more or less along the contours of the rounded hillocks and mounds that make up the site. While actually ploughing, a plough has a limited turning circle. At Rosal it is clear that whenever it had to turn any more tightly than a circle 130 m in diameter, it had to stop and start again on a new alignment. This provided furlongs or plough strips which varied from 30 to 150 m long, with headlands in-between for turning the plough round.

These rigs are very substantial, rather more so than many of those found at pre-clearance settlements in the north and west of Scotland. They typically range from 5.8 to 9.5 m wide, and 20 to 43 cm high. This puts them into the 'broad, high-backed, curvilinear rig' category (Halliday 2003: 70–2). Particularly in the eastern part of the area (Figure 8.2), they show the characteristic reverse-S shape of these rigs: the plough-driver widens out towards the end of the furlong while the share is still in the ground, to prepare for the turn at the end and so maximize the time spent ploughing.

The type of plough being used here was almost certainly the highland plough, a shorter and lighter version of the Old Scots Plough (Fenton 1999: 35–7). The long wooden sole that ran in the furrow was tipped with an iron share, and a flat wooden mouldboard turned the soil over onto the right-hand side. The plough-driver walked behind holding the two upright handles and steering the plough along beside the previous furrow. This required particular skill and concentration, as the plough had no wheels to support and guide it. An extra person drove the animals, usually four oxen in line abreast, and the plough was usually followed by a team of men and women breaking the clods with wooden mallets (Fenton 2000: 168–9).

The texture of the soil and the power of the oxen is transmitted through the sole and beam of the plough to the handles in your hands, and you push down for more depth, release pressure to ride over a rock or else decide to steer round it. The wind and rain are often a major part of the experience, but so is the warmth generated as you walk behind the plough and control it. You are accompanied by the pipits, lapwings and gulls, characteristic birds of farmland and moorland. The air is rich with the smell of the freshly-cut soil and the oxen, and your ears are filled with the daylong clunk and scrape of stones against the iron share (Lerche 1984–7; 2003).

The rigs are the material expression of generations of such experiences. You take the plough along the left-hand edge of the rig, throwing the soil up into the middle, then turn and come down the other side, again throwing the soil up into the middle. So the rig is created and maintained by the plough-ing, and the people driving the plough and the animals follow the same course and re-enact the same movements as their fellow members of the community, past and present. The decisions about where to stop and where to turn have been made collectively over the generations, and a boulder heaved out of the way and thrown onto the rock pile is another contribution to the long process of maintaining the rigs.

Such were the rhythms of rural life that were broken on Whitsunday 1814, when Patrick Sellar, sub-factor to the Sutherland estate, began the clearance of the Strathnaver townships.

The rhythms broken

Sharon Macdonald distinguishes two historiographical approaches to the highland clearances (1997: 73–80). The 'people's historians' dwell on the hor-rors of eviction, often using the bitter, vituperative accounts of eyewitnesses such as Donald Macleod (1892) and Donald Sage (1899) (e.g. Grigor 2000; Prebble 1963). The 'economic historians' see the actions of landlords in the context of Europe-wide processes of modernization, and use the inevitably pro-landlord estate papers as one of their principle sources (e.g. Devine 1994; Richards 2000).

This distinction, though a little overdrawn, is a useful introduction to the complexities of exploring and representing a past landscape which still evokes disturbing memories and passionate argument (Basu 2000). What archaeology can offer to this debate is an approach which sets communities firmly in their social and economic context, but can provide a very direct account of the material context of people's experience. This is particularly important in the search for resistance to the clearances and 'improvement', and especially the all-important everyday resistance (Dalglish 2003: 193–216; Symonds 1999).

The landlords were drawn into clearing their upland and inland townships by debt and Enlightenment. As state control, the market economy and the attractions of an aristocratic, urban lifestyle gradually encroached on the old chiefdoms of the Highlands, so did the old chiefs require new money (Dodgshon 1998: 102–18). Gone were the days of local feasting, feuding and identity between the chief and his real or supposed kinsmen. By the middle of the eighteenth century chiefs had become landlords, and demanded cash from what were now their tenants. For the tenants, selling a few cattle or distilling some surplus barley into whisky was not sufficient. Often they had no resources to do even that, when they were struggling to produce enough arable just for subsistence. Intensive commercial farms in the lowlands and vast sheep farms in the highlands, leased to ambitious southerners, were more able to produce the cash profits that landlords needed.

One example of the many ways in which landlords tried to increase their cash income is thirlage, the requirement for tenants to grind their corn at their landlord's mill and so pay mill dues (Dodgshon 1992: 179–80; Fenton 1999: 111–13). This is a characteristic example of the control over agricultural production with the purpose of obtaining income through dues and taxes (chapter 3). Litigation in the eighteenth century over 'out-grinding' was common, and it was even easier to continue using the small, portable hand querns, which were highly appropriate for small and remote plots of land (Dodgshon 1992: 183–4).

Remembering his childhood in South Uist in the 1870s and 1880s, Angus MacLellan relates a characteristic example of this. The millers were not receiving enough grain to keep the new mills operating, so the estate ordered that all hand querns should be destroyed and thrown into a loch. 'That loch has never been called anything since but 'Loch nam Bràithntean', 'the Loch of the Querns'; there are plenty of them yet in the loch' (MacLellan 1997: 7). The memory of the silencing of the querns lives on in the landscape.

During the eighteenth century Great Britain was nearing the fulfilment of its inevitable progression towards the Age of Commerce, according at least to Enlightenment ideology (Dalglish 2003: 129–51). Only the highlands of Scotland remained to be modernized, and in agricultural terms this meant above all 'improvement'. Landlords and factors were not committing deliberate acts of genocide: they firmly believed that the lives of their tenants would be greatly benefited by improved housing, lifestyle and above all agricultural work.

The ideology of improvement is best seen in the coastal and lowland farms and settlements where the tenants of the uplands and straths were resettled. In Kintyre in the south-west (Figure 8.4), the new farmsteads were built in neat ranges or round courtyards, in the midst of their rectilinear enclosed fields. Even within the houses, increased subdivision of domestic space showed the greater organization and regulation of the patterns of everyday life (Dalglish 2003: 103–23). Along the Dornoch coast in the northeast, the Sutherland estate set up a series of 36 mixed farms by 1829, with central yards and their own water wheels to drive the threshing machines. The new buildings, apparently designed en masse by the estate office, almost never incorporated their predecessors, so making a clean break with the unimproved past. The well-built and imposing stone facades were often marked with the Sutherland coat of arms (Martins 1996–7).

Order and tidiness were paramount in the improved structures and lifestyles. 'Whenever a tenant shall build a house on his lot', laid down the regulations of the Ardnamurchan and Sunart estate in about 1830, 'it shall be done in a straight line with adjoining houses' (Dodgshon 1993: 436). Such houses had to be built in stone, not woven saplings or turf, and often according to a specific plan (Dodgshon 1993: 422–3). This could cause major suffering among people who had no money to pay the masons for such an expensive and laborious building technique (Macleod 1892: 30–2). But for estate factors such as Patrick Sellar, writing about Sutherland in 1816, such

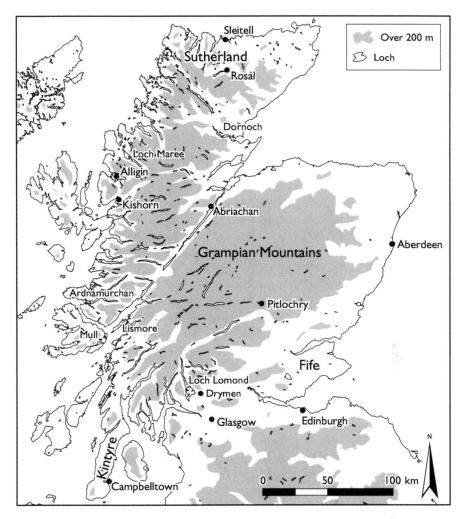

Figure 8.4 Map of northern and central Scotland.

settlements were the only means of producing an ordered, controlled and prosperous society:

> Nothing is more plain than that by an arrangement to be matured on a prudent considerate and systematic plan, the people may (as they ought) be brought from the inaccessible interior of the country where smuggling is the only possible means of life, where man is shut out from every rational pursuit to the accessible sea coast where all his motions are distinctly seen, where so many different

147

fields for his industry lie open, where his children are educated and bred to honest and useful trades and where the presence of people firmly knit together in the bond of one Society is necessary for any such things as scientific direction of labour wealth and prosperity in a country.

quoted in Adam 1972 I: 183

To the inhabitants of the inland townships, eviction from the homes and landscapes in which their lives were so deeply embedded was humiliating, traumatic and in social terms profoundly disruptive. The Sutherland clearances between 1807 and 1820 generally began with a standardized 'notice of removal' written in English, which most highland tenants, of course, could not read. On the declared day the removal party arrived, gave a little time for the family to remove its belongings, and then dismantled the roof and often burnt the house to discourage them from reoccupying it. The families, often with their young, old or sick, had to make their own way down the coast, where their newly allotted land awaited.

These new plots on the coast were often steep and thin-soiled, deliberately too small for a family to subsist on. This, Enlightenment theory ran, would encourage them to turn to new callings such as fishing or wage-labouring. The old rhythms of the seasons, the strath and the rig were suddenly replaced by the rhythms of the tide and the unpredictability of the winds and sea swell (Lelong 2000: 220–3). They needed new knowledge and skills to control a boat, read the shoreline and think like fish. They could not even teach their children in this new and unfamiliar environment.

Even where the old farming townships were replaced with modern commercial farms, the people and their landscape suffered a radical dislocation. Before improvement, the township, infields, outfields and shielings all made up a single, integrated landscape, with familiar paths and routes and regular movements carrying people through it. With the new commercial arable farms in the valley bottoms and coastal strips, and sheep farms in the uplands, this landscape was split into two completely separate and independent systems (J. Atkinson 2000: 159). Sellar's artificial division of these landscapes is clear in the quotation above, and in many ways the romantic stereotype of low-lying, manicured farmland versus the wild and free highlands still structures our thinking today.

Landlords and factors were happy to deride what they saw as the apathy and passiveness of their tenants in the face of eviction. Today's historians, by contrast, have been searching assiduously for evidence of resistance (e.g. Grigor 2000; Richards 2000: 315–16; cf. S. Macdonald 1997: 81). For this phase of the clearances, it has clearly been rather hard to find:

The traditional stereotype of the docile Highlander as passive and apathetic during the Clearances has been much qualified by recent research. Between 1780 and 1855 more than 50 acts of defiance against landlord authority occurred, and further intensive investigation will doubtless reveal even more intensive instances of collective protest.

Devine 1999: 425

Was the cultural trauma so great, and the underlying respect for those who had once been their chiefs so deep-seated, that people would not even contemplate resisting (Devine 1999: 182)? Was the power of the landlords and factors, and their allies the ministers, so strong that there was no point in trying? Or is there more to resistance than 'acts of defiance' and 'collective protest'? The role of evicted tenants in the highland clearances begins to look very different when we extend resistance to include everyday activities and routine practices which in their different ways contradicted the ideology of improvement and created pride and identity in the face of factors and landlords.

The most obvious means of resistance to eviction was to come back again once the removal party had moved on. The destruction of roofs and burning of houses was specifically intended to prevent this. Evidence for rebuilding and re-occupation is clearly something that can be found relatively easily by excavation, and offers an important alternative source to the usual estate papers and eyewitness accounts (Symonds 2000: 203). Shielings had long been used by outlaws and vagrants, especially in winter when the cattleherds were not in residence (Bil 1990: 233). While distributing food relief during the clearances of the 1810s, the Sutherland factor James Loch discovered to his surprise that there were 408 families living in remote parts of the estate, who 'held neither of landlord nor of any of the tacksmen; and who, in short, enjoyed the benefit of residing upon the property without paying any rent whatever' (Loch 1820: 81–2). Quite apart from the doubts this casts on using estate accounts as infallible historical sources, this shows the sheer size and significance of the hidden population.

The most famous documented example of a squatter who refused to be evicted was the 'tinker' William Chisholm, who had occupied the shielding of Badinloskin, 4.5 km south-east of Rosal. Archaeologically, it is clear that Chisholm had a substantial establishment at Badinloskin, with a long house, two stackyards, two outhouses and a grain-drying kiln (Fairhurst 1967–8: 163). After complaints by the new sheep farmers, Sellar had him evicted and the roof and turf walls removed from the house. In spite of the efforts to remove the roofing material, 'he presently found new birchen-boughs, set up one of their turff cabins as usual in a few hours and I understand is there to this day' (Sellar in 1815, quoted in Adam 1972 I: 161).

As Chisholm demonstrated so successfully, local materials and straightforward building techniques meant that houses could be easily constructed, dismantled and modified, and this fluidity was one of the characteristics of pre-improvement building (Holden *et al.* 2001: 30). Improved houses, by contrast, required specialist techniques, specified plans and imported materials. Even so, tenants found ways round this. Sleitell was a characteristic post-clearance settlement on a rocky, exposed beach on the north coast of Sutherland, 23 km north of Rosal (Lelong 2002: 269–70). The houses are well-built, of full-height dry stone construction easily capable of bearing the roof. Like the old wattle and turf long houses, however, they have vertical slots in the walls for crucks, the kneed roof support beams which rested on the ground. In spite of the compulsory improved architecture, the tenants kept what they saw as the solidity and security of the crucks.

At the other end of the country, Dalglish's analysis of post-improvement housing in Kintyre shows that many houses which appeared improved from the outside in fact retained the unpartitioned and communal character of their predecessors on the inside (2003: 200–10). There are clear patterns in the different levels at which improvement was accepted. Larger tenants tended to embrace it happily, as their continuing tenure depended on them supporting the estate's policies. Smaller tenants with shorter leases, by contrast, were much more likely to lose their own land and become wage labourers. To maintain communal family living within their houses gave them security in the face of such threats, and they had no reason to welcome the ideology of improvement.

Domestic architecture is just one field where people renegotiated their lifestyle and identity in the face of clearance, improvement and exploitation. The continuing use of the hand quern is another (Fenton 1999: 104–6), and much work remains to be done examining this type of resistance inherent in settlement patterns, agricultural practices, material culture and many other facets of social life. There were also some more specific activities where people quite deliberately set themselves up in opposition to the authorities. Some of these became so elaborate and widespread that they constituted entire landscapes of resistance.

One such activity was the smuggling of commodities such as tobacco, spirits, textiles and tea. This became rampant after the union of the Scottish and English parliaments in 1707, mostly because of the enormous rise in duty payments (Goring 1987: 53). It was particularly prevalent in Dumfries and Galloway in the south-west, with hundreds of miles of coastline facing England, Ireland and the largely tax-free Isle of Man. Stories abounded of the smugglers' cleverness and daring, and there was a complex landscape of routes, activities and meanings: the lookout point on the headland; the secret inlet for landing the goods; the caves and myriad ingenious 'brandy holes' for hiding them; the networks of tracks taken by the smuggling caravans in the back country (Dick 1919: 72–5; Goring 1987; McCulloch 2000: 418–20; McFadzean 1994: 151–5).

This is just one example of a landscape of resistance which is crying out for an archaeological analysis. I will look more closely at another related landscape, which at that period had the same name. In the eighteenth and nineteenth centuries, 'smuggling' also referred to illicit whisky distillation.

Landscape and whisky

Between the 1780s and 1820s whisky was distilled illicitly in the highlands of Scotland on a massive, almost industrial scale. In 1782, right at the beginning of the boom period, over 1,000 stills were seized in the highlands. By the early 1820s, some 4,000 were being confiscated each year in Aberdeenshire alone. These were just the ones that got caught. There were tens of thousands of such stills in the highlands, so much that the legal lowland distillers complained to the government that over half of the whisky drunk in Scotland was illegally produced (Devine 1975; 1994: 119–20, 126).

There were good political and economic reasons for this boom in illicit whisky distilling, most notably the punitively high taxes and duties imposed after the union of governments in 1707. As we shall see, at the level of the individual family it made excellent economic sense to convert bulky, low-value grain into high-value whisky. But there was more to it than national or family economics. Why did people choose to drink illicit whisky, even in the lowlands? Why were there so many stories of avoiding, outwitting or beating up the gaugers? What was the social role of illicit whisky in the highlands, particularly as it flourished at exactly the same time as the first wave of clearances?

Making whisky on a small scale required a relatively low outlay on equipment, a suitable working area hidden from the gaugers, and substantial amounts of skill and experience (Connell 1961: 59–62; Sillett 1965: 85–95). To begin the germination the sacks of barley were soaked in a burn or bog pool, and the germinating grain was then spread out on the floor of a cave or bothy and turned regularly for about ten days. Drying the malted grain in a kiln stops the germination process, and adds the aroma of the fuel, which was often but not necessarily peat. The malt was lightly ground with a hand-quern, and then added to boiling water and yeast to be fermented. The beer-like product of the fermentation was then heated in a copper or tin still. The alcohol evaporated off before the water, and rose into the cap or 'head' of the still. From there it passed into the distiller's most prized possession, the 'worm' or spiral tube immersed in cold running water to condense the alcohol vapour. The first distillation was returned to the still and distilled again, and this clear spirit was the whisky that could be drunk (often on the spot), sold, or in rare cases left to mature.

The most specialized requirement in all of this was the still and the worm, and the records of Robert Armour, a Kintyre coppersmith in the 1810s, show that these were easily and relatively cheaply obtainable (Glen 1970: 74–8). To a society which kiln-dried its grain as a matter of course, a kiln was easy to construct, and most people already owned movable items such as hand-querns

Figure 8.5 Illicit whisky still on Rannoch Moor. Source: Wilson 1850: 128.

and the numerous jugs and vessels required. A local historian in the 1880s describes the facilities of the whisky distillers of Abriachan, on the northern shore of Loch Ness:

> They had their bothies for making the malt under ground, and sometimes in the face of steep rocks where none but themselves and the goats could get into them. They had the kiln for drying the malt in the silent grove, or on the lonely moor. And they had a portable hand-mill for grinding the malt as well on the top of the hill as in the middle of the wood. They would distil their whisky in broad daylight, without raising any smoke from the fire. They gathered the old stumps of burnt heather and of juniper bushes for making a fire that would raise no smoke.
>
> T. Wallace 1880–3: 312–13

It is characteristic of Victorian romanticism that this is seen as taking place in the 'silent grove' and 'lonely moor' (Figure 8.5; cf. MacCulloch 1824: 367–8). Clearly, it was important to work in a discreet and private location, particularly in areas known for their energetic and enthusiastic gaugers, such as the hills west of Aberdeen in the 1810s. But it was equally important to work close to transport routes and to sources of grain and fuel. Distilling commonly took place actually in the house. A farm near Strathmiglo, Fife, has an illicit still dating to about 1830 cunningly incorporated into its basement (Butt 1967: 260). The inner room of the excavated long house at Rosal had a fragment of copper or brass tube, which most plausibly comes from a still (Fairhurst 1967–8: 165). Most of the stories tend to prefer the romance of moor and mountain, but Ian Macdonald, the retired exciseman, reported that distilling frequently took places in barns and outhouses (I. Macdonald 1914: 79).

This question clearly needs an archaeological distribution analysis. The archaeology of illicit whisky stills, unfortunately, is very much in its infancy. Apart from the Inchfad stills on Loch Lomond, which I will discuss in the next section, there are currently 14 archaeologically known illicit stills, most of them on the database of the Royal Commission on the Ancient and Historical Monuments of Scotland (Canmore 2003). These are typically no more than half an hour's walk from the nearest lochside, township or main road. Sheilings provided useful shelter in a familiar area well-connected with the settlement but away from the main roads, and so were regularly used for distilling (e.g. Michie 2000: 150–2; Wickham-Jones 2001: 62). Before agricultural improvement it had been the cattleherds and their beasts who passed regularly up and down between settlement and shieling; now it was the distiller.

The accounts of Robert Armour, the Kintyre coppersmith, allow a more systematic study of the location of illicit stills. Because he noted the names and addresses of his customers, it is possible to plot their approximate locations (Glen 1970: 79–80). This is clearly not an archaeological distribution map, and there is no guarantee that the distillers were working in or near their homes. But it does show very clearly that they were based primarily along the coast, in the river bottoms, and in and around Campbelltown itself. The correlation is with arable land, not with remote moorland and mountain.

The same link between still and settlement is apparent in the stories as well. A common theme is that when the gaugers arrive in a village, a boy is sent up the hill to warn the distillers, while the gaugers are given plentiful hospitality down in the village, often with the very product they were sent to confiscate (e.g. Macdonald I. 1914: 80; Thomson 1983: 114). The stills clearly had to be close enough for constant communication. Far from taking place in a remote and separate area, distilling was an integral part of the everyday landscape of settlement, agriculture and production.

Why was the production of illicit whisky so widespread between the 1780s and 1820s? There are two good economic reasons: the high levels of taxation on legal whisky; and the need for tenants to pay their rent in cash. The taxes and duties on whisky had been rising since the infamous malt tax of 1725, imposed on Scotland by the House of Commons in spite of the terms of the 1707 Act of Union. By 1786, the malt, the stills and the finished product were all being taxed at a highly punitive level, with some dispensations for the highlands provided their whisky was not sold south of the highland line. This came at a time when demand for whisky was rising exponentially, particularly after the outbreak of the Napoleonic Wars in 1793. As well as disrupting the importation of brandy and wine, both legal and illegal, the war turned educated tastes towards the more patriotic home-produced whisky (D. Brown 1999–2000; Devine 1994: 119–22; Dietz 1997).

The effect of this on the legal distilleries of the lowlands was a drastic reduction in quality. To avoid the malt tax they used high proportions of raw grain, in contrast to the malted grain regularly used by the illicit distillers of the highlands. The still tax was assessed according to the capacity of the still as measured by the excisemen, hence their name 'gaugers'. To get round this, new methods of rapid distillation were developed, which greatly increased the amount a still could produce in a day, again at the expense of quality (Dietz 1997: 61–3). The inevitable result was that any lowland drinker who could afford it turned to the much higher quality illicit whisky from the highlands. In the early 1820s King George IV himself favoured (illegal) Glenlivet.

At the other end of the social scale, tenants in poor agricultural areas regularly needed whisky in order to pay their rent (Dodgshon 1998: 111–12). As chiefs became landlords, they needed more and more cash in order to incorporate their estates into the commercial market, fund their aristocratic lifestyle and pay their debts. The provision of fighting kinsmen and contributions in kind was now useless, and instead they demanded cash from their tenants. The sale of cattle could raise some of this, particularly as they were able to transport themselves to the great markets of the lowlands. By the time low-value and high-bulk barley was transported out of the more remote glens, however, it was almost valueless. Thanks to the relatively straightforward distilling process, it could be readily turned into a high-value and low-bulk commodity, ideal for selling to middlemen and raising cash to pay the rent.

For this reason the great majority of landowners were in favour of the illicit whisky distilling of their tenants. How else would they obtain their rents? Because most landlords were also local Justices of the Peace, they were in an excellent position to make sure that the distillers were not unduly punished by the law. As Sir George Mackenzie of Coul, one such Justice of the Peace, said in 1822, 'We know and we feel, that when we inflict even the lowest penalty directed by law, if the tenant be able to pay he will not pay his rent' (quoted in Devine 1994: 125). It was only by policing local magistrates, as well as radically reducing the duties and licence fees, that the government finally began to stem the flow of illegal whisky by means of the Excise Act of 1823 (Devine 1994: 131).

So illicit whisky distilling was a direct result of excessive state taxation, and played an important economic role in highland communities. But there was more to it than that. Estate factors and the more scrupulous landlords were the first to connect whisky distilling with morality. This is abundantly clear in their commentaries on the highland clearances. For many landlords and factors, people's resistance to eviction was in direct proportion to the extent of their distilling (Richards 2000: 132). Patrick Sellar is characteristically unsubtle and outspoken on the link between distilling and morality:

His life becomes a continued struggle, how by lies, chicanery, perjury, cunning, midnight journeys, the midnight watching of his wife and family, debasing artifices, and sneaking to his superiors, he can obtain thro' theft a miserable livelihood. Debauchery and beggary follow the total absence of principle, *essential to his* trade.

quoted in Adam 1972 I: 177

The accounts of the coppersmith Robert Armour show a very different picture. Out of some 800 transactions over six years, there are remarkably few examples of bad debts, and many customers worked in cooperative groups, sharing the labour and equipment (Glen 1970: 78–9). This type of cooperation was relatively common. Different stages of the process could be done in different locations, which gave added security as well as sharing the labour. Partners and even communities would even share out the fines among themselves. In such cases distilling encourages solidarity and cooperation rather than individualism and mistrust.

In Sellar's conceptual division of the landscape, whisky distilling takes place in the 'inaccessible country', and can only be combated by bringing the people down to the model villages of the 'accessible coast' (quoted in Adam 1972 I: 179). The many stories that survive of outwitting the gaugers suggest that the distillers had a very different view. In particular, the landscapes of the whisky distillers were vibrant with meaning and memory, and very much integrated into wider landscapes of township, field and pasture.

Private knowledge was an important component of the experience of whisky distilling. The distillers and their community know the landscape, the activities and the language; the gaugers do not. One story tells of a bearded gauger arriving at the door of a bothy where a distiller and his daughter, Moll, were bagging the malt to take it to the drying kiln. When they barred the door against him, he put his head through the window, but Moll grabbed him by the beard and held him fast. 'The father, doubling his efforts to secure the malt, called to Moll, "*Cum greim cruaidh air a bheist!*" (Haud a hard grip of the beast!), but shouted in English, "Let the gentleman go, Moll!"' (I. Macdonald 1914: 92–3). The gauger is mocked for being an ignorant outsider, while the story celebrates the quick-thinking distiller and his tenacious daughter.

The hidden whisky stills of a highland landscape are only hidden to some. Many gaugers lamented the solidarity of communities such as Alligin and Diabaig in Wester Ross, whose members knew exactly where the stills were and combined to stop the gaugers finding them (I. Macdonald 1914: 84–7). The sites of whisky stills and associated markets were often widely known and easily recognisable. Clach a Mhail, the 'Rent Stone', is a large boulder on the eastern shore of Loch Maree in Wester Ross, where the landlord of the Letterewe estate collected his rent. The same stone was also the site for the periodic markets where the whisky distilled in large quantities on the Loch Maree islands was sold (Dixon 1886: 134, 343). The stone has a complex set of meanings: it was where you paid your rent, but also where you defied the authorities in order to gain the cash to pay your rent.

Such boulders are a good example of striking natural features being given local meanings which were often withheld from outsiders. We saw the same phenomenon with the boulder in Cyprus where the Virgin Mary ground a plague to death (chapter 2), or the rocks associated with Saint Mamas (chapter 7). Another huge boulder of gneiss above Abriachan on the shore of Loch Ness was a (locally) well-known spot for sheltering sheep or goats on a stormy night, and for hiding bags of malt for the distilling (T. Wallace 1880–3: 312). A distilling bothy north-east of Pitlochry with a 70-m long lade to bring in the water was constructed largely underground, but in the lee of a prominent pyramidal boulder (RCAHMS 1990: 146). To anyone with this sort of local knowledge, the landscape was not at all 'inaccessible' or 'wild', but well-known and full of the meanings, memories and stories which made it a landscape of resistance.

Whisky on Loch Lomond

The Highland Boundary Fault crosses the southern end of Loch Lomond, and makes it an excellent area for illicit whisky distilling. To the south are the rich agricultural areas of Drymen and the Vale of Leven, excellent sources of barley. In the central lowlands just beyond, the urban drinkers of Glasgow and the towns of the Clyde estuary created a huge demand for the illicit but higher-quality highland whisky. To the north of the fault, particularly on the east side, the pastures, steep hillsides and incised ravines provided many suitably discreet locations, as did the islands strung across the loch along the faultline.

There is a characteristic distilling landscape at Ardess, at the southern foot of Ben Lomond on the east side of the loch: 300 m from the edge of the loch are the remains of an eighteenth-century settlement, consisting of some nine houses in two clusters. Associated with them are two areas of rig and furrow, some substantial terracing, and a head dyke on the eastern side marking the edge of the cultivation. A trackway leads up the hillside to two groups of shielings, one of them 2 km to the north and 400 m higher in altitude, two-thirds of the way up Ben Lomond, and the other 1 km to the north-east and 250 m higher (Ellis 1997: 4–7).

A network of dykes across the settlement and arable areas suggests various stages of enclosure, and a large, drystone sheepfold in the midst of the northern cluster is evidence for the 'improved' economy which brought about the abandonment of the little settlement. This may be the township of Rowardennan recorded in 1759 as having four families, and parish records show that the population of this area fell by half between 1792 and 1881 (Ellis 1997: 2). Even though there was no dramatic clearance here of the kind that took place in Sutherland, the inhabitants of Ardess certainly experienced the stresses of falling population and a forced conversion from small-scale mixed cattle and arable farming to large, commercial sheep-farming.

Figure 8.6 Ardess, on the east shore of Loch Lomond, with the distilling site in the wooded gully in the foreground. Photograph: Michael Given.

Even after the shielings were abandoned with the arrival of the sheep, there were other reasons for taking the path leading from the settlement up the hillside along the side of the burn. The slope here is steep, rising 100 m in altitude over 300 m horizontally, and the burn is deeply incised (Figure 8.6). After about 20 minutes' climb, if you drop down into the gully of the burn at exactly the right point, you find a waterfall about 4 m high, with the peaty water forming clouds of spray when the burn is in spate. Beside the pool at its foot is a levelled platform 3 m across, supported on the downhill side by a short stretch of dry stone retaining wall. The alders grow thickly around it, and with 3 m high rock walls on each side, the waterfall above and the narrowing ravine below, it is entirely enclosed and hidden. If you looked down into the ravine 10 m above or 10 m below, you would miss it.

This is an unlikely place for a charcoal burners' platform, and with its secrecy, the plentiful supply of water, and its similarity with other better documented sites, it is most likely that this is the site of an illicit still (Ellis 1997: 5). It cannot be dated, of course, but as we shall see, illicit distilling was widespread in southern Loch Lomond in the late eighteenth and early nineteenth centuries.

The location by a waterfall was a well-known trick for hiding the smoke amid the spray (I. Macdonald 1914: 95), and as well as Ardess there are two illicit stills on Mull which exploit this (Batey 1992: 57). The noise of the waterfall in this enclosed space is thunderous when the burn is in spate, and was clearly central to the sensuous experience of those distilling whisky here, along with warm smell of the malt, the aromatic smoke from the peat or wood fuel, and the sharp pungency of the distillate. As any whisky connoisseur will tell you, these aromas from the production are the foundations of the flavour of the final product. To the distiller, the taste of the whisky carries within it the whole experience of avoiding the gaugers, resisting the new, oppressive rural economy, and reintegrating the settlement with its upland landscape.

Islands make excellent places for illicit distilling. On a fine day, you can see the gaugers coming for miles. On a stormy day, it is much harder for them to come, and even when they do you can submerge the equipment in the sea or loch and mark it with an innocent buoy. This is how Mary McKay, the *Cailleach an Eilean* or 'Old woman of the island', operated on Kishorn Island in Wester Ross in the mid-nineteenth century, with thirsty fishermen providing her market (Iain MacGregor and Helen Murchison, personal communication, September 2003). Enough whisky was produced on the islands of Loch Maree, as we have seen, for there to be a regular market on the shore. The island of Inchfad on Loch Lomond saw production at a similar scale (Figure. 8.7).

The illicit whisky distilling facilities at the northern end of Inchfad are on a completely different scale to the single, isolated stills at Loch nan Trì-Eileanan Beag or Ardess (F. Baker 1997: 83–7). Identifying and characterizing the remains is not easy, as they appear to have been deliberately destroyed. This could well be associated with the launch of a customs and excise cutter on Loch Lomond in the middle of the nineteenth century (F. Baker 1997: 77–8).

Most of the illicit distilling facilities lie in a 200 m strip along the north-western shore of the island. One of them is a complex, sub-rectangular building measuring 13.5 × 5.6 m, which is composed of six roughly circular structures with flues and clearly marked edges. These are clearly kilns, and were presumably for drying the malt. Others may have been fires and supports for the stills. There are three other such buildings in this group, made up of between two and four kilns. Another six kilns were free-standing, and a few other rubble piles are too amorphous to identify. Another smaller concentration in the south-western corner of the island includes two clear kilns

Figure 8.7 The island of Inchfad on Loch Lomond, from the east. Photograph: Michael Given.

and another five stone heaps which may be destroyed kilns, or could possibly just be clearance cairns.

Figure 8.8 shows one of the better-preserved structures in the south-western group (F. Baker 1997: 83). A burn runs down the north-eastern side, to provide the all-important supply of cold running water for cooling the worm. At the southern end there is one clear kiln with a flue, and there may be another collapsed one just north-west of it. The rough wall running off to the north-west is a feature of many of the Inchfad kilns. It may have been a support for a malting floor, presumably with some sort of roof or cover to keep it dry (F. Baker 1997: 78).

These structures raise the important issue of the morphology of illicit whisky stills. Most of the distilling stories describe the process as taking place in a bothy, such as the one at Loch nan Trì-Eileanan Beag. There are, however, mentions of distilling in the open. John MacCulloch, who partici-pated in an excise raid on a still on the island of Lismore in the early 1820s, commented that stills are 'frequently set up in the open air, under some bank or rock which permits a stream of water to be easily introduced into the tub' (1824: 371). This describes the Ardess and Mull stills perfectly. The flatter terrain of the Inchfad stills would have required more complex arrange-ments for the water, but even so, the principal structures were clearly the kiln for drying the malt, and the fireplace for heating and supporting the still.

With at least 12 complexes containing 24 kilns or fireplaces, the production

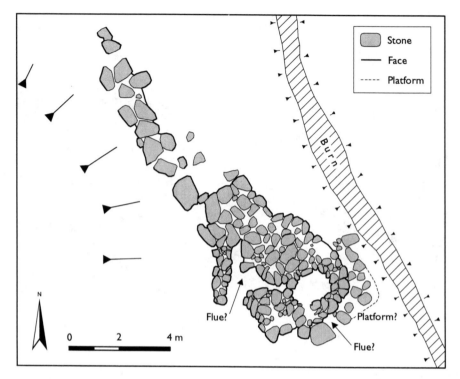

Figure 8.8 Plan of illicit whisky still on Inchfad, Loch Lomond. Source: F. Baker 1997: 96 (redrawn with the permission of Fiona Baker, Firat Archaeological Services).

of illicit whisky on Inchfad was a major operation. Government reports from the 1810s comment on the massive trade in illicit whisky being brought into Glasgow from the north (Devine 1994: 129). It was carried in heavily-armed convoys of up to 30 or 40 men, usually Irishmen or lowlanders, and sold to retailers at Cowcaddens, on the northern edge of the city. The Mac-farlanes on Loch Lomondside were particularly involved in this trade, and according to one of these reports, 'bands of lawless persons armed with defensive weapons, and even in some cases preceded by pipers unloaded vessels and carried off the smuggled spirits without molestation' (Woodbine Parrish in 1816, quoted in Devine 1975: 171). As the boats were unloaded and the pipers played, the whisky proclaimed its distillers' pride, identity and defiance of the authorities.

Conclusion

The highland clearances and the other processes of agricultural and social 'improvement' in the eighteenth and early nineteenth centuries caused enormous personal trauma and social dislocation. The deep-seated rhythms of everyday life and work were broken, and the intimate knowledge of a landscape rich in meanings and memories was lost. Some people were exiled to what was to them a hostile and unknown environment. Others saw their landscapes being decapitated, with their homes and arable land severed from their upland bodies.

The resistance to such trauma is still widely misunderstood. Some maintain the old stereotype of the conservative and fatalistic highlander, forced into accepting the changes imposed by the active and dynamic 'improver'. Even the people's historians tend to limit themselves to making lists of stone-throwings and deforcements. Thanks to the sensitivity of material culture to unwritten, often unspoken, attitudes and activities, a few archaeologists are beginning to investigate resistance to the highland clearances at a much broader and more nuanced level (Dalglish 2003: 193–216; Symonds 1999). People returned to their cleared houses and rebuilt their roofs, or lived entirely outside the control of the estate. Others were able to use house design and domestic space to negotiate their position within the newly 'improved' society.

There is also a wide range of activities which directly and explicitly defied the authorities, filled a variety of useful economic functions, and gave people the opportunity to regain some independence and pride. Poaching, smuggling and illicit whisky distilling are examples of these. They provided the hidden transcripts of everyday life and resistance, and allowed people to reaffirm their own agency and self-esteem in the face of humiliation, eviction, exploitation and what they saw as the violation of the social contract. Even amidst all their moralizing, a few commentators of the period saw this, as is clear from this report on illicit whisky distilling:

> It presents all the fascination of the gaming table . . . In smuggling, as in poaching, there is a spirit of adventure and hazard, which has a charm for the minds of the peasantry. An escape, or a successful resistance, is remembered, and related as an heroic achievement, men encouraging each other, and a fraternity of feeling is produced among them by a sense of common danger.
>
> Stewart of Garth 1828–9: 360

This is more than the chance to lend 'a certain colour to drab lives' (Devine 1994: 123). The activities, the cooperation and the stories are what make up resistance. People create new rhythms of everyday life and find new ways of forging pride and identity. The uplands are once again integrated with the low-lying settlements and fields, and new routines lead people from one to the other. And to the distillers and their friends and customers, the peat-reek of the whisky spoke of secret stills and malting floors, the waterfall's spray, and the story of how they outwitted the gaugers.

9

CONCLUSION

Archaeologists and the colonized

In the moonlight of a Cypriot summer's night two women sieve their grain, enjoying some quiet mockery of the tithe collector snoring on a nearby threshing floor. By the pounding roar of a highland waterfall 4,000 km away three men distil moonshine of a different kind, and taste the first results of their defiance with deep satisfaction. 1,500 years earlier, a family were struggling to carry their grain up the narrow steps of a state granary in Egypt, the first stage on its long journey to feed the people of Rome. 2,500 years before that, quarry workers were labouring in the heat and dust, dragging the huge stone blocks which would build the Pharaoh's pyramid and the new state machinery that controlled their lives. 45 centuries later and 3,000 km to the north-west, other quarry workers were staining the granite with their sweat and blood, building monuments to another totalitarian regime which arranged their death on the quarry steps. Meanwhile a muleteer and his son pause on the edge of a Roman-engineered road in western Anatolia and look up suspiciously at a huge inscription they cannot read.

Thanks to the archaeology of the colonized, it is possible to understand the lives and experiences of people like this. They were not statistics or the objects of some deeply implicated bureaucrat, but real people who used actual material culture in tangible contexts. The objects, structures and landscapes that enveloped their lives were the means of their repression and the tools of their resistance.

What does all this tell us about the colonized, or about the nature of colonial rule? Niall Ferguson puts the question in its baldest, most simplistic terms, asking 'whether the Empire was a good or bad thing' (N. Ferguson 2003: xii). This reduces the complexities of human dynamics and historical process to the level of the satirical *1066 and All That* (Sellar and Yeatman 1930). Ferguson's account of the British Empire is a resolute history of the colonizers, eulogizing the movement of goods and capital and the imposition of 'Western norms of law, order and governance' (N. Ferguson 2003: xxi). By ignoring the experience of the colonized and focusing on economic benefits to the colonizers, it is relatively straightforward to argue that apart from a few 'blemishes' (358), the British Empire was a 'good thing'. The oppression was very real. So was the pride, identity and independence of those people who are still being ignored by history.

The colonized

The huge machinery of taxation that characterized so many empires points to the core of imperial oppression: economic exploitation. Dismissed by Ferguson as a 'nationalist/Marxist assumption' (2003: xviii), the extraction of agricultural surplus was key not just to the imperial economy but to a farming family's direct experience of colonial rule (chapter 3). It was the loss of a third or a half of your food that brought the empire home.

To this was added the humiliation of dealing with self-important officials, tax collectors and judges, and seeing your produce removed from in front of you and your family and neighbours. The colonized were oppressed by means of mockery, arrogance and language switching, and intimidated by the architecture of public offices and state granaries, or by artefacts such as receipts, forms and unreadable inscriptions. Others felt it in their bodies, working in forced labour gangs in the quarries, building sites and road construction projects that built the tools and monuments of imperialism (chapter 6).

The worst part of the experience of colonial rule was the alienation. Those who were moved and resettled elsewhere were alienated from their own landscape, including their daily patterns of life and their memories of meaningful places (chapter 8). Many were alienated from their own past, not just by physical removal from the places that carried the associations but by the imposition of new ideologies and practices. The essential meaning of colonial rule is to be ruled by an alien society, whether alien in culture, language, social group, or place of origin. That is why I take such a broad view of the term 'colonized' in this book.

If oppression was a central part of the experience of colonial rule, so was resistance. The colonized were anything but passive, even if some archaeological accounts are still giving that impression (Dyson 2003: 493). It is archaeology which can get away from the elite-based written sources and show up the enormously wide range of activities and initiatives. Open rebellions and guerrilla warfare are only a small part of it. There were hidden economies on a vast scale, dealing in commodities such as secretly cultivated grain, smuggled goods or illicitly distilled whisky (chapters 7 and 8). These could involve complex networks of people, very specialized skills and huge amounts of produce.

At the most fundamental level of resistance, as I have been defining it, is the continuing process of people creating and maintaining their pride, independence and self-respect. People were proud of a particular skill, or of working in a team, or of the religious and historical associations of particular spots in the landscape. Stories of scoring a point over the taxman or factor, whether fictional or not, were always real, and contributed to people's respect for themselves and each other (chapter 7). However overwhelming the physical and ideological oppression, there is always space for a small amount of independence, as the Spanish prisoners in Mauthausen quarry demonstrated (chapter 6).

So resistance includes open rebellion, operating a hidden economy, and maintaining your self-respect (chapter 2). This is clearly so broad a definition that it is straining the usefulness of the term. In a way, it is just shorthand for the activities of an active and dynamic colonized people (Scham 2001: 199). In this sense, resistance is only one of the many aspects of social life which people continuously use to remake and negotiate their identities, along with age, gender, class, sexuality and ethnicity (Meskell 2002: 283). People's relationship to colonial rule becomes part of who they are.

Oppression and resistance, then, are only convenient markers for two aspects of the complex web of relationships and experiences that make up the lives of the colonized. Any nuanced study must be able to move between 'notions of blended or reworked articulations and the hard realities of repression' (Meskell 2002: 292). Perhaps the most important, if obvious, point to be made about the colonized is that they were complex. There are no absolute categories, with fixed lines dividing colonized from colonizers or domination from resistance. People could choose to accept, exploit, fight or ignore colonial rule, or else they remained utterly unaware of it. Even 'colonialism' is not an absolute category of analysis. As with resistance, it is more a set of processes, 'the dynamics of past behaviors, choices, and understandings' (Lyons and Papadopoulos 2002: 2). Our goal as archaeologists is to investigate and understand those dynamics.

The archaeologists

The archaeology of the colonized is not a merely academic issue, remote from the issues and concerns of contemporary life. Take Zimbabwe, for example. During 90 years of British rule, as well as almost five centuries of Portuguese, Boer and British intervention, its past was controlled by the colonizers. In a notorious act of appropriation, British archaeologists and colonizers in the late nineteenth and early twentieth centuries claimed that the monumental medieval stone zimbabwes were 'Phoenician', and therefore built by whites (Pikirayi 2001: 9–14). As recently as 20 years ago, the immediate predecessors of the Shona inhabitants were still being denigrated as the 'Refuge Culture', the decadent remnants of the Zimbabwe culture, on the basis of a handful of poorly investigated hilltop sites (Pikirayi 1993: 181–2).

The consequences of all this today are that the inhabitants of Zimbabwe are alienated from their past and their heritage, for all the symbolism of the country's postcolonial name. Some even think that the zimbabwes, whose ruins were once local cult centres, are so alien and irrelevant that they must indeed have been built by whites (Pwiti and Ndoro 1999: 151). The alienation is also physical. The zimbabwes were normally built in the best agricultural land – exactly that land which was appropriated for white farmers in 1930 (Pwiti and Ndoro 1999: 145–7). This means that most of them have become inaccessible as well as meaningless. What is the role of the archaeologist, whether Zimbabwean or foreign, who wants to help re-integrate people with their past and their landscape? This adds a highly problematic cultural dimension to the current economic and political struggle over the large white-owned commercial farms.

Archaeology has its own heritage of chauvinistic nationalism, colonialism and oppression, as is now widely accepted (Lyons and Papadopoulos 2002; Meskell 2002: 287–9). How successfully have we disassociated ourselves from our disciplinary forefathers (and a very few foremothers), such as those who created a white Great Zimbabwe? In chapter 2 I argued that people developed and maintained their identity and social relations through practice, the repeated everyday actions and decisions carried out in particular contexts and with particular groups of people. The same, then, must be true of archaeologists (Hamilakis 1999: 62). Ivory tower theorizing (such as this) is of little use, particularly if it is written so obscurely that it is only read by a handful of other ivory tower theorists. What about our field projects, international conferences, discussions with heritage managers, site tours and dealings with colleagues, students and the public? Challenging the metanarratives is all very well, but what about the details of our methods and practices (Scham 2001: 186)?

One recent development within archaeology that has been enormously productive is the 'loss of antiquity' (D. Hicks 2003). Historical archaeology has become an international discipline, rather than a parochial study of the mansions of 'great white men' in Australia and North America. Ethnoarchaeology has developed into something of interest in its own right, rather than just providing analogies for prehistory, and we are beginning to see a much-needed injection of theoretical debate into industrial archaeology.

Just because of the nature of world history over the last two or three centuries, much of this historical archaeology has by necessity been concerned with colonial situations and connections (D. Hicks 2003: 323). The immediacy and accessibility of most historical archaeological sites force the archaeologists to consider their role in contemporary communities. Plantation archaeology in North America, for example, is now an important means of encouraging discussion about power relations, racism and pride (Meskell 2002: 284). This is now well-established in the west, particularly when the memories and associations have not been wiped out as they were in Zimbabwe, and it is becoming increasingly so in postcolonial countries.

A key element of postcolonial archaeology is what Scham calls the 'archaeology of the colonized' (2001: 191–3), though a less ambiguous phrase might be 'archaeology by the colonized'. She sees postcolonial criticism and discourse as being 'the particular preserve of western educated nonwestern intellectuals' (191). This applies to some of the names in her list of references better than others, and it certainly does not apply to me . . . It is indeed essential that Zimbabweans should be involved in the interpretation and presentation of Great Zimbabwe. That allows the inclusion of the local mythology and oral traditions which make the site relevant to the local community, but might not be accessible or comprehensible to western academics (Ndoro 1994). But that should not exclude others with different perspectives from joining in the debate and dialogue.

There are many differences which fracture or connect society other than that between colonizer and colonized. If one group of a particular social class or religious background, for example, controls the presentation of the past, then that is no better than colonial rule. In a sense, it is actually a form of colonial rule. Archaeologists need to retain some authority, to provide a certain amount of coherence and comprehensibility, and to give the broader context and raise wider issues. But this still leaves room for other voices to give different stories which will be useful or meaningful to different people (Hamilakis 1999: 66; Louise and Hodder 1998).

This is the broader, philosophical reason behind my occasional use of narrative in this book. Its main purposes are to improve my communication with the reader, and to address academic issues of agency, decision-making, and the contingencies of everyday life. But narrative can also embrace a wider range of voices and identifications than the pseudo-objective monolith of academic pontification (Meskell 2002: 292). It includes different characters who by definition have different attitudes and trajectories through life. You, the reader, can choose which of these you want to identify with, and then lift your eyes from the page and take the story in your own direction.

This book is a cultural production based on my own circumstances and experiences, just as much as on the academic 'facts' cited in the references and bibliography. Perhaps I use narrative just because I have always enjoyed a good novel better than a good article. Perhaps all this multivocalism is just an expression of natural indecisiveness. Or is it because I suffered from a postmodern condition in late 1980s Cambridge? Doing archaeological fieldwork in Cyprus, Egypt, Turkey, Greece and Israel must have somehow influenced the path that I follow in this book. But that is only my path. I hope that I have pointed to enough junctions and signposts that you will be able to choose your own route through the archaeology of the colonized.

BIBLIOGRAPHY

MANUSCRIPT SOURCES

ARFD, *Annual Report of the Forest Department*, Nicosia: Government of Cyprus.

Confiscation and Prosecution Register for Makheras Forest, Lythrodontas Forest Station. Copyright remains with the Government of Cyprus.

SA1, unpublished Chief Secretary's minute papers, preserved in the State Archives of the Government of Cyprus. Copyright remains with the Government of Cyprus. 'Red' refers to the page number of the correspondence in the minute paper.

ANCIENT SOURCES

Cicero (1965–70) *Cicero's Letters to Atticus*, trans. D.R. Shackleton Bailey, 7 vols, Cambridge: Cambridge University Press.

Cicero (2002) *Cicero: Letters to Quintus and Brutus; Letter Fragments; Letter to Octavian; Invectives; Handbook of Electioneering*, trans. D.R. Shackleton Bailey, Cambridge, MA: Harvard University Press (Loeb Classical Library).

Herodotus (1996) *The Histories*, trans. A. de Sélincourt, revised edition, London: Penguin.

Pliny the Elder (1938–1962) *Natural History*, trans. H. Rackham, 10 vols, London: William Heinemann (Loeb Classical Library).

Pliny the Younger (1969) *The Letters of the Younger Pliny*, trans. B. Radice, Harmondsworth: Penguin.

Plutarch (1939) 'Whether the affections of the soul are worse than those of the body', in W. Helmbold (trans.) *Plutarch's Moralia* 6, 381–91, London: William Heinemann (Loeb Classical Library).

Seneca (1935) 'To Helvia on consolation', in J.W. Basore (trans.) *Seneca Moral Essays* 2: 416–89, London: William Heinemann (Loeb Classical Library).

Strabo (1917–1932) *The Geography of Strabo*, trans. H.L. Jones, 8 vols, London: William Heinemann (Loeb Classical Library).

Tacitus (1971) *The Annals of Imperial Rome*, trans. M. Grant, revised edition, Harmondsworth: Penguin.

MODERN PUBLISHED SOURCES

Abujaber, R.S. (1989) *Pioneers over Jordan: the frontier of settlement in Transjordan, 1850–1914*, London: I.B. Tauris.

167

Adam, R. (ed.) (1972) *Papers on Sutherland Estate Management 1802–1816*, 2 vols, Edinburgh: Scottish Historical Society.

Adas, M. (1986) 'From footdragging to flight: the evasive history of peasant avoidance protest in South and South-East Asia', *Journal of Peasant Studies* 13: 64–86.

—— (1995) 'The reconstruction of "tradition" and the defense of the colonial order: British West Africa in the early twentieth century', in J. Schneider and R. Rapp (eds) *Articulating Hidden Histories: exploring the influence of Eric R. Wolf*: 291–307, Berkeley: University of California Press.

Alcock, S.E. (1997) 'Greece: a landscape of resistance?', in D.J. Mattingly (ed.) *Dialogues in Roman Imperialism: power, discourse, and discrepant experience in the Roman Empire*: 103–15, Portsmouth, RI: Journal of Roman Archaeology (JRA Supplementary Series 23).

—— (2001) 'The reconfiguration of memory in the Eastern Roman Empire', in S.E. Alcock, T.N. D'Altroy, K.D. Morrison and C.M. Sinopoli (eds) *Empires: perspectives from archaeology and history*: 323–50, Cambridge: Cambridge University Press.

—— (2002) *Archaeologies of the Greek Past: landscape, monuments, and memories*, Cambridge: Cambridge University Press.

——, Cherry, J.F. and Davis, J.L. (1994) 'Intensive survey, agricultural practice and the classical landscape of Greece', in I. Morris (ed.) *Classical Greece: ancient histories and modern archaeologies*: 137–70, Cambridge: Cambridge University Press.

Allen, M.T. (1998) 'The banality of evil reconsidered: SS mid-level managers of extermination through work', *Central European History* 30: 253–94.

Anderson, B. (1991) *Imagined Communities: reflections on the origins and spread of nationalism*, 2nd edition, London: Verso.

Anderson, P.C. (2003) 'Observations on the threshing sledge and its products in ancient and present-day Mesopotamia', in P.C. Anderson, L.S. Cummings, T.K. Schippers and B. Simonel (eds) *Le Traitement des Récoltes: un regard sur la diversité, du néolithique au présent*: 417–38, Antibes: Éditions APDCA.

—— and Chabot, J. (2000) 'Functional analysis of glossed blades from Northern Mesopotamia in the Early Bronze Age (3000–2500 BC): the case of Tell Atij', *Recherches Archéométriques. Cahiers Archéologiques du CELAT, Université Laval, Québec*: 257–76.

Anschuetz, K.F., Wilshusen, R.H. and Scheick, C.L. (2001) 'An archaeology of landscapes: perspectives and directions', *Journal of Archaeological Research* 9: 157–211.

Arbel, B. and Veinstein, G. (1986) 'La fiscalité vénéto-chypriote au miroir de la législation ottomane: le qānūnnāme de 1572', *Turcica* 18: 7–51.

Ataman, K. (1999) 'Threshing sledges and archaeology', in P.C. Anderson (ed.) *Prehistory of Agriculture: new experimental and ethnographic approaches*: 211–22, Los Angeles: University of California at Los Angeles Institute of Archaeology.

Atkinson, D. (2000) 'Nomadic strategies and colonial governance: domination and resistance in Cyrenaica, 1923–1932', in J.P. Sharp, P. Routledge, C. Philo and R. Paddison (eds) *Entanglements of Power: geographies of domination/resistance*: 93–121, London: Routledge.

Atkinson, J.A. (2000) 'Rural settlement on North Lochtayside: understanding the landscapes of change', in J.A. Atkinson, I. Banks and G. MacGregor (eds) *Townships to Farmsteads: rural settlement studies in Scotland, England and Wales*: 150–60, Oxford: British Archaeological Reports (BAR British Series 293).

Avner, U. (1998) 'Settlement, agriculture and paleoclimate in Uvda Valley, Southern Negev Desert, 6th–3rd millennia BC', in A. Issar and N. Brown (eds) *Water, Environment and Society in Times of Climatic Change*: 147–202, Dordrecht: Kluwer Academic.

Baines, J. (1988) 'Literacy, social organization, and the archaeological record: the case of early Egypt', in J. Gledhill, B. Bender and M.T. Larsen (eds) *State and Society: the emergence and development of social hierarchy and political centralization*: 192–214, London: Unwin Hyman.

Baker, F. (1997) *Loch Lomond Islands Survey: an archaeological assessment commissioned by the Friends of Loch Lomond, Report of Phase 2*, Edinburgh: National Monuments Record of Scotland.

Baker, S.W. (1879) *Cyprus as I Saw It in 1879*, London: Macmillan.

Baram, U. (2000) 'Entangled objects from the Palestinian past: archaeological perspectives for the Ottoman period, 1500–1900', in U. Baram and L. Carroll (eds) *A Historical Archaeology of the Ottoman Empire: breaking new ground*: 137–59, New York: Kluwer Academic/Plenum.

Basso, K.H. (1996) 'Wisdom sits in places: notes on a Western Apache landscape', in S. Feld and K.H. Basso (eds) *Senses of Place*: 53–90, Santa Fe: School of American Research Press.

Basu, P. (2000) 'Sites of memory – sources of identity: landscape-narratives of the Sutherland Clearances', in J.A. Atkinson, I. Banks and G. MacGregor (eds) *Townships to Farmsteads: rural settlement studies in Scotland, England and Wales*: 225–36, Oxford: British Archaeological Reports (BAR British Series 293).

Batey, C.E. (ed.) (1992) *Discovery and Excavation in Scotland: an annual survey of Scottish archaeological discoveries, excavation and fieldwork*, Edinburgh: Council for Scottish Archaeology.

Beals, A.R. (1974) *Village Life in South India: cultural design and environmental variation*, Chicago: Aldine.

Bender, B. (1999) 'Subverting the Western Gaze: mapping alternative worlds', in P. Ucko and R. Layton (eds) *The Archaeology and Anthropology of Landscape*: 31–45, London: Routledge.

Bernand, E. (1975) *Recueil des Inscriptions Grecques du Fayoum, Tome I: La 'Méris' d'Hérakleidès*, Leiden: E.J. Brill.

Bhabha, H.K. (1994) *The Location of Culture*, London: Routledge.

Bil, A. (1990) *The Shieling 1600–1840: the case of the central Scottish Highlands*, Edinburgh: John Donald.

Bintliff, J.L., Howard, P. and Snodgrass, A. (1999) 'The hidden landscape of prehistoric Greece', *Journal of Mediterranean Archaeology* 12: 139–68.

Blanton, R.E. (2001) 'Mediterranean myopia', *Antiquity* 75: 627–9.

Boak, A.E. (1955) 'The population of Roman and Byzantine Karanis', *Historia* 4: 157–62.

Boivin, N. (1997) 'Insidious or just boring? An examination of academic writing in archaeology', *Archaeological Review from Cambridge* 14: 105–25.

Bourdieu, P. (1977) *Outline of a Theory of Practice*, trans. R. Nice, Cambridge: Cambridge University Press.

Bowman, A. (1996) *Egypt after the Pharaohs, 332 BC – AD 642*, 2nd edition, London: British Museum Press.

Boyle, S. (2003) 'Ben Lawers: an improvement-period landscape on Lochtayside, Perthshire', in S. Govan (ed.) *Medieval or Later Rural Settlement in Scotland: 10 years on*: 17–29, Edinburgh: Historic Scotland.

Bradley, R. (2000) *An Archaeology of Natural Places*, London: Routledge.

Brady, N. (1996) 'The Sacred Barn. Barn-building in Southern England, 1100–1550: a study of grain storage technology and its cultural context', unpublished PhD dissertation, Cornell University.

Brand, C.M. (1969) 'Two Byzantine treatises on taxation', *Traditio* 25: 35–60.

Brassley, P. (1999) 'Agricultural technology and the ephemeral landscape', in D.E. Nye (ed.) *Technologies of Landscape: from reaping to recycling*: 21–39, Amherst: University of Massachusetts Press.

Bresciani, E. (1967) *Missione di Scavo a Medinet Madi (Fayum – Egitto): rapporto preliminare delle campagne di scavo 1966 e 1967*, Milan: Istituto Editoriale Cisalpino.

Brown, D.J. (1999–2000) 'The politicians, the revenue men and the Scots distillers, 1780–1800', *Review of Scottish Culture* 12: 46–58.

Brown, M.F. (1996) 'On resisting resistance', *American Anthropologist* 98: 729–35.

Brück, J. (1998) 'In the footsteps of the ancestors: a review of Christopher Tilley's *A Phenomenology of Landscape: places, paths and monuments*', *Archaeological Review from Cambridge* 15: 23–36.

Brumfield, A. (2000) 'Agriculture and rural settlement in Ottoman Crete, 1669–1898: a modern site survey', in U. Baram and L. Carroll (eds) *A Historical Archaeology of the Ottoman Empire: breaking new ground*: 37–78, New York: Kluwer Academic/Plenum.

Brunt, P. (1975) 'The administrators of Roman Egypt', *Journal of Roman Studies* 65: 124–47.

Burton, G. (1975) 'Proconsuls, assizes and the administration of justice under the Empire', *Journal of Roman Studies* 65: 92–106.

Butt, J. (1967) *The Industrial Archaeology of Scotland*, Newton Abbot: David and Charles.

Cadogan, G. (1989) 'Maroni and the monuments', in E. Peltenburg (ed.) *Early Society in Cyprus*: 43–51, Edinburgh: Edinburgh University Press.

—— (1992) 'Maroni VI', *Report of the Department of Antiquities, Cyprus*: 51–8.

Calder, W. and Bean, G.E. (1958) *A Classical Map of Asia Minor*, London: British Institute of Archaeology at Ankara.

Callinicos, A. (1995) *Theories and Narratives: reflections on the philosophy of history*, Cambridge: Polity Press.

Canmore (2003) *Canmore: the national monuments record of Scotland database*. Online. Available http://www.rcahms.gov.uk/canmoreintro.html (accessed 20 June 2003).

Carr, D. (2001) 'Place and time: on the interplay of historical points of view', *History and Theory* 40: 153–67.

Carr, E.R. (2000) 'Meaning (and) materiality: rethinking contextual analysis through cellar-set houses', *Historical Archaeology* 34 (4): 32–45.

Casella, E.C. (2001) 'Landscapes of punishment and resistance: a female convict settlement in Tasmania, Australia', in B. Bender and M. Winer (eds) *Contested Landscapes: movement, exile and place*: 103–20, Oxford: Berg.

Caton-Thompson, G. and Gardner, E. (1934) *The Desert Fayum*, 2 vols, London: Royal Anthropological Institute of Great Britain and Ireland.

Census (1882) *Report on the Census of Population, 1881, Cyprus*, London: Colonial Office.

Chadwick, J. (1976) *The Mycenaean World*, Cambridge: Cambridge University Press.

Cherry, J. (1994) 'Regional survey in the Aegean: the "new wave" (and after)', in P.N. Kardulias (ed.) *Beyond the Site: regional studies in the Aegean area*: 91–112, Lanham: University Press of America.

Chevalier, R. (1976) *Roman Roads*, trans. N. Field, London: B.T. Batsford.

Christodoulou, D. (1959) *The Evolution of the Rural Land Use Pattern in Cyprus*, Bude: Geographical Publications (World Land Use Survey, Regional Monograph).

Christol, M. and Drew-Bear, T. (1987) *Un Castellum Romain près d'Apamée de Phrygie*, Vienna: Österreichischen Akademie der Wissenschaft (Ergänzungsbände zu den Tituli Asiae Minoris 12).

Clogg, R. (1986) *A Short History of Modern Greece*, 2nd edition, Cambridge: Cambridge University Press.

Cobham, C. (ed.) (1908) *Excerpta Cypria: materials for a history of Cyprus*, Cambridge: Cambridge University Press.

Cohn, B.S. (1961) 'The pasts of an Indian village', *Comparative Studies in History and Society* 3: 241–9.

—— (1996) *Colonialism and its Forms of Knowledge: the British in India*, Princeton: Princeton University Press.

Conkey, M.W. (2002) 'Expanding the archaeological imagination', *American Antiquity* 67: 166–8.

Connell, K. (1961) 'Illicit distillation: an Irish peasant industry', *Historical Studies: papers read before the Fourth Irish Conference of Historians* 3: 58–91.

Corbier, M. (1983) 'Fiscus and patrimonium: the Saepinum inscription and transhumance in the Abruzzi', *Journal of Roman Studies* 73: 126–31.

—— (1991) 'City, territory and taxation', in J. Rich and A. Wallace-Hadrill (eds) *City and Country in the Ancient World*: 211–39, London: Routledge.

Coulton, J. (1991) 'Balboura Survey 1988, 1990', *Araştırma Sonuçları Toplantısı* 9: 47–57.

—— (1998) 'Highland cities in south-west Turkey: the Oinoanda and Balboura surveys', in R. Matthews (ed.) *Ancient Anatolia: fifty years' work by the British Institute of Archaeology at Ankara*: 225–36, London: British Institute of Archaeology at Ankara.

Courtois, J.-C. (1983) 'Le tresor de poids de Kalavassos-Ayios Dhimitrios 1982', *Report of the Department of Antiquities, Cyprus*: 117–30.

Cuno, K.M. (1992) *The Pasha's Peasants: land, society, and economy in Lower Egypt, 1740–1858*, Cambridge: Cambridge University Press.

—— (1999) 'A tale of two villages: family, property, and economic activity in rural Egypt in the 1840s', in A.K. Bowman and E. Rogan (eds) *Agriculture in Egypt from Pharaonic to Modern Times*: 301–29, Oxford: Oxford University Press.

Dalglish, C. (2003) *Rural Society in the Age of Reason: an archaeology of the emergence of modern life in the southern Scottish Highlands*, New York: Kluwer Academic/Plenum (Contributions to Global Historical Archaeology).

Dalman, G. (1933) *Arbeit und Sitte in Palästina. Band III: Von der Ernte zum Mehl: Ernten, Dreschen, Worfeln, Sieben, Verwahren, Mahlen*, Gütersloh: C. Bertelsmann (Schriften des Deutschen Palästina-Instituts 6).

Dar, S. (1986) *Landscape and Pattern: an archaeological survey of Samaria 800 BCE – 636 CE*, 2 vols, Oxford: British Archaeological Reports (BAR International Series 308).

Darbyshire, G., Mitchell, S. and Vardar, L. (2000) 'The Galatian settlement in Asia Minor', *Anatolian Studies* 50: 75–97.

Davoli, P. (1997) *L'archaeologia urbana nel Fayyum di età ellenistica e romana*, Naples: Generoso Pracaccini (Missione Congiunta delle Università di Bologna e di Lecce in Egitto, Monografia 1).

de Laet, S.J. (1949) *Portorium: étude sur l'organisation douanière chez les Romains, surtout à l'époque du Haut-Empire*, Brugge: De Tempel.

Delle, J.A. (1999) '"A good and easy speculation": spatial conflict, collusion and resistance in late sixteenth-century Munster, Ireland', *International Journal of Historical Archaeology* 3: 11–35.

Devine, T. (1975) 'The rise and fall of illicit whisky-making in northern Scotland, c. 1780–1840', *Scottish Historical Review* 54: 155–77.

—— (1994) *Clanship to Crofters' War: the social transformation of the Scottish Highlands*, Manchester: Manchester University Press.

—— (1999) *The Scottish Nation 1700–2000*, London: Penguin Press.

Dick, C. (1919) *Highways and Byways in Galloway and Carrick*, London: Macmillan.

Dietz, V.E. (1997) 'The politics of whisky: Scottish distillers, the excise, and the Pittite state', *Journal of British Studies* 36: 35–69.

Dixon, J. (1886) *Gairloch in North-west Ross Shire: its records, traditions, inhabitants, and natural history*; reprinted, Gairloch (1974); Edinburgh: Cooperative Printing Company.

Dobres, M.-A. (2000) *Technology and Social Agency: outlining a practice framework for archaeology*, Oxford: Blackwell.

—— and Robb, J.E. (2000) 'Agency in archaeology: paradigm or platitude', in M.A. Dobres and J.E. Robb (eds) *Agency in Archaeology*: 3–17, London: Routledge.

Dodgshon, R.A. (1992) 'Farming practice in the western highlands and islands before crofting: a study in cultural inertia or opportunity costs?' *Rural History* 3: 173–89.

—— (1993) 'West highland and Hebridean settlement prior to crofting and the clearances: a study in stability or change?' *Proceedings of the Society of Antiquaries of Scotland* 123: 419–38.

—— (1998) *From Chiefs to Landlords: social and economic change in the western highlands and islands, c. 1493–1820*, Edinburgh: Edinburgh University Press.

Drury, M.D. (1972) 'Cyprus: ethnic dualism', in J.I. Clarke and W.B. Fisher (eds) *Populations of the Middle East and North Africa: a geographical approach*: 161–81, London: University of London Press.

Dunand, F. (1979) *Religion Populaire en Égypte Romaine*, Leiden: E.J. Brill (Études Préliminaires aux Religions Orientales dans l'Empire Romain 76).

Dyson, S.L. (2003) Review of *The Archaeology of Colonialism*, by C.L. Lyons and J.K. Papadopoulos (eds), *American Journal of Archaeology* 107: 493–4.

Eagleton, T. (1983) *Literary Theory: an introduction*, Oxford: Blackwell.

Ellis, P. (1997) *Ben Lomond Archaeological Survey*, Birmingham: Birmingham University Field Archaeology Unit (Project no. 465).

Ellis Burnet, J. (n.d.) *Forest Bioresource Utilisation in the Eastern Mediterranean since Antiquity: a case study of the Makheras*, Oxford: British Archaeological Reports (in press).

Engelmann, H. and Knibbe, D. (1989) 'Das Zollgesetz der Provinz Asia: eine neue Inschrift aus Ephesos', *Epigraphica Anatolia* 14: 1–206.

Ertuğ-Yaraş, F. (1997) 'An ethnoarchaeological study of subsistence and plant gathering in central Anatolia', unpublished PhD dissertation, Graduate School of Arts and Sciences of Washington University.

Eyre, C.J. (1987) 'Work and the organisation of work in the Old Kingdom', in M.A. Powell (ed.) *Labor in the Ancient Near East*: 5–47, New Haven: American Oriental Society (American Oriental Series 68).

Fairhurst, H. (1967–8) 'Rosal: a deserted township in Strath Naver, Sutherland', *Proceedings of the Society of Antiquaries of Scotland* 100: 135–69.

Fegan, B. (1986) 'Tenants' non-violent resistance to landower claims in a Central Luzon', *Journal of Peasant Studies* 13: 87–106.

Fenton, A. (1999) *Scottish Country Life*, East Linton: Tuckwell Press.

—— (2000) 'The adaptation of tools and techniques to ridge and furrow fields', in J.A. Atkinson, I. Banks and G. MacGregor (eds) *Townships to Farmsteads: rural settlement studies in Scotland, England and Wales*: 167–72, Oxford: British Archaeological Reports (British Series 293).

Ferguson, L. (1991) 'Struggling with pots in colonial South Carolina', in R.H. McGuire and R. Paynter (eds) *The Archaeology of Inequality*: 28–39, Oxford: Blackwell.

Ferguson, N. (2003) *Empire: how Britain made the modern world*, London: Allen Lane.

Fest, J. (1999) *Speer: the final verdict*, trans. E. Osers and A. Dring, London: Phoenix Press.

Finlayson, B. and Dennis, S. (2002) 'Landscape, archaeology and heritage', *Levant* 34: 219–27.

Fleming, A. (1999a) 'Human ecology and the early history of St Kilda, Scotland', *Journal of Historical Geography* 25: 183–200.

—— (1999b) 'Phenomenology and the megaliths of Wales: a dreaming too far?' *Oxford Journal of Archaeology* 18: 119–25.

Forbes, H. (1989) 'Of grandfathers and grand theories: the hierarchised ordering of responses to hazard in a Greek rural community', in P. Halstead and J. O'Shea (eds) *Bad Year Economics: cultural responses to risk and uncertainty*: 87–97, Cambridge: Cambridge University Press.

—— (1993) 'Ethnoarchaeology and the place of the olive in the economy of the southern Argolid, Greece', in M.-C. Amouretti and J.-P. Brun (eds) *La Production du Vin et de l'Huile en Méditerranée*: 213–26, Athens: École Française d'Athènes (Bulletin de Correspondance Hellénique, Supplément 26).

—— (1996) 'The uses of the uncultivated landscape in modern Greece: a pointer to the value of the wilderness in antiquity?', in G. Shipley and J. Salmon (eds) *Human Landscapes in Classical Antiquity: environment and culture*: 68–97, London: Routledge.

—— (1997) 'A "waste" of resources: aspects of landscape exploitation in lowland Greek agriculture', in P.N. Kardulias and M.T. Shutes (eds) *Aegean Strategies: studies of culture and environment on the European fringe*: 187–213, Lanham: Rowman and Littlefield.

Foucault, M. (1970) *The Order of Things: an archaeology of the human sciences*, London: Tavistock.

Frankfurter, D. (1998) *Religion in Roman Egypt: assimilation and resistance*, Princeton: Princeton University Press.

French, D.H. (1980) 'The Roman road-system of Asia Minor', in H. Temporini and W. Haase (eds) *Aufstieg und Niedergang der Römischen Welt: Geschichte und Kultur Roms im Spiegel der neuern Forschung*: 698–729, Berlin: Walter de Gruyter.

—— (1988) *Roman Roads and Milestones of Asia Minor. Fasc. 2: an interim catalogue of milestones*, Oxford: British Archaeological Reports (BAR International Series 392 (i); British Institute of Archaeology at Ankara, Monograph 9).

Gaffney, V. and van Leusen, M. (1995) 'Postscript – GIS, environmental determinism and archaeology: a parallel text', in G. Lock and Z. Stančič (eds) *Archaeology and Geographical Information Systems*: 367–82, London: Taylor and Francis.

Gallazzi, C. (1994) 'Tebtunis: piecing together 3,000 years of history', *Egyptian Archaeology* 5: 27–9.

Gardiner, A.H. (1927) 'An administrative letter of protest', *Journal of Egyptian Archaeology* 13: 75–8.

Gaudry, A. (1855) *Recherches Scientifiques en Orient Entreprises par les Ordres du Gouvernement, pendant les Années 1853–1854. Partie agricole*, Paris: Imprimerie Impériale.

Geertz, C.J. (1972) 'Deep play; notes on the Balinese cockfight', *Daedalus* 101: 1–37; reprinted in *The Interpretation of Cultures* (1973): 412–53, New York: Basic Books.

Gibb, J.G. (2000) 'Imaginary, but by no means unimaginable: storytelling, science, and historical archaeology', *Historical Archaeology* 34 (2): 1–6.

Giddens, A. (1979) *Central Problems in Social Theory: action, structure and contradiction in social analysis*, London: Macmillan.

Given, M. (1997) 'Star of the Parthenon, Cypriot mélange: education and representation in colonial Cyprus', *Journal of Mediterranean Studies* 7: 59–82.

—— (2000) 'Agriculture, settlement and landscape in Ottoman Cyprus', *Levant* 32: 215–36.

—— (2001) 'The fight for the past: Watkins vs. Warren (1885–6) and the control of excavation', in V. Tatton-Brown (ed.) *Cyprus in the 19th Century AD: fact, fancy and fiction*: 255–60, Oxford: Oxbow Books.

—— (2002) 'Maps, fields and boundary cairns: demarcation and resistance in colonial Cyprus', *International Journal of Historical Archaeology* 6: 1–22.

—— and Knapp, A.B. (2003) *The Sydney Cyprus Survey Project: social approaches to regional archaeological survey*, with 20 contributors, Los Angeles: University of California at Los Angeles Cotsen Institute of Archaeology (Monumenta Archaeologica 21).

—— and Seretis, K. (2003) 'Strangers in the landscape', in M. Given and A.B. Knapp (eds) *The Sydney Cyprus Survey Project: social approaches to regional archaeological survey*, with 20 contributors, Los Angeles: University of California at Los Angeles Cotsen Institute of Archaeology (Monumenta Archaeologica 21).

——, Kassianidou, V., Knapp, A.B. and Noller, J. (2002) 'Troodos Archaeological and Environmental Survey Project, Cyprus: report on the 2001 season', *Levant* 34: 25–38.

Glen, I. (1970) 'A maker of illicit stills', *Scottish Studies* 14: 67–83.

Gole, S. (1996) *Cyprus on the table: maps of Cyprus in British government papers, 1878–1920*, Nicosia: Bank of Cyprus Cultural Foundation (Cyprus Cartography Lectures 3).

Goring, R. (1987) 'Eighteenth-century Scottish smugglers: the evidence from Montrose and Dumfries', *Review of Scottish Culture* 3: 53–65.

Gosden, C. (1994) *Social Being and Time*, Oxford: Blackwell.

—— and Knowles, C. (2001) *Collecting Colonialism: material culture and colonial change*, Oxford: Berg.

Grenfell, B.P., Hunt, A.S. and Hogarth, D.G. (1900) *Fayûm Towns and their Papyri*, London: Egypt Exploration Fund, Graeco-Roman Branch.

Grigor, I.F. (2000) *Highland Resistance: the radical tradition in the Scottish north*, Edinburgh: Mainstream Publishing.

Grivaud, G. (1998) *Villages Désertés à Chypre (Fin XIIe – Fin XIXe Siècle)*, Nicosia: Archbishop Makarios III Foundation (Meletai kai Ipomnimata 3).

Guha, R. and Gadgil, M. (1989) 'State forestry and social conflict in British India', *Past and Present* 123: 141–77.

Gunn, N.M. (1943) *The Serpent*, London: Faber and Faber.

Gurova, M. (2001) 'Elements de tribulum de Bulgarie – références ethnographique et contexte préhistorique', *Archaeologia Bulgarica* 5: 1–19.

Haas, C. (1997) *Alexandria in Late Antiquity: topography and social conflict*, Baltimore: Johns Hopkins University Press.

Hackel, S.W. (1998) 'Land, labor and production: the colonial economy of Spanish and Mexican California', in R.A. Gutiérrez and R.J. Orsi (eds) *Contested Eden: California before the Gold Rush*: 111–46, Berkeley: University of California Press.

Hadjisavvas, S. (1992) *Olive Oil Processing in Cyprus from the Bronze Age to the Byzantine Period*, Nicosia: Paul Åströms Förlag (Studies in Mediterranean Archaeology 99).

Hall, M. (1992) 'Small things and the mobile, conflictual fusion of power, fear, and desire', in A.E. Yentsch and M.C. Beaudry (eds) *The Art and Mystery of Historical Archaeology: essays in honor of James Deetz*: 373–99, Boca Raton, Florida: CRC Press.

Halliday, S. (2003) 'Rig-and-furrow in Scotland', in S. Govan (ed.) *Medieval or Later Rural Settlement in Scotland: 10 years on*: 69–81, Edinburgh: Historic Scotland.

Halstead, P. (1992) 'Agriculture in the Bronze Age Aegean: towards a model of palatial economy', in B. Wells (ed.) *Agriculture in Ancient Greece: proceedings of the Seventh International Symposium at the Swedish Institute at Athens, 16–17 May 1990*: 105–17, Stockholm: Swedish Institute at Athens.

—— (1994) 'The north–south divide: regional paths to complexity in prehistoric Greece', in C. Mathers and S. Stoddart (eds) *Development and Decline in the Mediterranean Bronze Age*: 195–219, Sheffield: J.R. Collis Publications.

—— (1999) 'Towards a model of Mycenaean palatial mobilization', in M.L. Galaty and W.A. Parkinson (eds) *Rethinking Mycenaean Palaces: new interpretations of an old idea*: 35–41, Los Angeles: Cotsen Institute of Archaeology, University of California, Los Angeles.

—— and Jones, G. (1989) 'Agrarian ecology in the Greek islands: time stress, scale and risk', *Journal of Hellenic Studies* 109: 41–55.

—— and O'Shea, J. (1982) 'A friend in need is a friend indeed: social storage and the

174

origins of social ranking', in C. Renfrew and S. Shennan (eds) *Ranking, Resource and Exchange: aspects of the archaeology of early European society*: 92–9, Cambridge: Cambridge University Press (New Directions in Archaeology).

Hamilakis, Y. (1999) 'La trahison des archéologues? Archaeological practice as intellectual activity in postmodernity', *Journal of Mediterranean Archaeology* 12: 60–79.

Hawass, Z. (1997) 'Tombs of the pyramid builders', *Archaeology* 50 (1): 39–43.

—— and Lehner, M. (1997) 'Builders of the pyramids', *Archaeology* 50 (1): 30–8.

Hendon, J.A. (2000) 'Having and holding: storage, memory, knowledge and social relations', *American Anthropologist* 102: 42–53.

Hicks, D. (2003) 'Archaeology unfolding: diversity and the loss of isolation', *Oxford Journal of Archaeology* 22: 315–29.

Hicks, F. (1992) 'Subject states and tribute provinces: the Aztec empire in the northern Valley of Mexico', *Ancient Mesoamerica* 3: 1–10.

Hill, G. (1952) *A History of Cyprus, Volume IV: the Ottoman province, the British colony, 1571–1948*, ed. H. Luke, Cambridge: Cambridge University Press.

Hobsbawm, E. (1985) *Bandits*, 2nd edition, Harmondsworth: Penguin.

Hobson, D.W. (1993) 'The impact of law on village life in Roman Egypt', in B. Halpern and D.W. Hobson (eds) *Law, Politics and Society in the Ancient World*: 193–219, Sheffield: Sheffield University Press.

Hodder, I. (2000) 'Agency and individuals in long-term processes', in M.-A. Dobres and J.E. Robb (eds) *Agency in Archaeology*: 21–33, London: Routledge.

Holden, T., Dalland, M., Burgess, C., Walker, B. and Carter, S. (2001) 'No. 39 Arnol: the excavation of a Lewis blackhouse', *Scottish Archaeological Journal* 23: 15–32.

Hopkins, K. (1980) 'Taxes and trade in the Roman Empire (200 BC–AD 400)', *Journal of Roman Studies* 70: 101–25.

Hopwood, K. (1983) 'Policing the hinterland: Rough Cilicia and Isauria', in S. Mitchell (ed.) *Armies and Frontiers in Roman and Byzantine Anatolia*: 173–87, Oxford: British Archaeological Reports (BAR International Series 156; British Institute of Archaeology at Ankara, Monograph 5).

Horsley, G. and Mitchell, S. (eds) (2000) *The Inscriptions of Central Pisidia*, Bonn: Rudolf Habelt (Österreichische Akademie der Wissenschaft; Nordrhein-Westfälische Akademie der Wissenschaft: Inschriften Griechischer Städte aus Kleinasien).

Husselman, E.M. (1952) 'The granaries of Karanis', *Transactions of the American Philological Association* 83: 56–73.

—— (1979) *Karanis Excavations of the University of Michigan in Egypt, 1928–1935: topography and architecture*, Ann Arbor: University of Michigan Press.

Hutchins, D. (1909) *Cyprus: report on Cyprus forestry*, London: no publisher given.

Hutson, S.R. (2002) 'Built space and bad subjects: domination and resistance at Monte Albán, Oaxaca, Mexico', *Journal of Social Archaeology* 2: 53–80.

İnalcık, H. (1973) 'Ottoman policy and administration in Cyprus after the conquest', in T. Papadopoulos and M. Christodoulou (eds) *Praktika tou Protou Dhiethnous Kiproloyikou Sinedhriou*: 119–36, Nicosia: Eteria Kipriakon Spoudhon.

Ingold, T. (1993) 'The temporality of the landscape', *World Archaeology* 25: 152–74.

Ionas, I. (1998) *Pottery in the Cyprus Tradition*, Nicosia: Cyprus Research Centre (Publications of the Cyprus Research Centre 23).

—— (2000) 'Document sur les semailles et la moisson', *Epetiris tou Kendrou Epistimonikon Erevnon* 26: 319–38.

—— (2001) 'Le calendrier du paysan chypriote', *Epetiris tou Kendrou Epistimonikon Erevnon* 27: 367–98.

Jaskot, P.B. (2000) *The Architecture of Oppression: the SS, forced labour and the Nazi monumental building economy*, London: Routledge.

Jennings, R. (1986) 'The population, taxation, and wealth in the cities and villages of

Cyprus, according to the detailed population survey (defter-i mufassal) of 1572', *Journal of Turkish Studies* 10: 177–89.

Jocelin of Brakelond (1949) *The Chronicle of Jocelin of Brakelond concerning the Acts of Samson, Abbot of the Monastery of St. Edmond*, trans. H. Butler, London: Thomas Nelson and Sons.

Johnson, M.H. (1989) 'Conceptions of agency in archaeological interpretation', *Journal of Anthropological Archaeology* 8: 189–211.

Jones, C. (1978) *The Roman World of Dio Chrysostom*, Cambridge, MA: Harvard University Press.

Joyce, R.A. (2002) *The Languages of Archaeology: dialogue, narrative and writing*, Oxford: Blackwell.

Kana'an, R. and McQuitty, A. (1994) 'The architecture of Al-Qasr on the Kerak plateau: an essay in the chronology of vernacular architecture', *Palestine Exploration Quarterly* 126: 127–51.

Karageorghis, V. (1998) *Cypriote Archaeology Today: achievements and perspectives*, Glasgow: University of Glasgow, Glasgow Archaeological Society (Dalrymple Archaeological Monograph 4).

Kardulias, P.N. and Yerkes, R.W. (1996) 'Microwear and metric analysis of threshing sledge flints from Greece and Cyprus', *Journal of Archaeological Science* 23: 657–66.

Katsiaounis, R. (1996) *Labour, Society and Politics in Cyprus during the Second Half of the Nineteenth Century*, Nicosia: Cyprus Research Centre (Texts and Studies in the History of Cyprus 24).

Kehoe, D.P. (1988) *The Economics of Agriculture on Roman Imperial Estates in North Africa*, Göttingen: Vandenhoeck and Ruprecht (Hypomnemata 89).

Kelso, W.M. (1986) 'The archaeology of slave life at Thomas Jefferson's Monticello: "a wolf by the ears"', *Journal of New World Archaeology* 6 (4): 5–20.

Kemp, B.J. (1989) *Ancient Egypt: anatomy of a civilization*, London: Routledge.

Keswani, P.S. (1992) 'Gas chromatography analyses of pithoi from Kalavasos-Ayios Dhimitrios: a preliminary report', *Report of the Department of Antiquities, Cyprus*: 141–6.

—— (1993) 'Models of local exchange in Late Bronze Age Cyprus', *Bulletin of the American Schools of Oriental Research* 292: 73–83.

—— (1996) 'Hierarchies, heterarchies, and urbanization processes: the view from Bronze Age Cyprus', *Journal of Mediterranean Archaeology* 9: 211–50.

—— and Knapp, A.B. (2003) 'Bronze Age boundaries and social exchange in northwest Cyprus', *Oxford Journal of Archaeology* 22: 213–23.

Kiel, M. (1996) *Das Türkische Thessalien: etabliertes Geschichtsbild versus osmanische Quellen: ein Beitrag zur Entmythologisierung der Geschichte Griechenlands*, Göttingen: Vandenhoeck und Ruprecht (Abhandlungen der Akademie der Wissenschaften in Göttingen, Philologisch-Historische Klasse, Dritte Folge, 212).

—— (1997) 'The rise and decline of Turkish Boeotia, 15th–19th century', in J. Bintliff (ed.) *Recent Developments in the History and Archaeology of Central Greece*: 315–58, Oxford: British Archaeological Reports (BAR International Series 666).

King, A.D. (1976) *Colonial Urban Development: culture, social power and environment*, London: Routledge and Kegan Paul.

Kitromilides, P.M. (1982) 'Repression and protest in traditional society: Cyprus 1764', *Kypriakai Spoudhai* 46: 91–101.

Klirides, N. (1951) 'Prolegomena kai keimenon tis akolouthia tou ayiou endhoxou megalomartyros Mamandos tou thavmatourghou', *Kypriakai Spoudhai* 15: 91–145.

—— (1968) *25 Monastiria tis Kipro*, vol. 2, Nicosia: no publisher given.

Knapp, A.B. (1996) 'The Bronze Age economy of Cyprus: ritual, ideology, and the sacred landscape', in V. Karageorghis and D. Michaelides (eds) *The Development of the Cypriot Economy from the Prehistoric Period to the Present Day*: 71–106, Nicosia: University of Cyprus; Bank of Cyprus.

—— (1997) *The Archaeology of Late Bronze Age Cypriot Society: the study of settlement, survey and landscape*, Glasgow: Department of Archaeology, University of Glasgow.

—— and Ashmore, W. (1999) 'Archaeological landscapes: constructed, conceptualized, ideational', in W. Ashmore and A.B. Knapp (eds) *Archaeologies of Landscape: contemporary perspectives*: 1–30, Oxford: Blackwell.

——, Held, S.O. and Manning, S.W. (1994) 'The prehistory of Cyprus: problems and prospects', *Journal of World Prehistory* 8: 377–453.

Koşay, H.Z. (1951) *Das Dorf Alaca-Höyük: Materialien zur Ethnographie und Volkskunde von Anatolien*, Ankara: Türk Tarih Kurumu Başımevi (Türk Tarih Kurumu Yayınlarından 7/21).

—— (1976) 'Yeniköy Mound excavations, 1972', in S. Pekman (ed.) *Keban Project 1972 Activities*: 185–92, Ankara: Middle East Technical University Keban Project.

Lajoux, J.-D. (1966) *Les Fléaux en Cadence*, video, Centre National de la Recherche Scientifique, Diffusion Vidéothèque Photothèque.

Lane, B.M. (1985) *Architecture and Politics in Germany, 1918–1945*, 2nd edition, Cambridge, MA: Harvard University Press.

Lang, V. (1993–4) 'Prehistoric and medieval field systems in Estonia', *Tools and Tillage* 7 (2–3): 67–82.

—— (2002) 'Forest fields'. E-mail (30 January 2002).

Lehner, M. (1985) 'The development of the Giza necropolis: the Khufu project', *Mitteilungen des Deutschen Archäologischen Instituts, Abteilung Kairo* 41: 109–43.

—— (1997) *The Complete Pyramids*, London: Thames and Hudson.

Lelong, O. (2000) 'The prospect of the sea: responses to forced coastal resettlement in nineteenth century Sutherland', in J.A. Atkinson, I. Banks and G. MacGregor (eds) *Townships to Farmsteads: rural settlement studies in Scotland, England and Wales*: 217–24, Oxford: British Archaeological Reports (BAR British Series 293).

—— (2002) 'Writing people into the landscape: approaches to the archaeology of Badenoch and Strathnaver', 2 vols, unpublished PhD dissertation, University of Glasgow.

Lerche, G. (1984–7) 'Ridged fields and profiles of plough-furrows: ploughing practices in medieval and post-medieval times: a study in experimental archaeology', *Tools and Tillage* 5: 131–56.

—— (2003) 'Experience of ploughing'. E-mail (21 May 2003).

Lesquier, J. (1911) 'Fouilles à Tekhneh (1908)', *Bulletin de l'Institut Français d'Archéologie Orientale* 8: 113–33.

Lewis, N. (1983) *Life in Egypt under Roman Rule*, Oxford: Clarendon Press.

—— (1993) 'A reversal of a tax policy in Roman Egypt', *Greek, Roman and Byzantine Studies* 34: 101–18.

Lightfoot, K.G., Martinez, A. and Schiff, A.M. (1998) 'Daily practice and material culture in pluralistic social settings: an archaeological study of culture change and persistence from Fort Ross, California', *American Antiquity* 63: 199–222.

Lintott, A. (1993) *Imperium Romanum: politics and administration*, London: Routledge.

Loch, J. (1820) *An Account of the Improvements on the Estates of the Marquess of Stafford, in the Counties of Stafford and Salop, and on the Estate of Sutherland*, London: Longman, Hurst, Rees, Orme, and Brown.

Louise, A. and Hodder, I. (1998) 'Discussion with the Goddess community'. Online. Available http://catal.arch.cam.ac.uk/catal/goddess.html (accessed 24 October 2003).

Lyons, C.L. and Papadopoulos, J.K. (2002) 'Archaeology and colonialism', in C.L. Lyons and J.K. Papadopoulos (eds) *The Archaeology of Colonialism*: 1–23, Los Angeles: Getty Research Institute.

McCartney, C. (1993) 'An attribute analysis of Cypriot dhoukani "teeth": implications for the study of Cypriot chipped stone assemblages', *Report of the Department of Antiquities, Cyprus*: 349–64.

McCulloch, A. (2000) *Galloway: a land apart*, Edinburgh: Birlinn.

MacCulloch, J. (1824) *The Highlands and Western Isles of Scotland, containing descriptions of their scenery and antiquities, with an account of the political history and ancient manners, and of the origin, language, agriculture, economy, music, present condition of the people, &c. &c. &c.*, 4 vols, London: Longman, Hurst, Rees, Orme, Brown, and Green.

Macdonald, I. (1914) *Smuggling in the Highlands: an account of highland whisky with smuggling stories and detections*, Stirling: Eneas Mackay.

MacDonald, M. (1996) *Walking into the Past: historical walks in Torridon*, Evanton: Torridon Publishing.

Macdonald, S. (1997) *Reimagining Culture: histories, identities and the Gaelic renaissance*, Oxford: Berg (Ethnicity and Identity Series).

McFadzean, J. (1994) *Mochrum: a parish history 1794–1994*, Wigtown: G.C. Book Publishers.

MacLellan, A. (1997) *The Furrow behind Me*, trans. J.L. Campbell, Edinburgh: Birlinn.

Macleod, D. (1892) *Gloomy Memories in the Highlands of Scotland: versus Mrs. Harriet Beecher Stowe's Sunny Memories in (England) a Foreign Land: or a faithful picture of the extirpation of the Celtic race from the Highlands of Scotland*, Glasgow: Sinclair.

MacMullen, R. (1988) *Corruption and the Decline of Rome*, New Haven: Yale University Press.

McNeal, R. (ed.) (1993) *Nicholas Biddle in Greece: the journals and letters of 1806*, University Park, PA: Pennsylvania State University Press.

Makhairas, L. (1932) *Recital Concerning the Sweet Land of Cyprus Entitled 'Chronicle'*, 2 vols, trans. R. Dawkins, Oxford: Clarendon Press.

Malkides, F. (2001) 'Rayiadhes kai aghrotika kinimata stin Kypro tis othomanikis periodhou', *Epetiris tou Kendrou Epistimonikon Erevnon* 27: 149–61.

Manning, S.W. (1998a) 'Changing pasts and socio-political cognition in Late Bronze Age Cyprus', *World Archaeology* 30: 39–58.

—— (1998b) 'Tsaroukkas, Mycenaeans and Trade Project: preliminary report on the 1996–1997 seasons', *Report of the Department of Antiquities, Cyprus*: 39–54.

—— and Monks, S.J. (1998) 'Late Cypriot tombs at Maroni Tsaroukkas, Cyprus', *Annual of the British School at Athens* 93: 297–351.

——, Bolger, D.L., Ponting, M.J. and Swinton, A. (1994) 'Maroni Valley Archaeological Survey Project: preliminary report on 1992–1993 seasons', *Report of the Department of Antiquities, Cyprus*: 345–67.

——, De Mita, F.A.J., Sewell, D.A., Conwell, D.H., Creighton, J., Nakou, G., Ribeiro, E. and Steel, L. (1997) 'Cyprus, the Aegean, and Maroni-Tsaroukkas', in *Cyprus and the Aegean in Antiquity, from the Prehistoric Period to the 7th Century AD*: 103–42, Nicosia: Department of Antiquities, Cyprus.

——, Weninger, B., South, A.K., Kling, B., Kuniholm, P.I., Muhly, J.D., Hadjisavvas, S., Sewell, D.A. and Cadogan, G. (2001) 'Absolute age range of the Late Cypriot IIC period on Cyprus', *Antiquity* 75: 328–40.

Martin, M. (1698) *A Late Voyage to St Kilda*, reprinted in *A Description of the Western Islands of Scotland ca 1695 and A Late Voyage to St Kilda* (1999), Edinburgh: Birlinn.

Martins, S.W. (1996–7) 'A century of farms and farming on the Sutherland estate, 1790–1890', *Review of Scottish Culture* 10: 33–54.

Mattingly, D.J. (1988a) 'Megalithic madness and measurement: or how many olives could an olive press press?', *Oxford Journal of Archaeology* 7: 177–95.

—— (1988b) 'The olive boom: oil surpluses, wealth and power in Roman Tripolitania', *Libyan Studies* 19: 21–40.

Mee, C. and Forbes, H. (eds) (1997) *A Rough and Rocky Place: the landscape and settlement history of the Methana peninsula, Greece*, Liverpool: Liverpool University Press (Liverpool Monographs in Archaeology and Oriental Studies).

Mejelle (1901) *The Mejelle*, trans. C. Tyser, D. Demetriades and I. Haqqi Effendi, Nicosia: Government Printing Office.

Mendelssohn, K. (1971) 'A scientist looks at the pyramids', *American Scientist* 59: 210–20.

Meskell, L. (1998a) 'An archaeology of social relations in an Egyptian village', *Journal of Archaeological Method and Theory* 5: 209–43.

—— (1998b) 'The irresistible body and the seduction of archaeology', in D. Montserrat (ed.) *Changing Bodies, Changing Meanings: studies on the human body in antiquity*: 139–61, London: Routledge.

—— (2000) 'Cycles of life and death: narrative homology and archaeological realities', *World Archaeology* 31: 423–41.

—— (2002) 'The intersections of identity and politics in archaeology', *Annual Review of Anthropology* 31: 279–301.

Meyer, C. (1982) 'Large and small storerooms of the Roman villa', in D.S. Whitcomb and J.H. Johnson (eds) *Quseir Al-Qadim 1980*: 201–13, Malibu: Undena (ARCE Reports).

Michie, M.F. (2000) *Glenesk: the history and culture of an Angus community*, ed. A. Fenton and J. Beech, East Linton: Tuckwell Press.

Mitchell, S. (1976) 'Requisitioned transport in the Roman Empire: a new inscription from Pisidia', *Journal of Roman Studies* 66: 106–31.

—— (1990) 'Festivals, games, and civic life in Roman Asia Minor', *Journal of Roman Studies* 80: 183–93.

—— (1993) *Anatolia: land, men and gods in Asia Minor. Volume I: The Celts and the impact of Roman rule*, Oxford: Clarendon Press.

—— (1994) 'Termessos, King Amyntas, and the war with the Sandaliôtai. A new inscription from Pisidia', in D. French (ed.) *Studies in the History and Topography of Lycia and Pisidia in Memoriam A.S. Hall*: 95–105, London: British Institute of Archaeology at Ankara.

—— (1998) 'The cities of Asia Minor in the age of Constantine', in S.N. Lieu and D. Montserrat (eds) *Constantine: history, historiography and legend*: 52–73, London: Routledge.

—— (1999) 'The administration of Roman Asia from 133 BC to AD 250', in W. Eck (ed.) *Lokale Autonomie und Römische Ordnungsmacht in den Kaiserzeitlichen Provinzen vom 1. bis 3. Jahrhundert*: 17–46, Munich: R. Oldenbourg.

Mitchell, T. (1988) *Colonising Egypt*, Cambridge: Cambridge University Press.

Montserrat, D. and Meskell, L. (1997) 'Mortuary archaeology and religious landscape at Greco-Roman Deir-el-Medina', *Journal of Egyptian Archaeology* 83: 179–97.

Morgan, P.D. (1998) *Slave Counterpoint: black culture in the eighteenth-century Chesapeake and Lowcountry*, Chapel Hill: Omohundro Institute of Early American History and Culture; University of North Carolina Press.

Morrison, K.D. (2001) 'Coercion, resistance, and hierarchy: local processes and imperial strategies in the Vijayanagara empire', in S.E. Alcock, T.N. D'Altroy, K.D. Morrison and C.M. Sinopoli (eds) *Empires: perspectives from archaeology and history*: 252–78, Cambridge: Cambridge University Press.

Mueller, D. (1975) 'Some remarks on wage rates in the Middle Kingdom', *Journal of Near Eastern Studies* 34: 249–63.

Muhly, J.D. (1989) 'The organisation of the copper industry in Late Bronze Age Cyprus', in E. Peltenburg (ed.) *Early Society in Cyprus*: 298–314, Edinburgh: Edinburgh University Press.

Ndoro, W. (1994) 'The preservation and presentation of Great Zimbabwe', *Antiquity* 68: 616–23.

Needham, R. (1967) 'Percussion and transition', *Man* 2: 606–14.

Ohnefalsch-Richter, M. (1994) *Ellinika Ithi kai Ethima stin Kypro*, trans. A.G. Marangou, Nicosia: Laiki Trapeza Cultural Centre.

—— and Ohnefalsch-Richter, M. (1994) *Studies in Cyprus*, Nicosia: Cultural Centre, Cyprus Popular Bank.

Ortner, S.B. (1995) 'Resistance and the problem of ethnographic refusal', *Comparative Studies in Society and History* 37: 173–93.

O'Shea, J. (1981) 'Coping with scarcity: exchange and social storage', in A. Sheridan and G. Bailey (eds) *Economic Anthropology: towards an integration of ecological and social approaches*: 167–83, Oxford: British Archaeological Reports (BAR International Series 96).

O'Sullivan, A. (2001) 'Crannogs: places of resistance in the contested landscapes of early modern Ireland', in B. Bender and M. Winer (eds) *Contested Landscapes: movement, exile and place*: 87–101, Oxford: Berg.

Overy, R. (1994) *War and Economy in the Third Reich,* Oxford: Clarendon Press.

Paynter, R. and McGuire, R.H. (1991) 'The archaeology of inequality: material culture, domination, and resistance', in R.H. McGuire and R. Paynter (eds) *The Archaeology of Inequality*: 1–27, Oxford: Blackwell.

Pernigotti, S. (1999) 'Five seasons at Bacchias', *Egyptian Archaeology* 14: 26–7.

Pflaum, H.-G. (1975) 'Le bureau de la quadrigesima portuum Asiae à Apollonia de Pisidie', *Zeitschrift für Papyrologie und Epigraphik* 18: 13–14.

Piacentini, P. (1994) 'Lo scavo 1993, relazione preliminare', in S. Pernigotti and M. Capasso (eds) *Bakchias I: rapporto preliminare della campagna di scavo del 1993*: 39–70, Pisa: Giardini (Studi de Egittologia e di Antichità Puniche, Series Maior 1).

—— (1996) 'Excavating Bakchias', in D.M. Bailey (ed.) *Archaeological Research in Roman Egypt*: 57–60, Ann Arbor: Journal of Roman Archaeology (Supplementary Series 19).

Pikirayi, I. (1993) *The Archaeological Identity of the Mutapa State: towards an historical archaeology of northern Zimbabwe*, Uppsala: Societas Archaeologica Upsaliensis (Studies in African Archaeology 6).

—— (2001) *The Zimbabwe Culture: origins and decline of southern Zambezian states*, Walnut Creek: Altamira Press.

Pluciennik, M. (1999) 'Archaeological narratives and other ways of telling', *Current Anthropology* 40: 653–77.

Prebble, J. (1963) *The Highland Clearances*, London: Secker and Warburg.

Pwiti, G. and Ndoro, W. (1999) 'The legacy of colonialism: perceptions of the cultural heritage in southern Africa, with special reference to Zimbabwe', *African Archaeological Review* 16: 143–53.

Rackham, O. and Moody, J. (1996) *The Making of the Cretan Landscape*, Manchester: Manchester University Press.

Rathbone, D. (1996) 'Towards a historical topography of the Fayum', in D.M. Bailey (ed.) *Archaeological Research in Roman Egypt*: 51–6, Ann Arbor: Journal of Roman Archaeology (Supplementary Series 19).

Razola, M. and Constante, M. (1969) *Triangle Bleu: les républicains espagnol à Mauthausen 1940–1945*, Paris: Éditions Gallimard (Collection Témoins).

RCAHMS (1990) *North-east Perth: an archaeological landscape*, Edinburgh: Royal Commission on the Ancient and Historical Monuments of Scotland.

Richard, J. (1947) 'Casal de Psimolofo et la vie rurale en Chypre au XIVe siècle', *Mélanges d'Archéologie et d'Histoire Publiés par l'École Française de Rome* 59: 121–53.

—— (1950) 'Un évêque d'Orient latin au XIVe siècle: Guy d'Ibelin, O.P., et l'inventaire de ses biens', *Bulletin de Correspondance Hellénique* 74: 98–133.

Richards, E. (2000) *The Highland Clearances: people, landlords and rural turmoil*, Edinburgh: Birlinn.

Rickman, G. (1971) *Roman Granaries and Store Buildings*, Cambridge: Cambridge University Press.

Rizakis, A.D. (1997) 'Roman colonies in the province of Achaia: territories, land and population', in S.E. Alcock (ed.) *The Early Roman Empire in the East*: 15–36, Oxford: Oxbow.

Rodríguez, J.R. (1998) 'Baetican olive oil and the Roman economy', in S. Keay (ed.) *The Archaeology of Early Roman Baetica*: 183–99, Portsmouth, RI: Journal of Roman Archaeology (Supplementary Series 29).

Rodziewicz, M. (1998) 'From Alexandria to the west by land and by waterways', in J.-Y. Empereur (ed.) *Commerce et Artisanat dans l'Alexandrie Hellénistique et Romaine*: 93–103, Athens: École Française d'Athènes (Bulletin de Correspondance Hellénique, Supplément 33).

Rogan, E.L. (1999) *Frontiers of the State in the Late Ottoman Empire: Transjordan, 1850–1921*, Cambridge: Cambridge University Press.

Roth, A.M. (1991) *Egyptian Phyles in the Old Kingdom: the evolution of a system of social organization*, Chicago: Oriental Institute of the University of Chicago (Studies in Ancient Oriental Civilization 48).

Rowlandson, J. (1996) *Landowners and Tenants in Roman Egypt: the social relations of agriculture in the Oxyrhynchite nome*, Oxford: Clarendon Press (Oxford Classical Monographs).

Sage, D. (1899) *Memorabilia Domestica; or parish life in the north of Scotland*, 2nd edition, Wick: William Rae.

Said, E. (1978) *Orientalism*, London: Routledge and Kegan Paul.

Sant Cassia, P. (1986) 'Religion, politics and ethnicity in Cyprus during the Turkocratia', *Archives Européennes de Sociologie* 27: 3–28.

—— (1993) 'Banditry, myth and terror', *Comparative Studies in Society and History* 35: 773–95.

Sarpaki, A. (2000) 'Plants chosen to be depicted on Theran wall paintings: tentative interpretations', in S. Sherratt (ed.) *The Wall Paintings of Thera: proceedings of the First International Symposium*, 2 vols: 657–80, Athens: Thera Foundation and Petros M. Nomikos.

Scham, S.A. (2001) 'The archaeology of the disenfranchised', *Journal of Archaeological Method and Theory* 8: 183–213.

Schoep, I. (2002) 'Social and political organization on Crete in the Proto-Palatial Period: the case of Middle Minoan II Malia', *Journal of Mediterranean Archaeology* 15: 101–32.

Scobie, A. (1990) *Hitler's State Architecture: the impact of classical antiquity*, University Park: College Art Assocation; Pennsylvania State University Press.

Scott, J.C. (1990) *Domination and the Arts of Resistance: hidden transcripts*, New Haven: Yale University Press.

Scott-Stevenson, E. (1880) *Our Home in Cyprus*, London: Chapman and Hall.

Sellar, W.C. and Yeatman, R.J. (1930) *1066 and All That*, London: Methuen.

Sereny, G. (1995) *Albert Speer: his battle with truth*, London: Macmillan.

Sharp, M. (1999) 'Shearing sheep: Rome and the collection of taxes in Egypt, 30 BC–AD 200', in W. Eck (ed.) *Lokale Autonomie und Römische Ordnungsmacht in den Kaiserzeitlichen Provinzen vom 1. bis 3. Jahrhundert*: 213–41 (Schriften des Historischen Kollegs Kolloquien 42).

Shaw, B.D. (1984) 'Bandits in the Roman Empire', *Past and Present* 105: 3–52.

—— (1990) 'Bandit highlands and lowland peace: the mountains of Isauria-Cilicia', *Journal of the Economic and Social History of the Orient* 33: 199–270.

Silberman, N.A. (1995) 'Promised lands and chosen peoples: the politics and poetics of archaeological narrative', in P.L. Kohl and C. Fawcett (eds) *Nationalism, Politics and the Practice of Archaeology*: 249–62, Cambridge: Cambridge University Press.

Sillett, S. (1965) *Illicit Scotch*, Aberdeen: Impulse Books.

Silliman, S.W. (2001a) 'Agency, practical politics and the archaeology of cultural contact', *Journal of Social Archaeology* 1: 190–209.

—— (2001b) 'Theoretical perspectives on labor and colonialism: reconsidering the California missions', *Journal of Anthropological Archaeology* 20: 379–407.

Singer, A. (1994) *Palestinian Peasants and Ottoman Officials: rural administration around sixteenth-century Jerusalem*, Cambridge: Cambridge University Press.

Sivaramakrishnan, K. (1995) 'Colonialism and forestry in India: imagining the past in present politics', *Comparative Studies in Society and History* 37: 3–40.

Smith, A. (1998) 'Landscapes of power in nineteenth century Ireland', *Archaeological Dialogues* 5: 69–84.

Smith, T.J. (1997) 'Votive reliefs from Balboura and its environs', *Anatolian Studies* 47: 3–49.

Sophocleous, S. (1994) *Icons of Cyprus: 7th–20th century*, Nicosia: Museum Publications.

Sordinas, A. (1971) *Old olive mills and presses of the island of Corfu, Greece: an essay on industrial archaeology and the ethnography of agricultural implements*, Memphis: Memphis State University (Memphis State University Anthropological Research Center, Occasional Papers 5).

South, A.K. (1989) 'From copper to kingship: aspects of Bronze Age society as viewed from the Vasilikos Valley', in E. Peltenburg (ed.) *Early Society in Cyprus*: 315–24, Edinburgh: Edinburgh University Press.

—— (1992) 'Kalavasos-Ayios Dhimitrios 1991', *Report of the Department of Antiquities, Cyprus*: 133–46.

—— (1996) 'Kalavasos-Ayios Dhimitrios and the organisation of Late Bronze Age Cyprus', in P. Åström and E. Herscher (eds) *Late Bronze Age Settlement in Cyprus: function and relationship*: 39–49, Jonsered: Paul Åströms Förlag.

—— (1997) 'Kalavasos-Ayios Dhimitrios 1992–1996', *Report of the Department of Antiquities, Cyprus*: 151–75.

—— (2002) 'Late Bronze Age settlement patterns in southern Cyprus: the first kingdoms?', *Cahier du Centre d'Études Chypriotes* 32: 59–72.

—— (2003) 'Vasilikos Valley sites'. E-mail (15 June 2003).

Sparke, M. (1998) 'Mapped bodies and disembodied maps: (dis)placing cartographic struggle in colonial Canada', in H.J. Nast and S. Pile (eds) *Places through the Body*: 305–36, London: Routledge.

Speer, A. (1970) *Inside the Third Reich*, trans. R. Winston and C. Winston, London: Weidenfeld and Nicolson.

—— (1978) *Architektur: Arbeiten 1933–1942*, Frankfurt/Main: Propylaeen.

Stewart, M. (2003) 'Using the woods, 1600–1850. (1) The community resource', in T. Smout (ed.) *People and Woods in Scotland: a history*: 82–104, Edinburgh: Edinburgh University Press.

Stewart of Garth (1828–9) 'Observations on the origin and cause of smuggling in the Highlands of Scotland', *Quarterly Journal of Agriculture* 1: 358–66, 466–74.

Stoler, A.L. (1989) 'Rethinking colonial categories: European communities and the boundaries of rule', *Comparative Studies in Society and History* 31: 134–61.

Storrs, R. (1943) *Orientations*, definitive edition, London: Nicholson and Watson.

Strasser, T.F. (1997) 'Storage and states on prehistoric Crete: the function of the koulouras in the first Minoan palaces', *Journal of Mediterranean Archaeology* 10: 73–100.

Strudwick, N. (1985) *The Administration of Egypt in the Old Kingdom: the highest titles and their holders*, London: KPI.

Stylianou, A. and Stylianou, J.A. (1985) *The Painted Churches of Cyprus: treasures of Byzantine art*, London: Trigraph.

Symonds, J. (1999) 'Toiling in the vale of tears: everyday life and resistance in South Uist, Outer Hebrides, 1760–1860', *International Journal of Historical Archaeology* 3: 101–22.

—— (2000) 'The dark island revisited: an approach to the historical archaeology of Milton, South Uist', in J.A. Atkinson, I. Banks and G. MacGregor (eds) *Townships to Farmsteads: rural settlement studies in Scotland, England and Wales*: 197–210, Oxford: British Archaeological Reports (BAR British Series 293).

Tabet, P. (1979) 'Les mains, les outils, les armes', *L'Homme* 19: 5–61.

Tarlow, S. (1999) *Bereavement and Commemoration: an archaeology of mortality*, Oxford: Blackwell.

Tarsouli, A. (1963) *Kypros*, Athens: Ekdosis 'Alpha' I.M. Skaziki.

Taylor, W. (1976) *The Military Roads in Scotland*, Newton Abbot: David and Charles.

Theocharides, I.P. and Andreev, S. (1996) *Traghodhias 1821 sinekhia Othomaniki Piyi yia tin Kypro*, Nicosia: Kykko Monastery Research Centre.

Thirgood, J. (1987) *Cyprus: a chronicle of its forests, land, and people*, Vancouver: University of British Columbia Press.

Thompson, D.J. (1988) *Memphis under the Ptolemies*, Princeton: Princeton University Press.

Thomson, I.R. (1983) *Isolation Shepherd*, Beauly: Bidean Books.

Tilley, C. (1994) *A Phenomenology of Landscape: places, paths and monuments*, Oxford: Berg.

Todd, I.A. (1988) 'The Middle Bronze Age in the Vasilikos area', *Report of the Department of Antiquities, Cyprus* 1988 (1): 133–40.

—— (1989) 'The 1988 field survey in the Vasilikos Valley', *Report of the Department of Antiquities, Cyprus*: 41–50.

—— and South, A.K. (1992) 'The Late Bronze Age in the Vasilikos Valley: recent research', in G. Ioannides (ed.) *Studies in Honour of Vassos Karageorghis*: 191–204, Nicosia: Eteria Kipriakon Spoudhon (Kypriakai Spoudhai 54–55).

——, Wagstaff, J.M., Sallade, J.K., Hansen, J., Legge, A. and Cullen, T. (1978) 'Vasilikos Valley Project: second preliminary report, 1977', *Journal of Field Archaeology* 5: 161–95.

——, Croft, P., Gomez, B., Hordynsky, L., Kingsnorth, A., Photos, E., South, A. and Wagstaff, J.M. (1982) 'Vasilikos Valley Project: fourth preliminary report, 1978', *Journal of Field Archaeology* 9: 35–77.

——, South, A., Russell, P. and Keswani, P.S. (1989) *Vasilikos Valley Project 3: Kalavasos-Ayios Dhimitrios II: ceramics, objects, tombs, specialist studies*, Göteborg: Paul Åströms Förlag (Studies in Mediterranean Archaeology 71:3).

Trigger, B.G. (1990) 'Monumental architecture: a thermodynamic explanation of symbolic behaviour', *World Archaeology* 22: 119–32.

Tringham, R.E. (1991) 'Households with faces: the challenge of gender in prehistoric architectural remains', in J.M. Gero and M.W. Conkey (eds) *Engendering Archaeology: women and prehistory*: 93–131, Oxford: Blackwell.

Unwin, A. (1928) *Goat-grazing and Forestry in Cyprus*, London: Crosby Lockwood and Son.

van Alfen, P.G. (1996) 'New light on the 7th-c. Yassi Ada shipwreck: capacities and standard sizes of LRA1 amphoras', *Journal of Roman Archaeology* 9: 189–213.

van Andel, T.H., Runnels, C.N. and Pope, K.O. (1986) 'Five thousand years of land use and abuse in the southern Argolid, Greece', *Hesperia* 55: 103–38.

van Dommelen, P. (1998) *On Colonial Grounds: a comparative study of colonialism and rural settlement in first millenium BC west central Sardinia*, Leiden: Faculty of Archaeology, University of Leiden (Archaeological Studies Leiden University).

—— (2002) 'Ambiguous matters: colonialism and local identities in Punic Sardinia', in C.L. Lyons and J.K. Papadopoulos (eds) *The Archaeology of Colonialism*: 121–45, Los Angeles: Getty Research Institute.

Vanhaverbeke, H. (2003). 'The evolution of the settlement pattern', in H. Vanhaverbeke and M. Waelkens (eds) *The Chora of Sagalassos: the evolution of the settlement pattern from prehistoric until recent times*: 149–326, Turnhout: Brepols (Studies in Eastern Mediterranean Archaeology 5).

—— and Waelkens, M. (eds) (2003) *The Chora of Sagalassos: the evolution of the settlement pattern from prehistoric until recent times*, Turnhout: Brepols (Studies in Eastern Mediterranean Archaeology 5).

Waelkens, M. and Loots, L. (eds) (2000) *Sagalassos V: report on the survey and excavation campaigns of 1996 and 1997*, Leuven: Leuven University Press (Act Archaeologica Lovaniensia Monographiae 11).

Wallace, S.L. (1938) *Taxation in Egypt from Augustus to Diocletian*, Princeton: Princeton University Press.

Wallace, T. (1880–3) 'Archaeological notes by Mr Wallace', *Transactions of the Inverness Scientific Society and Field Club* 2: 307–15.

Webb, J.M. and Frankel, D. (1994) 'Making an impression: storage and staple finance at Analiondas Paleoklichia', *Journal of Mediterranean Archaeology* 7: 5–26.

Whittaker, J.C. (1999) 'Alonia: ethnoarchaeology of Cypriot threshing floors', *Journal of Mediterranean Archaeology* 12: 7–25.

Wickham-Jones, C. (2001) *The Landscape of Scotland: a hidden history*, Stroud: Tempus.

Wilson, J. (1850) *Scotland Illustrated in a Series of Eighty Views from Drawings by John C. Brown and Other Scottish Artists*, London: A. Fullarton.

Winkler, J. (1980) 'Lollianos and the desperadoes', *Journal of Hellenic Studies* 100: 155–81.

Winter, F. (1966) 'Notes on military architecture in the Termessos region', *American Journal of Archaeology* 70: 127–37.

Wolf, E.R. (1966) *Peasants*, Eaglewood Cliffs, NJ: Prentice-Hall.

Wörrle, M. (1988) *Stadt und Fest im Kaiserzeitlichen Kleinasien: Studien zu einer agonistischen Stiftung aus Oinoanda*, Munich: C.H. Beck'sche Verlagsbuchhandlung.

Yadin, Y. (1966) *Masada: Herod's fortress and the zealots' last stand*, London: Weidenfeld and Nicolson.

Yakar, J. (2000) *Ethnoarchaeology of Anatolia: rural socio-economy in the Bronze and Iron Ages*, Tel Aviv: Emery and Claire Yass Publications in Archaeology, Institute of Archaeology, Tel Aviv University.

Zeller, T. (1999) '"The landscape's crown": landscape, perceptions, and modernizing effects of the German Autobahn system, 1934–1941', in D.E. Nye (ed.) *Technologies of Landscape: from reaping to recycling*: 218–38, Amherst: University of Massachusetts Press.

INDEX